Women, Ethnics, and Exotics

Look at modern TV Advertising + go back...

Methodology:

[Bkgd. Hist. myth. socio. Psych.]

Austen   Jones
Bronte
Hawthorne   Faulkner
Hemingway   Steinbeck
Woolf   Gilman
Plath
                          Atwood?
McCullers
Mailer

Women, Ethnics, and Exotics

*Images of Power
in Mid-Nineteenth-Century
American Fiction*

BY KRISTIN HERZOG

THE UNIVERSITY OF TENNESSEE PRESS
KNOXVILLE

Library of Congress Cataloging in Publication Data
Herzog, Kristin, 1929-
    Women, ethnics, and exotics.
    Bibliography: p.
    Includes index.
    1. American fiction—19th century—History and
criticism. 2. Women in literature. 3. Minorities in
literature. 4. Primitivism in literature. 5. Exoticism
in literature. 6. Ethnocentrism in literature.
I. Title.
PS374.W6H45   1983   813'.3'099287   82-15881
ISBN 0-87049-372-8

Preface

The substance of this study grew out of a quest of many years. R.W.B. Lewis's work *The American Adam: Innocence, Tragedy, and Tradition in the Nineteenth Century* evoked many questions about an American Eve. Leslie Fiedler's *Love and Death in the American Novel* aroused my curiosity about the relationship of women and black, Indian, or Oriental characters, and Richard Harter Fogle's studies of Hawthorne and Melville focused my interest on images. In the early seventies I had been concerned with the strong individualism of twentieth-century American poetry, black as well as white. In tracing it back to its roots, I looked at the origins of the American novel as well and found it not only intensely individualistic but also very masculine and ethnocentric. At the same time, I discovered that during the American novel's first flowering several mainstream writers overcame this narrow focus, sometimes by using the traditional images of fair and dark lady, noble and ignoble savage in a new and even subversive way. Surprisingly, such writers could also be found outside the canon of "great" American literature. Thus I began to question the presuppositions of a canon that ignores the contributions of many women and ethnic authors.

Other questions followed: How did certain authors portray characters different in sex and race from themselves or the average male Anglo-Saxon hero? What images did they use for women on the one hand and for "savages," noble or ignoble, on the other? Do the characters of women show "primitive" traits, and are ethnic or exotic characters of nonwhite groups seen to have feminine qualities? Are the images different when the author is a woman or an ethnic writer?

I have used the terms "savage" and "primitive" in the romantic sense of being closer to nature, less intellectual, and more determined by instinct and passion than more "civilized" characters. Many writers located this primitivism in persons different from the average writer and reader in race or nationality, and they either denigrated or admired it. The term "ethnic" in this work includes blacks and Indians and is not limited to strictly immigrant groups definable by nationality. The term "exotic" refers to characters such as Melville's South Sea natives, Donatello of *The Marble Faun,* and Rappaccini of Hawthorne's tale, among others, and does not mean exclusively "of a foreign nation or race" but also "strikingly out of the ordinary" or "excitingly strange." Thus spiritists or witches can be exotic. These exotic characters have much in common with the "ethnic" blacks and Indians in the view of the nineteenth century.

In examining the portrayal of women and ethnic characters, this study compares works of completely different origin, aim, and artistic achievement. Considered here are two "great" writers of the American Renaissance, a widely read female novelist, the first two black authors publishing in the United States, and an American Indian oral narrative. The fusion of black and white literary studies of the nineteenth century has yet to happen, and many women writers are still overlooked. To an even lesser extent has American Indian literature, in its transition from oral to written form, been taken seriously as part of what is academically known as "American Literature." The writing of women and blacks in the nineteenth century has been considered artistically deficient, and American Indian literature has been regarded at best as good folklore. Actually some North American tribes had developed a highly sophisticated culture long before Columbus's heirs equated culture and literacy. Our "fictions" about Native Americans and about the essence of good literature have led us often to see aboriginal American literature as merely functional rather than purely fictional, when in fact its religious, political, educational, and psychological functions express a wholeness that "civilized" fiction has frequently lost.

In black literature and women's literature the function of fiction, for example, as a protest novel or as a partly autobiographical account, has prevented readers from considering these works for their artistic merit. As these works are admitted into the canon of American literature, our perception of fictional art will be altered, its definition expanded. Excellence in art is not tied to the absence of its social function. Where art is lacking in works by women and ethnic writers, it is lacking for other reasons: they had extremely limited opportunities for education, for leisure, and for acquaintance with the personal ties and technicalities of writing and publishing.

It is my hope that this book will contribute to the intensifying discussions about the new shape of courses, anthologies, and literary criticism in American literature. As long as Women's Studies and Multi-Ethnic Studies are tacked on to old academic structures as exotic electives, they will remain sterile. If they can be integrated at the very core of American literary studies as revitalizing points of view, they will emerge as genuinely American and therefore indispensible.

I am grateful to many scholars at Duke University and the University of North Carolina at Chapel Hill who stimulated my research in American literature. Among the first were Bernard I. Duffey, Victor H. Strandberg, and Louis J. Budd. I owe the greatest debt to Richard Harter Fogle. Robert A. Bain, Louis D. Rubin, Jr., and Blyden Jackson gave valuable advice, and Margaret A. O'Connor supported my work in professional as well as personal ways. Marjorie Pryse and H. Bruce Franklin, readers for the University of Tennessee Press, helped me greatly by their criticism and encouragement. Franklin's incisive comments and suggestions opened significant perspectives even where I disagreed with him. Karl Kroeber provided the expertise for a special evaluation of the American Indian chapter. Carol Orr and her editorial board handled the manuscript in an exemplary way. Special research questions were efficiently and kindly answered by William G. McLoughlin, Theda Perdue, and Elizabeth Marx. I am also grateful to Alfreda Kaplan whose superb skills in typing I have admired many times.

My work would have been impossible without the inspiration and support of my husband, Frederick Herzog, whose thoughts have shaped mine in innumerable ways, and of our daughter, Dagmar, whose zest for life and learning is infectious. It is to them and to our common vision of the Word's humanizing power in the global village that this book is dedicated.   K. H.
Durham, North Carolina March 1982

Contents

Introduction

Her intellect and heart had their home, as it were, in desert places, where she roamed as freely as the wild Indian in his woods. For years past she had looked from this estranged point of view at human institutions, and whatever priests and legislators have established; criticizing all with hardly more reverence than the Indian would feel for the clerical band, the judicial robe, the pillory, the gallows, the fireside, or the church.[1]

In Hester Prynne, Hawthorne portrayed a woman as independent of civilized institutions and as irreverent toward their authority as a "wild Indian." Melville, similarly, compares a savage to a woman in a scene in *Moby-Dick*. The exotic Queequeg, hugging Ishmael in his sleep, reminds the narrator of his stepmother, whom he cannot think of without a mixture of awe and fear. Although she often beat him, she was "the best and most conscientious of stepmothers." Only once, when he woke up from sleep after being punished by her, he felt a hand like that of a frightening phantom in his own; so the grown-up Ishmael feels very uneasy in the "matrimonial" embrace of the harmless Queequeg.[2]

What do the images of women in the literature of the mid-nineteenth century have in common with the images of "Noble Savages" and other nonwhite people? In many instances women are considered more "natural" and therefore either more innocent or more inscrutably demonic than men, more divine but also more terrifying, like all divinities, and the same type of imagery is used for them as for many Indians, blacks, Orientals, and Mediterranean Europeans. The comparing of women and primitives was certainly nothing new in the nineteenth century. From earliest times until today, women have been described, like the nonwhite races, as more passive, less logical; more imaginative, less technically inclined; more emotional, less incisive; and more religious, less scientifically oriented. This ancient tradition, however, appeared in a new light in the Romantic era.

During the Romantic revolution the traditional idea of the Great Chain of Being was transformed. No longer was the higher place on the ladder of Being the better, but surprisingly the lower preceded the higher in value. This inversion became possible because the idea of God had become secularized and merged with the idea of nature. The Chain of Being was converted into the Chain of Becoming because the fact of evolution could no longer be overlooked. "The world-generating process starts not at the top but at the bottom."[3] This transvaluation became important for the Romantic writers in England as well as America. "The eighteenth century faith in common sense gave to the Romantics a rational justification for holding up the primitive mind as the lamp of truth; to the savage, the peasant, the child, even to the idiot and the lunatic, they went for revelation."[4] Most readers and many writers in the eighteenth and nineteenth centuries also went to women for revelation. Woman was considered "a purer and brighter being, an emanation of some better world, irradiating like a rainbow of hope, the stormy elements of life."[5] The highly popular sentimental novels fostered the idea that women civilized, refined, and spiritualized men, whether this was stated in a tame, traditional way or with a feminist vengeance. Americans created the idea of the "Secular Manly" instead of going to church:

> Practical men who were occupied with the problems of settling and operating a new society—with Congress, Indians, canals—later simplified the whole matter by adopting an easy convention: good women embodied a living victory of the spirit over the flesh. Conviction of this sort did not require attendance at church. America itself became a cathedral. Womanliness came to mean sexlessness and in the 1840's and later, fiction relied on this conviction whenever it presented an ideal woman.[6]

Such facetious comments, of course, do not pertain to a figure like Hester Prynne but to the "ideal" women of the "average" genteel novel.

Frequently the same ideals were projected upon Noble Savages as upon women. In Lydia Maria Child's novel *Hobomok*, the

Indian sacrifices his own happiness to that of others as "naturally" as any ideal woman. But in the primitive native, as in woman, the demonic was constantly lurking. This double image had developed much earlier:

> In the symbolic psychology invented in the eighteenth century, the "heart" does not correspond precisely to what we would call the "id," but only to its benign aspects. The sexual and demonic components of impulse and unreason . . . are later allowed for by splitting the basic "heart" symbols into polar opposites: woman becomes the Fair Virgin and the Dark Lady, the Indian becomes Mingo and Mohawk, Pawnee and Sioux—Good Indian and Bad Indian! In each case, the Dark Double represents the threat of sex as well as that of death; the bad Indian is a rapist as inevitably as the Dark Lady is a sexual aggressor. [7]

A more precise expression of the eighteenth-century notion of the Noble Savage, sometimes seen as more noble and sometimes more savage, is found in Rousseau. He did not simply propose that man turn "back to nature" and did not hold up the primitive savage as the ideal person. He suggested instead that humans have to use reason and will provided by nature to create an artificial moral and political environment reproducing, as far as possible, the conditions of the original state of nature. They must contract positively into the true social state what they have "contracted out" by civilization's processes of acquiescence. Instead of "back to nature," Rousseau says rather: forward to the fulfillment of human nature as it was meant to be. For him, the state of nature is the state of the brute which has to be overcome. Especially the older Rousseau did not believe in the Noble Savage as representative of the cult of the subrational. [8] Nevertheless, the Indians, for Rousseau as for Crèvecoeur, were nobler than civilized people because they were free of the evils of civilization.

Among the early followers of Rousseau, Chateaubriand was not a naive admirer of Indians either. He, too, changed his opinion in the course of his life. By the time he wrote *Les Natchez,* he was convinced that the qualities of human nature which divide classes and races are immutable. In his earlier works, however, he had painted an idealistic picture of the noble Indian which expressed the popular American and French notions of the time.

Besides these foreign influences, America had its own tradition of the Noble Savage. In the sentimental novel Indians were mostly considered noble, while in the novels of Charles Brockden Brown they appeared more savage because Brown combined the traditional description of Indian captivities and Indian warfare with an exploration of the subconscious. Brown did not use stereotypes. He offered, for example, in *Edgar Huntley* a "complex version of the frontier experience, charged with troubling ambiguities that suggest unexplored significances hidden deep within that experience."[9]

How, then, should the Noble Savage be defined against the background of these foreign and native traditions? In H.N. Fairchild's classic study he is described as any free and wild being who draws directly from nature virtues which raise doubts as to the value of civilization. The term may even be applied metaphorically to romantic peasants and children. Although Fairchild does not include women in his definition, the fictional image of women is very close to that of other "natural" characters who are supposed to live by instinct more than by reason, and who express power, threatening or saving.

The concept of the "primitive" is closely related to the idea of the Noble Savage. Arthur O. Lovejoy and George Boas, in their outstanding work on *Primitivism and Related Ideas in Antiquity* published in 1935, distinguish "chronological" and "cultural" primitivism. The former pertains to "a theory, or a customary assumption, as to the time—past or present or future—at which the most excellent condition of life . . . must be supposed to occur"; the latter concerns "the discontent of the civilized with civilization, or with some conspicuous . . . feature of it. It is the belief of men living in a relatively highly evolved and complex cultural condition that a life far simpler and less sophisticated . . . is a more desirable life."[10] Cultural primitivism is not an invention of the Romantic era but is as ancient as humankind. Some cave men probably "discoursed with contempt upon the cowardly effeminacy of living under shelter." An early form of primitivism is the Golden Age myth. In at least one version of it, as recorded by Hesiod, there were no women in this age, "Pandora being the first of her sex and the immediate source of human misery." From ancient times on, racial differences have been connected with cultural discontent: "At least from the fourth century B.C. on . . . the Scythians apparently were to the ancients very much what the North American Indians were to the primitivists of the sixteenth to the eighteenth centuries in modern Europe."[11]

Nineteenth-century Romanticism finally changed the focus of these ancient traditions. Primitivism no longer implied a concern with analyzing how various cultures ennobled or corrupted human beings; it became instead a state of mind. In Wordsworth, for example, primitivism shifted from a conventional location (a rural retreat or a paradise of Pacific races) to a mode of sensibility. The Romantic writers saw certain life situations (such as the peasant's life or life stages such as childhood) as favorable to a primitive state of mind, but this different mode of feeling and response was a universal potentiality of human nature and was expressed, for example, in natural piety or animism.[12] While primitivism in all its manifestations is related to what is closest to "nature," there are innumerable differences in the understanding of this term. Lovejoy and Boas listed sixty-six meanings of "nature," some of them antithetical to each other. "Nature" is a key word for rationalists as well as "irrationalists." It can pertain to a set of "natural laws," understandable by every person's *lumen naturale*, or, as in the German *Sturm und Drang* and in English Romanticism, to the irrational dynamic process of the universe in which one may yearn to be immersed and made whole.[13] Returning to nature in the latter sense does not mean returning to another stage in human history or another level of culture but to one's inward, essential, "natural" self—in modern terms, to the unconscious. By this return one does not affect a primitive pose like Chateaubriand, but one is able to say like Melville's Ishmael: "I myself am a savage."[14]

The mid-nineteenth-century fiction which I will discuss is concerned with recovering the essential wholeness of human nature and human relations, with healing the split of mind and body, reason and emotion, white and nonwhite, civilized and primitive, man and woman. This happens in various ways: by repudiating a cold, scientific, mechanical intelligence in favor of a vitality and spiritual sensitivity, as embodied in many of Hawthorne's women; by turning to the Orient as the source of all religion and finding in some aspects of Eastern life a revitalization of Western Christianity, as in Melville's portrayal of Oriental characters; by finding in representatives of the "African race" and in women primitive values which the white man can suppress only at the price of his own debasement, as in Stowe's *Uncle Tom's Cabin;* and by defining the essentially noble character of black people considered primitive by their masters, as in the novels of Brown and Delany. The American Indian epic likewise speaks of the vital power of Native Americans, male and female. The Iroquois Confederacy, as envisioned by the mythical Dekanawida, gives women power in the political affairs of the tribes. The rites that belong to the Great Law, which is part of the Iroquois epic, express the spiritual strength underlying the political insights. In all these works, then, women and nonwhite people are considered to harbor an innate power—however demonic it might sometimes appear—which the civilized white male has lost or suppressed.

The question arises, why was American fiction "white-centered" as well as male-centered, or, to use R.W.B. Lewis's famous designation, determined by the American Adam? To answer this question, we have to consider how this figure differs from the savage as well as the "American Eve." According to Lewis, the American Adam is "an individual emancipated from history, happily bereft of ancestry, untouched and undefiled by the usual inheritances of family and race; an individual standing alone, self-reliant and self-propelling."[15] Daniel G. Hoffman describes the American folk hero in a very similar way. He explains how egalitarianism in America casts the individual in a lonely role without heritage or tradition. The American Adam has to achieve everything he does or becomes. Unlike heroes of myths and Märchen in other countries, the American folk hero has "no parents, no past, no patrimony, no siblings, no family, no life cycle, because he never marries or has children. He seldom dies."[16] In spite of the simplification inherent in this definition, Hoffman makes an interesting point. He counts among folk heroes not only Crocket, Fink, and Johnny Appleseed, but sees as also deriving from them Hawthorne's peddler Dominicus Pike of "Mr. Higginbotham's Catastrophe", Holgrave of *The House of the Seven Gables,* Robin of "My Kinsman, Major Molineux", Melville's Ishmael, Ahab, Delano, and the whole cast of *The Confidence Man.*

Neither Lewis nor Hoffman, however, is concerned with the American Eve. Lewis mentions several times Francis Parkman's severe masculinity of spirit, but when he interprets *The Scarlet Letter*, for example, he simply sees Hester Prynne as another American Adam, not mentioning that Hawthorne's fictional women represented a significant change from masculine heroes and sentimental heroines to a new conception of an American Eve. The existence of a black or Indian American Adam is also ignored. The black American Adam in the slave narratives, for example, had something in common with his white counterpart. He was by force as bereft of ancestry, patrimony, or sponsorship of any kind as the white Adam was by choice or by chance, and he showed an even greater self-reliance when he propelled himself out of slavery; but he was never seen to be as individualistic as the white protagonist in ignoring, subduing, or fearing women and "primitive" people. In American Indian narratives, the protagonists were seen as even more tied to their group, whether family, clan, or tribe, and in contrast to the white as well as the black Adam, a Hayonwatha (Hiawatha) was ever conscious of his ancestors. Fiction simply reflected the circumstances of the time: nonwhite people, like women, were dependent on their own kind for support, and frequently the two groups supported each other.[17]

There are several reasons for the extreme individualism and masculinity of white Amerian fiction in the nineteenth century, from the Leatherstocking Tales and *Arthur Gordon Pym* to *Moby-Dick* and *Huckleberry Finn*. Ian Watt, in *The Rise of the Novel*, finds the origins of modern individualism in the rise of democracy and the spread of industrial capitalism and Protestantism, especially introspective Puritanism. All these conditions were fulfilled in America on a much larger scale than in the England of Defoe or Richardson. These elements combined with the theological interpretation of America as the new Eden and the popular experience of a seemingly endless frontier gave the myth of the American Adam its peculiar shape. German idealism was also influential in the forming of American individualism.[18] The frontier, however, more than any other influence, made the American novel more individualistic and more male-centered than English fiction of the nineteenth century. American authors stood outside their society much more than English writers because American society was still more fragmentary and less structured, and the audience was a fluctuating, uncertain entity. This difference between American and English fiction, however, is not an absolute one. Even the great women figures in English novels by Jane Austen, George Eliot, and the Brontës submit in the end to a life of self-restraint or sacrifice in a male-dominated world; or they are doomed, as in Hardy's novels.[19] The male traits of American fiction merely show a different accent. The violence and vigor of the frontier world and the lack of a native cultural tradition fostered the American Adam's disregard for persons different from himself as well as his "innocence" and hopefulness.

Why, then, has the American literature of the mid-nineteenth century been labeled "feminine"? The thesis of the predominant emotionalism and "femininity" of the 1850s simply does not fit the major writers.[20] It appropriately describes only the upsurge of women authors during this time and their tremendous popular appeal. The alliance between women and the liberal-optimistic clergy fostered the emergence of a popular and sentimental literature which constitutes the beginning of modern mass culture. The concept of femininity in much of the writing about women authors of the 1850s is understood primarily as sentimental weakness. This unfortunate usage is widespread.[21]

The sentimental women's novels and their popularity have been studied intensively in recent years. There were, of course, various reasons for the "wrong" taste of the public during the 1850s. The era of frontier masculinity and aristocratic values was ending, and the era of feminine popular values had taken its place and had given women more opportunities for education and leisure. The educational system prescribed only professional or classical curricula for boys whereas girls studied whatever was an enrichment of life, such as modern fiction and the fine arts.

Several critics have found an overt or covert, intentional or unintentional feminism in the sentimental novels by women authors. Helen Papashvily finds these works meek and mild only on the surface; underneath they expressed the discontent of women who were frustrated by the limitations and injustices of their position which they could neither understand nor change.[22] Nina Baym sees the women's novels as representing "a moderate, or limited, or pragmatic feminism, which is not in the least covert but quite obvious." She also opposes the label "sentimental novel" or "novel of sensibility" for nineteenth-century women's novels because she considers them as a turning against the Richardsonian novel of sensibility; the heroine who lives entirely within her feelings is criticized. For the heroine as sexual prey of a Lovelacian monomaniac the women writers substitute female figures in whom personality and spirit are rated above physical perfection.[23]

Whatever the motive behind the fiction of the sentimental women novelists (in many cases the motive was simply economic necessity), these novels expressed the "Cult of True Woman-hood" pervasive in society at large. The cardinal virtues of True Womanhood were piety, purity, submissiveness, and domesticity. Spiritual woman was expected to be the salvation of sensual man. Women were passive responders in a love-centered domestic world; men were the movers and doers in a greedy commercial world. Woman was to work in silence and without regard for earthly reward. As Elizabeth Cady Stanton observed, "[I]t requires philosophy and heroism to rise above the opinion of the wise men of all nations and races, that to be unknown is the highest test-imonial woman can give to her virtue, delicacy and refine-ment."[24] The women's magazines of the time provided a modi-cum of intellectual refinement while espousing the virtues and abilities of the housewife. Even as talented a woman as Harriet Beecher Stowe described the virtues of the homemaker in religious terms: the Christian home is the "appointed shrine for woman, more holy than cloister, more saintly and pure than church or altar. . . . Priestess, wife, and mother, there she ministers daily in holy works of household peace."[25] Horace Greeley, in his preface to Margaret Fuller's *Woman in the Nineteenth Century* (1855), regarded the evasion of domestic duties as inexcusable, but their fulfillment not impossible to combine with intellectual endeavors: "It is often supposed that literary women, and those who are active and earnest in promoting great intellectual, philan-thropic, or religious movements, must of necessity neglect the domestic concerns of life. It may be that this is sometimes so, *nor can such neglect be too severely reprehended;* yet this is by no means a necessary result." He then testified to the fact that Margaret Fuller in her own life never "slighted or shunned" even the most humble of domestic duties.[26]

Although many readers and writers have ridiculed the ste-

reotypes of True Womanhood and the glorification of domesticity in the popular fiction of the time, domesticity in the 1850s
represented for many women a tremendous advance over the
drudgery of pioneer times when they had to work hard outdoors,
often fighting for the survival of their families and homesteads.
Moreover, in the sentimental novels, such as *Uncle Tom's Cabin*,
stereotypes were often turned into powerful symbols. For the
overall point of this study, the sentimental women's novel contributes essentially three aspects: it represents the foil for those
works in which stereotypes of True Womanhood were partly or
wholly overcome; it shows the popular imagery which rang certain
bells in the average reader's mind when a woman was described;
and, most important, it demonstrates the combination of characteristics found in women and Noble Savages. The first of these
points needs no great elaboration. We simply have to keep in
mind that the sales of all the works by Hawthorne, Melville,
Thoreau, and Whitman in the 1850s did not equal the sales of
Susan Warner's *The Wide, Wide World*, to name only one example. Only against the background of a host of clichés can we
appreciate the achievement of the more discerning writers. The
second point is related to the repetitious style of the domestic
novels. The imagery for husband and wife frequently includes the
opposites of sun and moon, oak and vine, eagle and dove, lion and
lamb. A favorite source of imagery is the world of flowers. Pervasive is the "clinging vine" theory of female conduct. In her novel
The Heiress of Greenhurst, Mrs. Ann Sophia Stephens warns a man
that the woman who belongs to him can be molded in any way he
determines: "She is in your hands; make of her what you will, a
gazelle or a tiger, the thing you call an angel, or the thing you fear
as a fiend. That which you make her she will be, a blessing or a
curse, which will cling to you for ever and ever."[27] Domestic
imagery, of course, prevails. Women are "chosen vessels." Even
women reformers use domestic images like "sweep Uncle Sam's
kitchen clean" and "tidy up our country's house."

The domestic novel's third contribution to my topic is its
combination of the images of women and Noble Savages. The
simplicity and innocence of "natural man" were taken for granted.
"With the perfectability of man as a favorite article in their creed,
they found generosity in pirates, chivalry in rustics, humanity in

Negroes, and nobility in savages, West Indians, and Algerines."[28]
Mrs. Stephens and some other women writers had no qualms
about miscegenation. "Gypsies, as well as Sicilians, Corsicans,
and Arabs, were imagined to have formed societies based on
passion rather than self-control, and novels in which these supposed races are featured contain a crude rebellion against Victorian values."[29] While exotics were seen as passionate, however,
ethnic characters closer to home were more likely to be considered
submissive. Noble Indians could be as self-sacrificing as true
women. For example, the heroine in Mrs. Stephens's novel
Malaeska: The Indian Wife of the White Hunter (1860) appears as
the noblest of all savages. She possesses all the requirements of the
beautiful Indian: a laugh as musical as a birdsong, hair that glowed
like a raven's wing, and motion as graceful as an untamed gazelle.
"Her language was pure and elegant, sometimes even poetical
beyond . . . comprehension, and her sentiments were correct in
principle, and full of simplicity. . . . She was never seen to be
angry, and a sweet patient smile always hovered about her lips
. . . . , the poetry of intellect and of warm, deep feeling, shed a
loveliness over her face seldom witnessed on the brow of a savage."
She spent her life "in piling up soft couches for those she loved,
and taking the cold stone for herself. It was her woman's destiny. . . . Civilization does not always reverse this mournful picture of womanly self-abnegation."[30]

It would be a mistake to assume that women and savages had so
much in common only in the superficial diction which provided
the bestsellers. "Like the very gentle perfect knight of the middle
ages and the noble savage of the eighteenth century, the saintly
heroine came to be accepted as fact."[31] It is the merit of Hawthorne and Melville, however, that they describe heroines and
primitive people as neither saints nor demons but as ambiguous
human beings. Where they do take over the old images of dark and
fair lady, noble and evil savage, they do so with a special purpose:
to question or reinterpret the images or even to reverse their values
completely. Two cases in point are Melville's *Pierre* and Hawthorne's *The Marble Faun*.

Isabel in Melville's *Pierre* has an extremely primitive mind:
"She cannot understand abstract language; she conceives only of
physical objects; she thinks many inanimate objects are alive and

talks to them; she has difficulty distinguishing between cats, stones, trees, and people; she is childlike; she was once thought to be mad and has spent part of her life in a madhouse."[32] These are obviously the traits of an uncivilized character. There is hardly any white male figure in Melville's work who is primitive in a similar way, but many nonwhite males can be found who are childlike and emotional, in the best as well as the worst sense.

Miriam in Hawthorne's *The Marble Faun* is not a primitive savage in the way her friend Donatello is, but she is as inscrutable and potentially demonic as any American Indian in fiction. She acts impulsively, not rationally, when with just one look she incites Donatello to murder. If she is as dark and dangerous as many exotic characters in fiction, she is also as victimized and helpless as any lamia in Romantic literature.

Thus Hawthorne and Melville show us the similarities of women and primitive people, but in each work the similarities are evaluated in a way very different from the sentimental novelist's use of the same images. Isabel saves Pierre from his superficial childhood utopia, but she also represents his destruction. Her opposite is not the typical fair lady but a rather good girl with many self-delusions. Miriam and Hilda in *The Marble Faun* are both ambiguous women. Hawthorne and Melville often see primitiveness as strength, not docility; as culturally conditioned, not innate.

These similarities between Hawthorne and Melville are the more surprising as their political and social opinions were quite different. Melville's views on race and war were very progressive; he was thoroughly democratic and sensitive to the issue of racism and slavery. Hawthorne, on the other hand, wrote a campaign biography for the conservative Franklin Pierce which catered to the pro-slavery forces and cost Hawthorne many friends. He also showed no sympathy for the reformers he got to know at Brook Farm. Hawthorne, however, did know something about freedom and oppression in personal and local situations. He lacked Melville's wide range of experience and the close acquaintance with other races, but his psychological sensitivity enabled him to draw fictional portraits of strong, complex women. He lacked political acumen but knew history, especially Puritan history.

Writing at the same time as Hawthorne and Melville were

authors who were themselves different from the average author and reader in either sex or race. They were less concerned with primitive psychological forces than with the social dimensions of primitive images. These two dimensions are closely interwoven. Whenever individuals have disowned primitive vitality and claimed cultivated intellect as the essential human quality, they will project that primitiveness onto some Other, either glorifying or degrading it, but in either case regarding the Other as nonequal. This process occurs on the personal level as well as on a massive social scale.

At first reading, many characters in *Uncle Tom's Cabin* might be considered primitives, but a closer examination shows that their primitiveness is different from the clichés of sentimental novels. They can best be understood as figures of a folk-epic or national myth,[33] and they share all the boon and bane that such a myth entails. Some of the women as well as some of the black characters are rather realistically portrayed. The black race is characterized by epithets commonly used to describe women. Uncle Tom had the "soft, impressible nature of his kindly race, ever yearning toward the simple and childlike." Black people are sensitive, religious, tactful, humble, obliging, patient, "impassioned and imaginative," "not naturally daring and enterprising," and talented in cooking.[34] All of these terms, however, are part of the rhetoric of Stowe's time, and her character portraits transcend these popular notions by far. There are strong black characters in the novel, and many of the women are convincing in their individuality. The author did not equate the Christian spirit of Uncle Tom with weakness and accommodation; his response to degradation is only one of many different responses in other characters who show subversive strength. Stowe tries to revamp a male-oriented Christianity that justifies slavery by inserting feminine values into the Christian faith.

William Wells Brown as the first black novelist in America could hardly avoid taking over the patterns of white fiction. "At a crucial time for black people, when the novelist should have been engaged in redefining definitions, in moving to rebut both Mrs. Stowe and her detractors, Brown is found lacking. His solution to the problem of images is to offer counter-images, more appealing to whites and the black middle class than to those on the slave plantation."[35] Brown's *Clotel,* however, like Stowe's *Uncle Tom's Cabin,* does present new types of characters, even if they are tinged with gentility and rely more on rational endeavor than primitive instinct. *Clotel* is significant because it portrays the one fictional type which combines the traits of the female and the Noble Savage more than any other: the tragic mulatto, a figure extremely popular in fiction for about fifty years in the mid-nineteenth century. Mulattoes, quadroons, and octoroons "would claim the morals, images and symbols of whites . . . as their own,"[36] yet as members of an ethnic minority they give these images a different value. For example, Brown depicts mulatto women who vigorously overcome the victimization which is their lot in the sentimental novels.

Though Martin R. Delany may not be "the most important African-American novelist in the nineteenth century,"[37] Delany's *Blake* is a very surprising achievement in its time, in many ways anticipating twentieth-century black fiction. Delany depicts black people in a greater diversity of color and class stratification than any writer, black or white, before him. The characters in *Blake* include mulattoes, poor blacks, middle class blacks, intellectuals, house slaves, field slaves, a black Cuban poet, and an Indian chief. Delany also portrays women in various strata of society, from the poorest to the most aristocratic, and in spite of their inferiority of education, they show much of the Delany hero's strength and resistance. That this hero is an all-black man, and not one of the intelligent mulattoes of abolitionist fiction, determines the progressive character of the novel.

All the authors mentioned present powerful images of women and primitive characters, and yet there are great differences in their presuppositions. If even Hawthorne's and Melville's world views are vastly different on some points, the distance between Hawthorne and Delany is, of course, even greater. Hawthorne, an American consul in Liverpool serving an administration which favors the South and Southern aspirations of Caribbean expansion; Delany, a revolutionary black leader writing about violent slave rebellion fomented in Cuba—the two figures hardly seem comparable. Yet these two authors, like Melville, Stowe, and Brown, are empathizing with aboriginal power, whether lodged in Indians, Typees, common laborers, poor ethnics, mad people, religious sectarians, black slaves, mulattoes, or women. They defend this power over and against the overwhelming mechanization and rationalization of a progress-loving society dominated by white males of Anglo-Saxon Protestant origin. They plead for social community instead of laissez-faire individualism. They have visions of a New Adam and Eve and a new social order.

This same romantic vision informs the American Indian narratives. The myth of Dekanawida is a reaction against centuries of intertribal warfare. The ideal of the male warrior was superseded by the figure of the wise peace leader who embodied physical as well as spiritual strength and mystical healing powers. The vision of a new society and the development of the Great Law for the Iroquois League would unite the warring tribes, and women would have a substantial role in the process. It is one of the ironics of history that a people whom Americans considered one of the most brutish had developed at least by the sixteenth century (if not much earlier) a concept of government, an understanding of psychological states, and a model for balancing power and rights between the sexes that can be ranked higher than any similar concepts flourishing at the same time in Europe. The story of the League and its Great Law was not written down before 1880, but ethnologists of the mid-nineteenth century recorded its importance for Iroquois culture at that time as in the earlier centuries. It still constitutes an essential nucleus of Iroquoian rites today.

Dekanawida's spirit of peace was not the spirit of white America, North or South, in the 1850s. The two parts of the country grew steadily more hostile toward each other. Northerners considered the South backward, decadent, primitive, and endangering the industrialization and free westward expansion of their growing multitudes. Southerners saw the North as money-grabbing, uncultured, and cold-natured. Neither society realized fully the deeper problems each had at home: slums and industrial exploitation in the North, slavery and a sexual double standard in the South. The underlying causes of these problems were not very different. In both parts of the country a disregard for the Native American, the nonwhite slave, or the non-Protestant, non-Anglo-Saxon immigrant created tremendous social tension. The failure to see women as equals was reflected, in the South, in the abstract adoration or benign neglect of white women and the sexual exploitation of black slave women; and in the North it engendered a glorification of the home as women's realm, since the men were eager to keep the realm of finance, politics, industrial progress, and academic achievement to themselves. The vital power of those who were "other," and therefore frightening—illiterate slaves, unbaptized Indians, and legally unrecognized women—was not tapped anywhere. Instead, comforting images of these "primitive" groups were used to justify slavery, paternalism, and "property rights."

Marshall McLuhan in his book *War and Peace in the Global Village* sees violence, whether in the form of war or in some other shape, as an involuntary quest for identity among people who lack a holistic, mythical sense of self and society.[38] The United States, in the decade culminating in the Civil War, was immersed in a painful search for identity. It learned only gradually that "alien" elements had to be acknowledged as powerful and equal in their claims to humanity. The violence of slavery bred the violence of war, an agony which not only liberated slaves but gave women a chance to prove, especially in the South, that they could grow beyond the images which had been imposed upon them.[39]

This study takes seriously those works of American literature that were reshaping old images of women and nonwhite people and humanizing them. It takes note of the "imperial self" and the Adamic egocentrism of American literature pointed out by various critics, but, more important, it examines those writers who "tried with a noble generosity to imagine a world in which other people really counted."[40] Wherever women and other classes and races really count, individual human beings have balanced primitive instinct and guiding reason, and human societies have balanced the rights and responsibilities of different sexes, races, and nationalities.

Women, Ethnics, and Exotics

1
Primitive Strength
in Hawthorne's Women

Powerful Victims of Science: Georgiana and Beatrice

*There is something truer and more real, than what we can see with the eyes,
and touch with the finger.* [1]

The primitive vitality of many of Hawthorne's women is frequently symbolized by their association with Oriental, Mediterranean,
Indian, or other ethnic or exotic elements, but it is also portrayed
indirectly by contrasting the women with idealistic, Faustian,
science-possessed men who wield unnatural power over them and
reject woman's earthiness.

The most playful version of bookish man, materialistic in his
appetites and idealistic in his goals, is Adam in "The New Adam
and Eve," a sketch Hawthorne wrote during the blissful first year
of married life with Sophia Peabody. The author imagines here
that Father William Miller's doomsday vision of 1843 has become
reality. Of all humankind, only a young couple is left to roam the
deserted streets. When Adam feels the urge to spend some time
among the tomes of the Harvard library, the narrator warns him:
"Oh Adam, it is too soon, too soon by at least five thousand years,
to put on spectacles, and bury yourself in the alcoves of a library!"
And Eve feels the same way: "Let us talk with one another, and
with the sky, and the green earth, and its trees and flowers. They

will teach us better knowledge than we can find here" (265). The narrator is even bold enough to suggest that "the downfall of a second Adam" would have taken place had Adam then and there stayed in the library.

Hawthorne's humorous point goes beyond the romantic commonplace that intellectualism is related to sin and decay. It says something about the distinctive nature of man and woman, and Hawthorne comes back to this idea many times in his fiction. The Eve in this sketch has been considered "an archconservative" and "a bit of a Philistine."[2] But it is Adam who is an archconservative when he talks condescendingly of Eve's "little head" that should not trouble itself too much about things she cannot understand (251). He is "unconscious" of the symbolic import of his placing Eve in the speaker's chair in an empty legislature, whereas the narrator is certain that "Man's intellect, moderated by Woman's tenderness and moral sense" would make all legislature superfluous. It is only through Eve's influence that Adam avoids "all the specious theories, which turn earth into cloud-land, and men into shadows" (265).

The image of woman as closer to nature and instinctually less warped by civilization than man is continued in "The Birth-mark" and "Rappaccini's Daughter." Aylmer in "The Birth-mark" still retains a faint remnant of natural emotion—he kisses Georgiana's hated birth-mark "by a strange and unaccountable impulse" before his experiment kills her—but Rappaccini is an altogether evil figure. Both men strive for ultimate control over nature. While they wield the power of life and death in scientific terms, Georgiana and Beatrice show love and trust and are thereby more powerful in human terms. The warm integrity of Beatrice has often been overlooked in favor of her exotic luxuriance and fatal charm. The latter are only the characteristic traits of the Dark Lady, and Hawthorne reverses their impact by pointing in the end to Rappaccini's scientific deviltry, Baglione's jealous hatred, and Giovanni's poisonous mistrust which stand in contrast to Beatrice's original integrity.

Georgiana is not an exotic figure like Beatrice, but she is unusually beautiful except for the ambiguous birth-mark which in the end is symbolic of her life-force. Aylmer cannot bear to see or touch the mark. Beauty to him is merely something physical to be fixed up to optical perfection, not something to be lived or touched. His primitive helper Aminadab symbolizes the savageness he rejects in himself, not realizing that his lofty idealism under the guise of science is the greater savagery. Woman's sexuality, emotion, soul, and earthiness are so abhorrent to him that he arrives at the point where "the only good woman is a dead one."[3] Imperfection is the very essence of being human; in eradicating it Aylmer extinguishes Georgiana's life. But Georgiana remains the stronger person even in the face of death. A passing reference to a marble sculpture by Hiram Powers as the "Eve of Powers" (38) may be a unique pun. Georgiana is definitely an Eve of power. She is open and frank, even in her deepest anxiety, while Aylmer conceals his emotions (40). Although she worships her husband's scientific miracles, she gradually senses the illusory aspect of his successes (49), while he remains blind to the workings of nature, "our great creative Mother," even in his wife. She demands no proof of his skill and intentions—"I joyfully stake all upon your word" (53)—while he tries to prove the efficacy of his procedure by a plant experiment. She dies without hatred or accusation, merely with pity for the man who "failed to find the perfect future in the present."

The power of Beatrice is more complex than that of Georgiana. From birth on, Rappaccini worked to turn her into an artifact, like the brilliant shrub in his garden. Her whole life therefore was spent in a polluted atmosphere; she is indeed filled with poison and her touch is fatal, as the images of the dying reptile and insect, the withering flowers, and the "infected" Giovanni indicate. But the narrator leaves no doubt that without Rappaccini's poisoning influence her nature would express love and trust. The poison has not penetrated completely into her soul. Her real emblem is the shattered fountain in the garden, not the artificial shrub which she outwardly resembles. When she began to love Giovanni, "the pure fountain had been unsealed from its depths, and made visible in its transparency" (122). "Giovanni," she begs him to believe, "though my body be nourished with poison, my spirit is God's creature, and craves love as its daily food" (125).

Giovanni, however, has moments of distrust from the very beginning (97), although he is dazzled by Beatrice and curious to figure her out. He is a "sexually confused Victorian male,"[4] but he also lacks depth and integrity. He "had not a deep heart" (105). He wonders gradually whether his feeling for Beatrice might not be a matter of the heart at all but a mere fantasy of his brain (109). The slight confidence in her which has grown in him is based rather on "the necessary force of her high attributes" than on "any deep and generous faith, on his part" (120). Like Aylmer, Giovanni longs for scientific proof: he wants to test Beatrice's integrity by watching whether a flower will be blighted by her touch. He expresses "a certain shallowness of feeling and insincerity of character" as he contemplates himself in the mirror and is too sure of his own strength: "I am no flower to perish in her grasp!" (121) As he realizes that Beatrice's touch is about to kill him, he reacts with deep hatred and murderous thoughts (122), while she shows "faith in his tenderness" and blushes for having doubted even an instant (123). His words are "blighting" (126), and she dies with the ambiguous question, "Oh, was there not, from the first, more poison in thy nature than in mine?"

Georgiana and Beatrice, then, are strong in their instinctual dependence on "something truer and more real than what we can see with the eyes, and touch with the finger" (120). They are not images of rough, amoral nature like Aminadab, Aylmer's helper. They retain the mystery of nature which the men in the stories are driven to decipher and dissect. The power of primitive forces is evident when even the savage Aminadab declares in looking at Georgiana, "If she were my wife, I'd never part with that birthmark" (43). The Faustian intellectual lacks such primitive instinct. Like Aylmer, Rappaccini cannot tolerate woman's life-giving force. Projecting his own destructive powers, Rappaccini sees in Beatrice a formidable enemy.

> "What mean you, foolish girl? Dost thou deem it misery to be endowed with marvellous gifts, against which no power nor strength could avail an enemy? Misery, to be able to quell the mightiest with a breath? Misery, to be as terrible as thou art beautiful? Wouldst thou, then, have preferred the condition of a weak woman, exposed to all evil, and capable of none ?"
>
> "I would fain have been loved, not feared," murmured Beatrice. (127)

To Giovanni, too, she is a femme fatale. But Hawthorne knows better. He chides young Giovanni for lack of trust and ultimately blames only Rappaccini and his jealous colleague Baglione, not Beatrice, for her death.[5] When Beatrice dies, the fountain in Rappaccini's garden is shattered, but the water continues "to gush and sparkle into the sunbeams as cheerfully as ever" (94). In Hawthorne's vision, the primitive power of love and trust does not die.

The Scarlet A: Aboriginal and Awesome

It might be that a sluggish bond-servant, or an undutiful child . . . was to be corrected at the whipping post. It might be, that an Antinomian, a Quaker, or other heterodox religionist was to be scourged out of the town, or an idle and vagrant Indian, whom the white man's fire-water had made riotous about the streets, was to be driven with stripes into the shadow of the forest. It might be, too, that a witch, like old Mistress Hibbins, the bitter-tempered widow of the magistrate, was to die upon the gallows.[6]

The Scarlet Letter is a story set at the rough edge of civilization. The dark forest is still ominously near, and the dark dangers from foreign servants, untamed children, stubborn heretics, idle Indians, or hell-bound witches seem to threaten the progress of Puritan civilization's sacred new orders. The passage quoted above foreshadows in a variety of images Hester Prynne's emergence from the prison: while she is not a bond-servant, she is bound by the bonds of marriage to an unloved, old husband who sent her alone to a foreign continent. She also binds herself in love to a man whose name she will not utter. She is certainly no child, but the gruff English-born matrons who gossip about her fate and her character call her "brazen hussy" (54) and "naughty baggage" (51), and the image of the "undutiful child" prepares us for getting to know Pearl. Her lonely exile at the border of the town will later make her an Antinomian in thought, and the author has already reminded us of another freethinker, "sainted Ann Hutchinson," with whom Hester is symbolically identified through the wild rosebush at the prison door (48). Hester herself might have become the foundress of a religious sect or a prophetess if she had not borne a child and had lived a purer life (165, 263). She certainly is as much an outcast as any Quaker in the Puritan

7

colony, and she bears public abuse with a Quaker's dignity. Her freedom of speculation makes her as dangerous as any "heterodox religionist" who was "then common enough on the other side of the Atlantic" (164).

The image of the Indian appears at the beginning and at the end of the novel, and throughout the story a certain wildness and passion in Hester's character is, directly or indirectly, identified with the American Indian. This "aboriginal" aspect of Hester's femininity is not the only trait, however, which separates her from the Puritan women around her. She is also an alien with a touch of the exotic, in spite of her apparently uneventful childhood in rural England. "She had in her nature a rich, voluptuous, Oriental characteristic,—a taste for the gorgeously beautiful" (83). In her "otherness," she is a woman of awesome power.

Hester's Indian or "aboriginal" characteristics have been strengthened by social isolation which caused her to wander "without rule or guidance, in a moral wilderness; as vast, as intricate and shadowy, as the untamed forest" (199). Arthur Dimmesdale, after the climactic union in the forest, is filled not only with hope and joy, but "with fear betwixt them, and a kind of horror at her boldness." In part Hester's attitude grew out of her "native courage and activity," but it was also a consequence of her outlaw existence. "Her intellect and heart had their home, as it were, in desert places, where she roamed as freely as the wild Indian in his woods" (199). At the beginning of the novel, she is described as "impulsive and passionate" (57) and yet showing a "natural dignity and force of character" (52). The "desperate recklessness of her mood" (53) is hidden behind a "serene deportment" (55). This description parallels a portrayal of the Indians toward the end of the story, when they have flocked to town at the New England holiday.

> A party of Indians—in their savage finery of curiously embroidered deer-skin robes, wampum belts, red and yellow ochre, and feathers, and armed with the bow and arrow and stone-headed spear—stood apart, with countenances of inflexible gravity, beyond what even a Puritan aspect could attain. Nor, wild as were these painted barbarians, were they the wildest feature of the scene. This distinction could more justly be claimed by some mariners. (232)

Inwardly passionate, outwardly composed—this describes Hester as well as the Indians. Her garment is "curiously embroidered" like theirs, and she stands apart, like them, from the crowd (232, 234). A "combative energy" in her character enables her to turn the scene of her public ignominy "into a kind of lurid triumph" (78). She is free to return to her birthplace, and she has "the passes of the dark, inscrutable forest open to her, where the wildness of her nature might assimilate itself with a people whose customs and life were alien from the law that had condemned her" (79), but she decides to stay at the place of her shame, to submit "uncomplainingly to the worst usage of the public" (160). She gives an impression of "marble coldness" (164) and, at times, of humility, even though it might actually be pride (162); like the Indians she keeps her emotions to herself.

The primeval forest, an image of the "moral wilderness in which she had so long been wandering" (183), and an image always connected with the Native Americans, also expresses Hester's deepest hope and joy. "That wild, heathen nature of the forest, never subjugated by human law, nor illuminated by higher truth" harbors a "heart of mystery" which at the reawakening of love between Hester and Dimmesdale becomes a "mystery of joy" (203). But the joy is transient. "In itself good, Nature is not a sufficient support for human beings."[7]

The most splendid image for the wild, untamed aspect of Hester's nature is her "elf" child, Pearl. In her dress, her looks, and her behavior she is a part of wild nature.

> A fox, startled from his sleep by her light footstep on the leaves, looked inquisitively at Pearl, as doubting whether it were better to steal off, or renew his nap on the same spot. A wolf, it is said,—but here the tale has surely lapsed into the improbable,—came up, and smelt of Pearl's robe, and offered his savage head to be patted by her hand. The truth seems to be, however, that the mother-forest, and these wild things which it nourished, all recognized a kindred wildness in the human child. (204–5)

This description of the child expresses a part of Hester's nature as well. Among the crowds at the holiday,

Pearl, who was the gem on her mother's unquiet bosom, betrayed, by the very dance of her spirits, the emotions which none could detect in the marble passiveness of Hester's brow.

This effervescence made her flit with a bird-like movement. . . . She broke continually into shouts of a wild, inarticulate, and sometimes piercing music. (228)

The Puritans are inclined to consider Pearl a "demon-offspring" (244), just as they consider the Indians to be "powerful enchanters" skilled in the "black art" (127). At the holiday, when Pearl runs to look a wild Indian in the face, he becomes "conscious of a nature wilder than his own" (244). Just like Hester, Pearl combines "native audacity" with "a reserve as characteristic" (244). The vivid natural images that describe her confirm her as a part of nature. Besides being repeatedly compared to a bird, she is associated with an April breeze and a brook, and likened to a nymph-child or infant-dryad, a fairy, and an elf. She is so "aboriginal" that she declares in public "she had not been made at all, but had been plucked by her mother off the bush of wild roses that grew by the prison-door" (112).

Pearl is not only an image of her mother's passionate, yet restrained, "Indian" nature; she is also a picture of Hester's "taste for the gorgeously beautiful" (83), of her rich, Oriental, luxurious traits that make her awesome among Indians as well as Puritans. Pearl's garments are the product of the "fertility and gorgeous luxuriance of fancy" expressed in Hester's needlework (53) and make the child look as exotic as "a wild tropical bird" (111). Hester's exquisite needlework is her art, an outlet for her passion and imagination. Through it she converts her badge of shame into a symbol of triumph and defiance.

Hester's exotic Oriental traits contribute also to her awe-inspiring elevation and isolation. Throughout the novel she is repeatedly seen as pedestaled on the scaffold.[8] With her child in her arms she seems an "image of Divine Maternity" (56) as the crowd beholds her for the first time. At the end, after having stood "statue-like" at the foot of the scaffold (244), she appears almost like a Pietà at the moment of Dimmesdale's death of "triumphant ignominy" (357), although the scene is ambiguous: "Then, down he sank upon the scaffold! Hester partly raised him, and supported his head against her bosom. Old Roger Chillingworth knelt down beside him" (255).

As an image of Divine Maternity Hester is, in archetypal terms, not the aboriginal adulteress but the awesome, adored, and redeeming Magna Mater. She inspires a vague "horror" in Dimmesdale (199) as well as in Chillingworth (61), and yet she is Dimmesdale's "better angel" (201). In the forest scene, he is exhilarated by breathing the same "wild, free atmosphere of an unredeemed, unchristianized, lawless region" as Hester (201), and yet the flood of sunshine brightening the "magic circle" of this hour (202) indicates that their love is also redeeming and healing, even if it will not in the end prevent Dimmesdale's death or Hester's suffering.

Again it is Pearl who images most clearly the redemptive aspect of Hester's nature, just as she also expressed her untamed, precivilized life-force. In spite of her wild elf nature, "there was love in the child's heart" (115). Had the authorities taken Pearl away from her mother, Hester might have been lost to the Black Man. "Even thus early had the child saved her from Satan's snare" (117). In the forest scene, Dimmesdale and Pearl for the first time really meet each other. There was "an awe about the child as she came onward" (207). She shares in Hester's alien, exotic nature. Dimmesdale "dreads this interview, and yearns for it" (207). When Pearl has decked herself out with flowers, her "brilliant picturesqueness" is intensified. The sunshine is "attracted thitherward as by a certain sympathy" (208). But the germ of love in her does not grow prematurely. She withholds her affection as long as she detects falsehood, which she scorns bitterly (180). She senses that Hester's throwing off the scarlet letter means throwing off part of what has shaped her identity, and she might also sense that the minister is not ready as yet to "go back with us hand in hand, we three together, into the town" (212). And so she throws a temper tantrum which for Dimmesdale has as "preternatural" an effect as Mistress Hibbins's "cankered wrath" (210). This is the "aboriginal" trait of the "witch-baby" in Pearl, a name the shipmaster gives her (245). The same potentially demonic force unites Hester herself with weird Mistress Hibbins. The witch-baby Pearl becomes an image of love and liberation at the scaffold when she flies to the staggering Dimmesdale with "bird-like motion" and when just before his death she kisses his lips and breaks the spell of guilt and estrangement. Redemption comes from the very forest powers which the Puritans considered fiendish.[9]

Pearl is not the only evidence of Hester's identity as a redemptive figure. The aura of Divine Maternity is reflected in various ways. To some of the townspeople, "the scarlet letter had the effect of a cross on a nun's bosom. It imparted to the wearer a kind of sacredness. . . . It was reported, and believed by many, that an Indian had drawn his arrow against the badge, and that the missile struck it, but fell harmless to the ground" (163). Hester is a "self-ordained Sister of Mercy"; her nature "showed itself warm and rich: a well-spring of human tenderness, unfailing to every real demand, and inexhaustible by the largest" (161). At the turning point of the novel, when Hester, Dimmesdale, and Pearl meet during the night at the scaffold, there seems to appear in the sky an A which some observers take as standing for "Angel"; and although they refer to Governor Winthrop who was "made an angel that night" (158), the reader knows that the A refers first of all to Hester Prynne, adulteress as well as "angel of mercy."

Hester, then, is described in images that form two clusters: the aboriginal and the awesome (to spin out farther the mystical meaning of the letter A). In the first aspect, she represents subhuman nature, as it is usually associated with the American Indian, with wild forest places, and with witch-like persons such as Mistress Hibbins. In the second, she represents an almost supernatural figure of Divine Maternity, exotic beauty, Oriental richness, and angel-like mercy. The two clusters of imagery merge and overlap. Pearl, for example, is in the end the humanizing force which unites the subhuman and the superhuman in a redeeming center. She is both the witch-baby and the child mediating divine grace.

Hester's inner spiritual and emotional struggle shows the same polarity. On the one hand, she is a typical romantic heroine who can say after a meeting with her husband, "Be it sin or no . . . I hate the man" (176). She can remind Dimmesdale that what they did had "a consecration of its own" (195). When she broods about the dilemma of womanhood, she wanders "without a clew in the dark labyrinth of her mind." At times, a fearful doubt strives to possess her soul "whether it were not better to send Pearl at once to heaven, and go herself to such futurity as Eternal Justice should provide" (166). When she finds new hope after the reunion with Dimmesdale in the forst, she is ready to flee with him on a ship that significantly is an outlaw vessel with a crew of "rough looking desperadoes" who are guilty of "depredations on the Spanish commerce" (233). Hester is at times a "Fausta," boldly or desperately overstepping all boundaries of faith and tradition.[10]

But there is a self-restraining side to Hester also. She upbraids herself for hating Chillingworth, though she cannot overcome her hate (176); she patiently bears insults, even from the poor whom she is helping; she is "a martyr indeed," although she does not pray for her enemies "lest, in spite of her forgiving aspirations, the words of the blessing should stubbornly twist themselves into a curse" (85). Before as well as after Dimmesdale's death, she is free to go back to England but remains to do of her own free will what society had forced her to do. She becomes a Mary figure to whom people bring "all their sorrows and perplexities" (263).

Thus Hester is not just a fallen Eve; she is a divine mother, a Sister of Mercy, a nun, a saint, an angel, a potential prophetess or foundress of a religious sect, and a martyr. Hester is an "able woman" (161), a woman of strength "almost majestic in . . . despair" (173). She is a queenly figure who may have gotten her name from the biblical Esther. Queen Esther is a woman of courage, beauty, dignity, and selflessness. Hester Prynne has all these qualities. In contrast to many pliable, submissive women figures in the fiction of the 1850s, Hester has "combative energy" (78), a "desperate recklessness of . . . mood" (53), "freedom of speculation" (164), and "a mind of native courage and activity" (199). She explores realms unimagined by Dimmesdale and by her society.

Dimmesdale lacks the strength which had borne up Hester under the burden of the scarlet letter (171), and he begs her, "Twine thy strength about me! Thy strength, Hester" (253). In contrast to her, Dimmesdale is often described in feminine terms. He "kept himself simple and childlike; coming forth . . . with a freshness, and fragrance, and a dewy purity of thought, which, as many people said, affected them like an angel" (66). "The creator never made another being so sensitive as this" (171). Dimmesdale himself admits his weakness in the forest scene: "Think for me,

Hester! Thou art strong. Resolve for me!" (196). And she urges him desperately: "Preach! Write! Act! Do anything, save to lie down and die!" Although Dimmesdale agrees to flee with Hester, he returns immediately and guiltily, "pitiably weak" (215), to his public duties after their meeting.

Hester combines the strength of a Squaw Sachem (described earlier in Hawthorne's historical sketch "Mainstreet") with the awesomeness of a Hebrew queen, but the primitive strength of these two types is tempered by Hester's suffering and faith which convince her that a life of loving service will give her existence new meaning.[11] While she appears at first as a kind of Arminian who wants to expiate her sins by quiet good works without public confession, her final views amount in effect to the same public confession which Dimmesdale felt urged to make as a true Puritan. The important difference between the two, however, is that Hester embodies a life-force and creativity whereas Dimmesdale exemplifies "mere" spirituality. In her maturity, Hester represents an early, lively Puritanism that emphasized the heart's turning away from itself toward others and discovering God's grace in human action.[12]

Romantic primitivism tempered by suffering and faith—this aspect of the novel's meaning is also reflected in its structure. Of Hawthorne's works, it has been said that "theme . . . is structure."[13] In *The Scarlet Letter* the scaffold is the central symbol and, like the scarlet A, it stands for shame as well as elevation. The action of the first three chapters and the last three (except for part of the Conclusion) is centered around the scaffold, and in the central chapter 12 Hester, Dimmesdale, and Pearl mount the scaffold in the night. During the procession at the New England holiday, when Hester stands "statue-like" at the scaffold, she has "a sense within her . . . that her whole orb of life, both before and after, [is] connected with this spot, as with the one point that gave it unity" (244). This "scaffolding" in structure and theme of the novel is related to its concern with divine and human law. It could be summarized by James Russell Lowell's simple line, "Truth forever on a scaffold." Divine truth is forever crucified on the scaffolds of human authorities. The same paradox of theme and structure is mirrored in the stylistic scaffolding of romantic and realistic elements. Hawthorne and Melville use the romance pattern in its primitive or archetypal form. They do not make use of a realistic "displacement" of the basic romance but consciously write "a more primitive and archaic sort of fiction."[14] In *The Scarlet Letter* Hawthorne uses allegory, witchcraft, superstitions, Indian Black Art, or the popular assumption that dark Oriental or European heroines are fallen or dangerous women.[15] Hawthorne, however, weaves a measure of realism, in setting and psychological detail, into this romantic primitivism and so makes the reader aware of an element of illusion. He thereby invites us to use our own imagination and draw our own conclusions. If we are told of the folk belief that an Indian had drawn his arrow against Hester's badge, but that it struck and fell harmless to the ground, we are compelled to think about the incredible power of a social stigma.[16]

Hester's "lawless passion," then, "turns her into a kind of white Indian, and she becomes in Hawthorne's mind a focus for all those associations of knowledge with sexual power which we have . . . observed in Cooper's mythic red men and dark ladies."[17] But besides her "Indian" or primitive side, Hester has a Puritan side. As a member of a Puritan colony and in love with a Puritan minister, she fights the demonic forces of the forest in herself when she tries hard not to hate or curse, not to take her own life or that of her child, not to join in with Mistress Hibbins's insane forest rites, and to keep love and mercy alive in her. Her Indianness, however, is also her strength. Her return to her old abode and her taking up the scarlet letter again of her own free will are the best expression of the two forces in her: an aboriginal freedom and an awesome power of commitment.

In the early Puritan tradition, the colonist is either a captive or a destroyer of Indians; he has to oppose the primitive elements of human experience he sees expressed in the Indian enemy. Later in the history of the Puritan colonies, this attitude changes. After the threat of the real Indian is removed from the more established American civilization, Indian life and lore turns into myth, and the colonists adopt "a more favorable attitude toward the Indians, beginning with a more objective treatment of them and ending (in 1773–1800) in the advocacy of a systematic imitation of the Indian way of life." The transformation of Indian culture into myth culminates in Thoreau's work and in Longfellow's "Hiawatha."[18] Hawthorne, especially in his tales, describes the early Puritan view of the Indian, but as a romantic writer he cherishes the vitality of the primitive life-force expressed in the American Indian. Therefore, on the one hand, Chillingworth's worst traits, according to Puritan rumors, were intensified by his contact with the Indians' Black Art (127), and Hester wanders in a "moral wilderness" like the Indian who roams in desert places; on the other hand, Hester's Indian-like qualities of strength, passion, endurance, dignity, and independence are deemed admirable and are contrasted with the narrow-mindedness of the Puritan system and the weakness of Dimmesdale. The Indian of the nineteenth century was alternately the symbol of humanity's childhood and Golden Age innocence and the lustful, cruel violator of American pastoral peace. But to Hawthorne, the Puritans are the more cruel violators. Throughout the Hawthorne canon, the Puritans' martial prowess against the Indian is exposed as inhuman.[19]

Hester, then, is an example of a new American Eve. Her similarity to primitive Indians is not, as it would be in popular sentimental novels, a similarity in terms of childlike behavior, docility, and self-effacing nobility. It is instead a kinship on grounds of an unquenchable thirst for freedom, a vital power of imagination, as expressed in her needlework art, and a strength in endurance which looks merely stoic on the outside but allows her to turn the prejudices of society, the images of the "old" Eve, into symbols of victory. Hester does not use her inner freedom in an individualistic fashion; she builds community instead of destroying it, as her final way of life indicates.[20] No American writer before Hawthorne had described a woman as powerful as Hester Prynne.

The Home-based Power of Women and Maules

In a passage in *The American Notebooks* Hawthorne speaks of the human heart as a gloomy cavern to be passed through before one can find beauty and sunlight. His seven-gabled house is connected with the heart. "To pass into the house is necessary; yet the human heart decays when it lingers there. To pass out of the house is necessary; yet the heart is hardened when it abandons those inmost meanings which the house contains. But to pass into and through and then *out* of the house . . . herein lies . . . the way toward redemption."[21]

An intangible world of superstitions and chimney-corner traditions forms the essential substructure of *The House of the Seven Gables.*[22] This world is associated with the original Maule and his grandson. In their primitive folk strength and their wizard powers they represent a kind of ethnic as well as exotic strand of the story. Unless the proud Pyncheon spirit admits the primitive Maule spirit into the house and bends down to its level, it can only decay; and the expelled Maules, personified by the jack-of-all-trades Holgrave, from their exile have to find a way back into the house, or else they abandon "those inmost meanings which the house contains." A decaying Hepzibah can be revitalized and a too sunny Phoebe become mature by contact with the Maule forces, and the Maule spirit, by being granted its right of place, can lose its curse and hate: "herein lies . . . the way toward redemption," the way *"into* and *through* and then *out* of the house." Certainly, the book leaves us only with a qualified and personal hope.[23] The liberation through and from the house ends with the inheritance of another house. The Pyncheon curse may only be arrested. But the hope for redemption is found in primitive elements: in women who emerge from the realm of ghosts, fairy tales, and myth, and in ethnic characters who had been enslaved and made homeless.

The characterization of Hepzibah represents an important milestone in American literary history since *The House of the Seven Gables* is "the first notable American novel in which a single woman is a major character."[24] Hawthorne follows the traditional depiction of single women by giving Miss Pyncheon a very quaint name, but he does not take over the stereotype in other ways. Single women were usually minor characters who did the prattling or gossiping necessary for the denouement of the plot. They were usually middle-aged or older. They had some altruistic ambitions but no specific goals, so they did not fail in life. They were frequently dressmakers, school teachers, or domestics. They were conventional, well liked, and not dynamic enough to clash with anyone. If they were suffragettes, they were ridiculed.

Two voices are used in the description of Hepzibah: one speaks with the "cruel humor of the jaunty listener," and the other is "a more omniscient narrator" who can see her inner emotions and feel compassion. "At the end the tone, the attitude to be taken toward Hepzibah, itself becomes [Hawthorne's] subject."[25] The characterization of Hepzibah is not at all a parody or an abusive portrait, as some critics have suggested. Hawthorne refuses to bestow on Hepzibah the dignity of a tragic heroine, which could easily have led to a sentimental or glorifying characterization, but he gives her dignity by making us aware of the truly human quality of her heart and by indicating that the social context of the Pyncheon family and her society at large made her what she is.

In *The House of the Seven Gables,* as in *The Scarlet Letter,* an isolated woman dramatically emerges from a door to be publicly exposed. But the description of Hepzibah before she opens the shop door of the seven-gabled mansion is mock-heroic rather than somber.[26] "Far from us be the indecorum of assisting, even in imagination, at a maiden lady's toilet! Our story must therefore await Miss Hepzibah at the threshold of her chamber; only pre-suming, meanwhile, to note some of the heavy sighs that labored from her bosom, with little restraint as to their lugubrious depth and volume of sound, inasmuch as they could be audible to nobody save a disembodied listener like ourself. The Old Maid was alone in the house" (30). This passage sounds like a comic description of the stereotypical old maid if read out of context. Within the framework of the whole novel, however, the narrative voice achieves a different effect. In the first chapter we are introduced to the house itself which had been willed to Hepzibah for her lifetime and which is likened to a "great human heart" (27). Judge Pyn-cheon, whom we get to know in the same chapter as an eminently respectable, generous person had "repeatedly offered [Hepzibah] all the comforts of life" (24). But there is a casualness in the juxtaposition of the respectable judge and the ridiculous old maid that is suspicious. Much later in the story we learn that the judge has no part in the house at all and has no share in any human heart either. Hepzibah's love turns out to be as real as her scowl is innocent, and the judge's smile and social eminence prove decep-tive. The careful reader senses very early that the serious depiction of the judge is not to be taken seriously and the ridiculous portrait of Hepzibah is not meant to ridicule her.

There are, then, two sides to Hepzibah, and two narrative voices trying to combine the two sides in a focused image which does justice to her as a whole human being. There is something ludicrous, ambiguous, and ghostlike in her character as in the Maules, because she has been denied a proper place in society as much as they. That as a Pyncheon she participates in some of the pretensions of her forebears makes her even more ludicrous. She is a living example of the psychological warping that results from social injustice. But like Holgrave, the last Maule descendant, she has not lost the potential for human tenderness in her ghostlike existence. The "disembodied listener," as the narrator calls himself, can sense, besides the old maid's "gusty sighs" and "creaking joints," the "almost agony of prayer—now whispered, now a groan, now a struggling silence" (30–31). He even realizes there is a sole "strong passion" in her life, an "undying faith and trust" and "continual devotedness" (32). "Her heart never frowned. It was naturally tender, sensitive, and full of little tremors and palpitations. . . . Nor had Hepzibah any hardihood, except what came from the very warmest nook in her affections" (34). After we are given these glimpses of her real self, the narrator quickly distances himself again in drawing his humorous portrait of Hepzibah: when she sighs, her breast is "a very cave of Aeolus" (36), when she arranges toys, the "deeply tragic character" of this old figure contrasts "irreconcilably with the ludicrous pettiness of her employment." At the close of this description the half-sympathizing, half-mocking narrator draws the reader into his difficulty of adequately portraying a person like Hepzibah: "Heaven help our poor old Hepzibah, and forgive us for taking a ludicrous view of her position!" (37).

We soon understand the narrator's problem: his democratic world view clashes with the decaying gentility that is Hepzibah's world. He can only smile at her shadowy, upper-class pretentiousness, and yet he sees Hepzibah's humanity. (Harriet Beecher Stowe, William Wells Brown, and Martin Delany face a similar problem in depicting slave-holding women who participate in an inhuman system while they try to keep their humanity and are themselves victimized by prejudice.) Hepzibah needs to come down to the Maule level to be democratized, to become a social being, to join, in Holgrave's words, "the united struggle of mankind" (45). But for the time being she appears like the ancient Maules who wield unseen wizard powers and who are ghostlike, absent and present at the same time. She ventures into the shop but straightway vanishes back into the dusk, as though she wanted to minister to the community "like a disembodied divinity, or enchantress" (40). Just as "life is made of marble and mud" (41), the ludicrous and the divine are mingled in her.

> What tragic dignity . . . can be wrought into a scene like this! How can we elevate our history of retribution for the sin of long ago, when, as one of our most prominent figures, we are compelled to introduce—not a young and lovely woman, nor even the stately remains of beauty, storm-shattered by affliction—but a gaunt, sallow, rusty-jointed maiden, in a long-waisted silk gown, and with the strange horror of a turban on her head! . . . What is called poetic insight is the gift of discerning, in this sphere of strangely mixed elements, the beauty and the majesty which are compelled to assume a garb so sordid. (41)

Gradually Hepzibah takes on the ghostlike aspect of the Maule wizards: when the shop bell gives a "tinkling alarum," she is startled and rises "as pale as a ghost at cock-crow, for she was an enslaved spirit, and this is the talisman to which she owed obedience" (42). Her enslavement resembles that of Alice Pyncheon or, indeed, of all Pyncheons who, according to town rumors, were "no better than bond-servants to these plebeian Maules, on entering the topsy-turvy commonwealth of sleep" (26), because the curse of dying Matthew Maule seems to haunt the Pyncheons in their dreams. Old Matthew, a victim of Cotton Mather's witch delusions, himself "was known to have as little hesitation or difficulty in rising out of his grave as an ordinary man in getting out of bed" (189). When later in the story Clifford and Hepzibah rouse themselves to go to church again, Clifford holds back his sister at the last moment with the words "We are ghosts! We have no right among human beings" (169). In *The House of the Seven Gables* the proud aristocrats who are haunted by plebeian ghosts become ghosts themselves. Hepzibah becomes "Maulish" when the ill-gotten property of the family has finally evaporated. She is as poor, shadowy, and ludicrous as the Maules ever appeared to those around them.

Hepzibah has a counterpart in the ethnic New Englander Uncle Venner, who is a part of the primitive folk elements associated with the house. He "had studied the world at street corners" (155), goes around in his "patched coat and rusty beaver" (221), and has a vein of poetry in him (61). He belongs to a different world, and yet he is a lonely outsider like Hepzibah, an "immemorial personage" (60) and, in his own way, as simple-minded as she is. While she is still secretly hoping for some "harlequin trick of fortune" which might restore to her the former Pyncheon wealth and status (64), he is dreaming of his "farm" as a utopian refuge.

Hepzibah's simple-mindedness is also an admirable single-mindedness. She shows "warmth of heart" (95), "much love" (96), "tenderness" (101), "natural dignity, mingled with deep emotion" (113), "heroism" (133), and "courage" (228) whenever she takes care of her victimized brother Clifford or responds to the sunny nature of Phoebe. With all these benevolent and noble traits, she could easily have turned into the stereotype of the do-good Old Maid. But Hawthorne keeps the reader from feeling sentimental about her. She looks so horrid that she is a "grief" to Clifford (136); her exotically strange "horror of a turban" is "oddly and wickedly analogous" to the crest on the degenerate Pyncheon hens (89); she appears to the shop customers like a "real old vixen" (54); she counts nothing higher than to be born a lady (45, 79); and she protects her brother against his evil cousin like "the dragon which, in fairy tales, is wont to be the guardian over an enchanted beauty" (126). With "princess-like condescension" she does not yield an inch of her own gentility (155). In short, her seclusion has made her into a "kind of lunatic" (174). Her life is made up of "marble and mud" (41), the marble of Alice Pyncheon's exotic pride and the mud of Maulish poverty and ghostlike existence, but also the marble of unfailing love and the mud of victimization.

Alice Pyncheon is the woman in the novel who represents the first connecting link between the greed and pride of the Pyncheons and the vengeance and remorse of a Maule. She is the most exotic figure in the story: "At an open window of a room in the second story, hanging over some pots of beautiful and delicate flowers—exotics, but which had never known a more genial sunshine than that of the New England autumn—was the figure of a young lady, an exotic, like the flowers, and beautiful and delicate as they. Her presence imparted an indescribable grace and faint witchery to the whole edifice" (191). Alice is of "foreign education," her mother having been an English "lady of fortune" and her father having lived for some time in England and Italy where his mind became "industriously stored with foreign ideas, and elaborated into artificial refinement" (193). Alice thus fits the pattern of other Hawthorne women who are Europeans and at the same time either proud or dangerous or both:

> The guilty men [in Hawthorne] may be Europeans (Chillingworth, Donatello) or Americans (Dimmesdale, Hollingsworth). But when guilt is personified in a woman, she is a European with a rich emotional experience. She belongs to his glamorous type. We already find this tendency in his short stories. Lady Eleanor, who carries a gorgeous mantle containing the germs of a deadly disease, and with it a burden of personal pride, comes from the other side of the Atlantic. Beatrice, whose beauty is a deadly menace, is an Italian. Hester . . . is a European immigrant, and Zenobia . . . is a cosmopolitan. Miriam, finally, is of mixed European descent. All these daughters of the Old World are beautiful, intelligent, and passionate women with a past.[27]

Alice is "a lady born, and set apart from the world's vulgar mass by a certain gentle and cold stateliness," but she also has "tender capabilities." Her voice is "sweet and harp-like," and she is passionate enough to be suddenly "struck with admiration" when she sees the "remarkable comeliness, strength, and energy" of carpenter Maule's figure. Alice has only one flaw: "She was very proud. . . . This fair girl deemed herself conscious of a power—combined of beauty, high, unsullied purity, and the preservative force of womanhood—that could make her sphere impenetrable" (203), but the carpenter overpowers her with his mesmerism.

Witchcraft in *The House of the Seven Gables* is in a state of decay. There are no sexual orgies, as in "Young Goodman Brown," no compacts with the Black Man. Witchcraft is only a generalized dread and an exercise of personal vengeance, not a search for the Unpardonable Sin, and it will be even further reduced to mere modern psychology in *The Blithedale Romance*.[28] Whatever the state of the Maules' wizardry, Alice is powerless against it because she is too proud of her strength and purity. She has to pay dearly: "While Alice Pyncheon lived, she was Maule's slave" (208). He keeps humiliating her until finally she wastes away in body and spirit, yet not before she is "penitent of her one earthly sin, and proud no more!" Now it is Matthew Maule's turn to repent, and he becomes "the darkest and wofullest man. . . . He meant to humble Alice, not to kill her" (210). Alice's spirit lives on in the house of the seven gables, in haunting music which emanates, ghostlike, from her harpsichord—"it looked more like a coffin" (73)—and in "Alice's posies" which, as legend has it, grew from exotic seeds Alice had flung up in sport into the nook between two of the gables (28). At the end of the story they are in full bloom. The rich beauty of the "crimson-spotted flowers" seems to be "a mystic expression that something within the house was consummated" (286). What is consummated, through the death of Judge Pyncheon, is the union of a Pyncheon offspring who is neither proud nor exotic and a Maule offspring who no longer uses vengeful wizard powers.

Phoebe, a kind of sunshine girl, has troubled many Hawthorne critics. She has neither the great flaws nor the tragic depth of Hepzibah, neither the refined beauty nor the education of Alice. Phoebe represents simple reality in contrast to the shadowy existence of Clifford and Hepzibah, but what her "real substance" lacks is "the modifying influence of tragic insight. While she fails as a character—fails because Hawthorne is only partially capable of demonstrating her maturation—Phoebe is like Donatello or the bridal pair at Merrimount, an innocent whose defect is her very innocence."[29] Yet Hawthorne must have admired many traits in Phoebe because she has much in common with his wife, Sophia, whom he repeatedly called Phoebe in his love letters and in his notebooks. Phoebe, like Sophia, is sunny, birdlike, and churchgoing. Both can make comfortable quarters in an old, musty house.[30] She is called "a young rosebud of a girl" (117), a playful, gushing fountain (138), a fragrant garden flower (143), a girl "like a prayer," "a Religion in herself, warm, simple, true, with a substance that could walk on earth, and a spirit that was capable of heaven" (168). She is an "angel" to Clifford as well as to Uncle Venner (142, 221), a bringer of "hope, warmth, and joy" to Holgrave (306), a singing bird (138). Her youthful and pleasant nature throws "a cheerfulness about the parlor, like the circle of reflected brilliancy around the glass vase of flowers that was standing in the sunshine" (104). Phoebe and the fire that boiled the teakettle are described as "equally bright, cheerful, and efficient," and she shows a "magnetism of innate fitness" in contrast to the clumsy Hepzibah.

But Phoebe has definite limitations, and Hawthorne was evidently conscious of them. When Hepzibah implies that Judge Pyncheon is an evil man, Phoebe, who belongs to the "trim, orderly, and limit-loving class," reacts with naiveté: "A wider scope of view, and a deeper insight, may see rank, dignity, and station, all proved illusory, so far as regards their claim to human reverence, and yet not feel as if the universe were thereby tumbled headlong into chaos. But Phoebe, in order to keep the universe in its old place, was fain to smother, in some degree, her own intuitions as to Judge Pyncheon's character" (131). Phoebe always keeps within the limits of the law (85); anything mysterious annoys her (143, 218, 302); she loves no riddles (144); all extravagance is a horror to her (166). "Significantly, she knows little concerning the family's past, has forgotten most of what she once was told, remains profoundly incurious about Clifford's identity, Jaffrey's motives, the meaning of Maule's curse."[31]

Phoebe in her innocence and naturalness belongs to the real world and to the realm of myth at the same time. "Finding the new guest there—with a bloom on her cheeks, like the morning's own, and a gentle stir of departing slumber in her limbs, as when an early breeze moves the foliage—the Dawn kissed her brow. It was the caress which a dewy maiden—such as the Dawn is, immortally—gives to her sleeping sister" (70). Phoebe belongs to the realm of Eden. When she has gathered roses before the first breakfast with Clifford, "the early sunshine—as fresh as that which peeped into Eve's bower while she and Adam sat at breakfast there—came twinkling through the branches of the pear-tree" (101). At the end of the story, the love of Holgrave and Phoebe makes life an Eden again; the flower of Eden is present in Alice's posies; the one golden bough of the Pyncheon elm is "like the golden branch that gained Aeneas and the Sybil admittance into Hades" (285). Hawthorne breaks down all distinctions between inner and outer facts, myth and reality. Aeneas and the Sybil, Alice Pyncheon,

Holgrave, and Phoebe, are all on the same level or ontological plane.[32] Just as Hepzibah is occasionally described in mock-heroic terms, just as Alice Pyncheon is partly a fairy-tale figure, so Phoebe is sometimes lifted into the realm of nature myth. She has even been called an "apostle of nature," a feminine Phoebus who comes and goes with the sun, a country cousin wearing a straw bonnet, bringing country butter, and making better "Indian cakes" than Hepzibah.[33]

Phoebe as a simple representation of nature brings back into the Pyncheon house what has been kept out ever since a greedy Pyncheon outwitted a Maule. Her down-to-earth character revives the old ethnic Maule element as it lived before it turned ghostlike by being deprived of its place and its natural rights. The story of *The House of the Seven Gables* is, on one level, a story of romantic primitivism: all the main characters have to go through the dark cavern of the house, the dark mystery of primitive nature, to gain human wholeness and also a concrete right of place. Only then can they pass out of the house into sunshine and the new Eden of a "thunder-smitten" Adam and Eve (150).

Hepzibah has to undergo a more agonizing change than Phoebe because she has inherited the whole Pyncheon legacy of unnatural pretensions. She first takes on the ghostly traits of the deprived Maules before Phoebe's natural simplicity and Clifford's childlike need for love and care revive her love and devotion. Having been unable to pray even in a moment of greatest need (245), she is finally able to say like a child, "Oh God—our Father—are we not thy children? Have mercy on us!" (267).

Phoebe's change is not as dramatic as Hepzibah's. She simply matures by being immersed in the dark mysteries of the house. Gradually, she is no longer "constantly gay"; she grows "less girlish, but more a woman" (175). "I shall never be so merry as before I knew Cousin Hepzibah and poor Cousin Clifford. I have grown a great deal older, in this little time. Older, and, I hope, wiser, and—not exactly sadder—but, certainly with not half so much lightness in my spirits! I have given them my sunshine, and have been glad to give it; but, of course, I cannot both give and keep it. They are welcome, notwithstanding!" (214–15). In the end, she is no longer afraid of Holgrave's "oscillating tendency" (307). She grows to understand what Hepzibah, having "gnashed her teeth against human law," understood much earlier: Holgrave, the lawless mystic, may have a "law of his own" (85).

The happy ending of the story leaves many questions unanswered. Will the Pyncheon money eventually perpetuate the Pyncheon curse? Will Hepzibah again be a lady and isolated? Will Clifford live only for beauty? Does Holgrave end up a sad man, transformed to take up the stance of the former Pyncheons only without their ruthlessness? The text does not really point in any of these directions and, as usual, Hawthorne does not give us a clear-cut opinion. "A man's bewilderment is the measure of his wisdom," as Holgrave says (178). But the portraits Hawthorne draws of Hepzibah, Alice, and Phoebe and of their relationship to the other characters make one thing sure: each of them has to pass into and then out of some seven-gabled Hades to become more fully human. For Hepzibah and Alice that means coming down to the Maule level of "ethnic" life to be humbled. For Phoebe it means outgrowing her natural simplicity to the extent that she can understand exotic characters like Holgrave, the vagabond wizard; Clifford, the sybarite and lover of beauty; and Alice, the ghostly memory of a too-proud family. In the end she is able to sympathize with their sufferings and sense the depth of evil inherent in men like Judge Pyncheon. Her maturation is not fully developed by Hawthorne, but it is in the interaction of all the characters that she comes alive, since only "together they make up a design."[34] When justice has been done and the curse forgotten, the strong ethnic Maule element emerges like Alice's posies, no longer exotic but homegrown, from the chinks between the gables, and under the sun of Phoebe's simple humanity bursts into bloom.

In *The Scarlet Letter*, Hester, compared to the Indians, shows their vigor, endurance, and imagination. In *The House of the Seven Gables*, the main women figures, having gone through the ordeal of humiliation or at least close contact with suffering, show the common-sense wisdom and down-to-earth strength of the Maules. In neither case are the "primitive" people idealized. On the contrary, Indians and ethnic Maules harbor a demonic potential. But their demonic power becomes destructive only when they are repressed and deprived of their rights by Puritan authority or aristocratic pretension. The women likewise are flawed characters, but their ambiguous potential becomes demonic (as in Hester) or ghostlike (as in Hepzibah) only when their natural place in society is not acknowledged, or when they are plainly over-powered like Alice. Phoebe represents only the simple, down-to-earth aspect of the primitive; she lacks its dark depth. But when she accepts the love of Holgrave, she is "permitting Maule Im-agination to become a part of the fully integrated and harmonious personality at last,"[35] and only in this way can human community be built.

If we disregard the fairy-tale ending, the story of the Maules symbolically seems to anticipate the rising up of oppressed people as envisioned in "Benito Cereno," *Uncle Tom's Cabin*, and *Blake*, and Hawthorne's novel, like these other works, expresses the interdependence of personal and social wholeness. But Haw-thorne was too much of a secularized Calvinist to believe in a radical transformation of society based on human effort. What has been redeemed might easily regress to the old pattern of exploita-tion. The reader may speculate whether Hepzibah, instead of selling "Jim Crow" gingerbread men, might simply regain her old pride along with her old wealth, and whether Holgrave might soon build a house of stone because the Judge's wooden mansion is not good enough for him (314). After all, the luck of the Pyn-cheons is "pretty good business," as the Yankee named Dixie and his unnamed companion conclude in the end. Hawthorne leaves us to wonder whether the Pyncheon curse of ill-gotten wealth and various forms of enslavement may simply be an ineradicable ori-ginal sin.[36]

Although Hawthorne certainly opposes the equation of mate-rial prosperity with "the will of Providence" (318), and his fairy-tale ending of the novel is ambiguous, he does provide a glimpse of redemption in the vitality of women and of Maulish forces who are home-based, but not home-bound. There is an "enchantment of origins" in Hawthorne, but also a disenchantment.[37] Displaced, alienated, houseless human beings have to draw strength from a home base, the mysteries of the heart, the shadows of the past, the Hades of earth-bound instinct. Yet they cannot linger there, as Clifford Pyncheon's passionate indictment of domesticity indi-cates: "The greatest possible stumbling-blocks in the path of human happiness and improvement are these heaps of bricks and stones, consolidated with mortar, or hewn timber, fastened together with spike-nails, which men painfully contrive for their own torment, and call them house and home! The soul needs air; a wide sweep and frequent change of it. Morbid influences, in a thousand-fold variety, gather about hearths, and pollute the life of households" (261). Clifford is lost, however, in a prison or in a faceless crowd in the street, if he is not invigorated by the powers of the house, the "enchantment of origins," which the women and the Maules have kept alive. Whether they can sustain it in Jaffrey Pyncheon's soulless, pretentious mansion remains uncertain. Hawthorne locates hope within human history without denying the power of the past. His ending of the story challenges us to grapple with a problem, not to consider it solved by the author or his protagonists.[38]

The Blithedale Sisters: Nature Queen and Spirit Medium

With *The Blithedale Romance*, Hawthorne turned to women characters very different from those in *The House of the Seven Gables*. But they express the same innate power, this time derived from an exotic richness of nature in one woman and from ethnic social forces, bred in poverty and neglect, in the other. As a rendering of the Brook Farm experiment, *The Blithedale Romance* is a dismal failure. This is ironic since almost all of the incidents of the novel derive, sometimes verbatim, from Hawthorne's notebook entries during his Brook Farm sojourn ten years earlier. As a psychological study of men and women trying in vain to recoup the primitive power of nature and human wholeness, the novel maintains its value today. Hawthorne never intended to mirror the actual Brook Farm, although he knew that everybody would be looking for pieces in the puzzle of a *Schlüsselroman*. Occasionally he would fool the curious: when readers begin to assume that Margaret Fuller is, at least in part, the model for Zenobia, the author lets his narrator connect Fuller's image with Priscilla (52).

Hawthorne did not join the Brook Farm community with very high ideals. He went there hoping to find a place where he could settle after marriage. When he realized that his financial investment did not bear the expected fruit and that he actually disliked farm work because it did not leave him sufficient time and strength for writing, he was disillusioned. His lifelong distrust of professional reformers was nourished by the experience, and as early as September 3, 1841, he wrote to his fiancée: "It already looks like a dream behind me," and "the real Me was never an associate of the community."[39] Hawthorne's later fictional criticism of Brook Farm is not surprising in view of Emerson's similar indictment. He had called George Ripley's experiment the hotel approach to reform, "a perpetual picnic," "a French Revolution in small; an Age of Reason in a patty-pan," an effort supported by "narrow, self-pleasing, conceited men." "They miss the fire of the moral sentiment with personal and party heats, with measureless exaggerations and the blindness that prefers some darling measure to justice and truth."[40] Neither Hawthorne nor Emerson understood in the least the positive force hidden under the ambiguous procedures of the experiment, and Hawthorne was unable to draw more than a psychological lesson from his sojourn at the farm. He turned it, however, into creative fiction, portraying an attempt at Romantic primitivism that failed.

Hawthorne may have wanted to exorcise, in his narrator Coverdale, his own feelings of failure, his preference for distanced observation instead of vital involvement.[41] The use of Coverdale as a sometimes obtuse, sometimes unreliable narrator effects the active involvement of the reader.[42] Thus Zenobia as well as Priscilla has a very different effect on different readers. "What a wicked woman Hawthorne meant Zenobia to be," suggests Marius Bewley, and D.H. Lawrence had little more than a sneer for Priscilla, "the little psychic prostitute" and "degenerate descendant of Ligeia." The sisters can also be seen in a very positive way. According to Nina Baym, Zenobia stands for creative energy of both nature and the self, while Priscilla is seen by Randall Stewart as "a woman of delicate refinement." Peter B. Murray thinks that both women are "partial people, two aspects of the feminine personality."[43]

Certainly the text does not suggest that Zenobia is "wicked," though Coverdale considers her as amoral as nature itself. Phoebe, depicted through imagery of sunshine, country butter, garden flowers, and kitchen skills, represented nature in its ethnic and domestic aspect. Zenobia, however, stands for nature as exotic beauty and irresistible life-force pressed by civilization into artificial or deadening channels. The flower in her hair is a hothouse flower, natural and "of rare beauty" but forced in its splendor (15). Zenobia, like Phoebe, is compared to Eve, but instead of the idyllic image of "Eve's bower," we find Zenobia's suggestive witticism, "As for the garb of Eden . . . I shall not assume it till after May-day!" and Coverdale's predictable reaction of imagining Zenobia in "Eve's earliest garment." "One felt an influence breathing out of her such as we might suppose to come from Eve, when she was just made, and her creator brought her to Adam, saying, 'Behold, here is a woman!' " (17). Coverdale becomes slightly disturbed when she flings away her faded hothouse flower "as unconcernedly as a village girl would throw away a faded violet" (21). His fears or doubts are echoed in the fire imagery in chapter 4 ("The Supper Table"). The "warm and radiant luxury" of the fire (23) illuminates Zenobia's nature, but this positive image is immediately qualified: the peat added to the fire bestows a "yet sultrier warmth"; the fire is "somewhat too abundant"; the "beacon-fire kindled for humanity" is just a short blaze of brushwood, and its light "will draw stragglers, just as a candle draws dorbugs" (23, 25). In the most ambiguous image of fire Zenobia is compared to a glowing Pandora, "fresh from Vulcan's workshop, and full of celestial warmth by dint of which he had tempered and moulded her" (24).

Priscilla, though often interpreted as Zenobia's opposite, is also associated with nature. Her mythic counterpart is Persephone, who shares with Aphrodite (Zenobia) her love for Adonis (Hollingsworth). Priscilla brings spring to Blithedale; the major crisis of the romance occurs in searing mid August; the story concludes with the coming of autumn and decay.[44] In each half of the book a seasonal ritual takes place, a rescue of Priscilla by Hollingsworth, once from the city tenement existence and once from Westervelt's power. Throughout most of the novel, Priscilla seems destined to be "sacrificed," but she is not merely a victim, a "leaf floating on the dark current of events" (168, cf. 171). She exhibits "wildness," "animal spirits," and stubbornness (59, 73, 78). She can even be compared to a choking vine: "A wild grape-vine, of unusual size and luxuriance, had twined and twisted itself up into the tree, and, after wreathing the entanglement of its tendrils almost around every bough, had caught hold of three or four neighboring trees, and married the whole clump with a perfectly inextricable knot of polygamy. . . . A hollow chamber of rare seclusion had been formed by the decay of some of the pine branches, which the vine had lovingly strangled with its embrace" (98).[45] At first sight it seems doubtful that this description of the vine at Coverdale's hermitage points to Priscilla, because the images of "luxuriance" and "polygamy" seem to fit Zenobia better and the passage seems to describe the intertwining fates of the two women and the other Blithedale characters. But later when Priscilla's life story is told, she is explicitly compared to a grapevine. "Out of the loneliness of her sad little existence, Priscilla's love grew, and tended upward, and twined itself perseveringly around this unseen sister; as a grape-vine might strive to clamber out of a gloomy hollow among the rocks, and embrace a young tree standing in the sunny warmth above. It was almost like worship" (186). Zenobia herself in her utter defeat calls Priscilla the "victorious one" (219). In the final scene Priscilla seems to be the protector and guardian of Hollingsworth (242).

A gradual transformation takes place in Priscilla when she comes to Blithedale. The "ghost-child" (187), the "slim and unsubstantial girl" (26), the "shadowy snow-maiden" (33), the sprite (35, 173), the plant growing on scanty soil without sunlight (50) becomes a "flowery May Queen." Her smile is "like a baby's first one," and her weaknesses and clumsy pranks are "bewitching" and "pleasant" (73–74). She is as "impressible as wax" and yet shows persistence (78); her "impalpable grace" lies "so singularly between disease and beauty" (101). She is a "gentle parasite" (123) and yet she learns to exhibit a "singular self-possession" (142). A "forlorn dove" is her image (152), and yet her experiences teach her a "remarkable decisiveness" (201). And so the "shadow-like girl," who is repeatedly described in images of melting and floating and who appears to Coverdale like a "figure in a dream," will fulfill Zenobia's grotesque, ironic prophecy: she will "melt away at my feet in a pool of ice-cold water and give me my death with a pair of wet slippers!" (33).

Zenobia's transformation is the inversion of Priscilla's. The imagery of fire in the early scenes gives way to coldness, darkness, and death in the final tragedy (227–37). The "lioness" (171), the truly "magnificent woman" whose queenliness seems to destine her for the stage (44), becomes a dethroned queen, a queen "discrowning herself" (226). The very image of natural passion and creative energy becomes, like the flower in her hair, a piece of lifeless art: "Zenobia now looked like marble" (213, cf. 235). Her power, however, is not extinguished in her death. She will haunt Hollingsworth for the rest of his life.

The images used to describe the two women overlap in many instances, even in such a trivial matter as their both being bad cooks (48, 74). Not only is Zenobia queenlike but occasionally Priscilla can be so (126, 61). Even Zenobia can be called a "sprite" (48). On one occasion Zenobia's behavior reminds Coverdale of a murderess with a concealed dagger (78), but it is Priscilla who finally causes Zenobia's death, even though innocently. Both women are blind to Hollingsworth's egotism and would give all for his love. Both show traits of Margaret Fuller: Priscilla resembles her in Coverdale's opinion (52), and most readers find an implied resemblance in Zenobia. Both women can be seen as Pandora figures. Pandora is the equivalent of the Hebrew-Christian Eve, a troublemaker. She is given to men as a punishment for the invention of fire. Zeus ordered Hephaistos to make Pandora and carry her to a place where men were sitting around their fire. So Moody sends Priscilla with Hollingsworth to the fireside at Blithedale.[46] The classical image of Pandora is that of a "shy maiden" to whom all the gods gave gifts, "silvery raiment and a broidered veil, a wonder to behold, and bright garlands of blooming flowers and a crown of gold. . . . From her, the first woman, comes the race of women, who are an evil to men, with a nature to do evil."[47] While Hawthorne directly links Pandora with Zenobia through the fire imagery, other aspects of the image—shyness, the veil, flower garlands, bringing gifts (74)—fit Priscilla.

An important image cluster uniting Zenobia and Priscilla suggests their exotic mysteriousness which can be fatal to those who come close to them. Zenobia is an "enchantress," a "witch" (45, 48), a "sorceress" (214), a serpent (170); there can be "deviltry" in her eye (59). Priscilla, too, can be "bewitching" (73, 126). She is compared to a "riddle" (35), a "Medusa" (110), a Sibyl (111), a "mystery" like her hard-to-open silk purses, and a sprite "who had haunted the rustic fireside" (35). Zenobia sees Priscilla as doomed, "whether by her own will or no," to fling a blight over her half-sister's life (115, cf. 220), and in this fatedness she resembles the lamia figures of Romantic poetry who are mysteriously victims and agents of evil at the same time. Coverdale sees her as "a little prophetess" (142). She is said to have grown up with the gift of second sight (187). When she is the Veiled Lady, anybody lifting her veil without "holy faith" is doomed (113).

There is a difference, however, in the exotic mysteriousness of the two sisters. As we see her through Coverdale's eyes, Zenobia may express the mystery of nature, and Priscilla that of the spirit. The Blithedalers fail the test of harmonizing nature and spirit.[48] The passionate, exotic nature queen looks down upon the pale ethnic seamstress who emerges from an Irish immigrant tenement, just as she looks down upon Silas Foster—his brain may be a Savoy cabbage in her opinion! (67)—who is a primitive, but very kind person (74). The whole "knot of visionary transcendentalists" (115) has joined the community to come closer to nature, but "the clods of earth . . . were never etherealized into thought. Our thoughts, on the contrary, were fast becoming cloddish" (66). Blithedale turns out to be a "masquerade, a pastoral, a counterfeit Arcadia" (21), since the members "by and large neglect Spirit,"[49] especially the spirit of true brotherhood and sisterhood. Hollingsworth and Zenobia sacrifice Priscilla to the devil Westervelt; Coverdale does not have the courage to save her. Brotherhood fails even between Coverdale and Hollingsworth. But the Blithedalers also neglect nature. Hollingsworth prefers a scheme, or a pile of money for his scheme, to either one of the women. Coverdale fantasizes about Zenobia's sex life and idly decks out Priscilla with the "fancy-work" of his imagination (100) without committing himself to either woman.

The crew of Comus represents a comically exaggerated version of the Blithedalers' attempt at primitivism. The community's outdoor revelry, which occurs just before the crisis point of the novel, highlights the theatrical aspects of its enterprise. Ironically, the clumsy, timid Coverdale, having long been absent from Blithedale, sees himself spying around the community "as craftily as the wild Indian before he makes his onset" (207). Coverdale plays at being primitive and comes upon others acting as primitives, divinities and demons. Among the crew are an Indian chief, the goddess Diana, a Bavarian broom girl, a Negro of the Jim Crow order, foresters of the Middle Ages, a woodsman, a Shaker elder, shepherds from Arcadia, a gypsy, a witch, a fiendish fiddler, and an Oriental princess. These exotic characters might seem enchanting were not Silas Foster standing by with his "look of shrewd, acrid, Yankee observation" (210). Silas realizes that the Blithedalers' efforts to achieve human brotherhood and sisterhood and to return to nature have been a masquerade. In fantasy the different sexes, races, and classes celebrate life together and are full of jollity; in real life the community members cannot see each other as equals.

The men and women at Blithedale are not blamed equally, however, for failing to harmonize nature and spirit. The men—Coverdale, Hollingsworth, and Westervelt—lack natural strength, and they see women as either nature or spirit, but never as both. The women, in all their ambiguity, harbor the primitive power which the men have denied in themselves and projected onto two different types of women. Coverdale has a faint inkling of this process at the end of the story. At the sight of Zenobia's grave he reflects on the strength of the spirit beyond death; at the sight of Priscilla at Hollingsworth's side he is amazed at her natural strength in comparison with the broken man. The images of Nature Queen and Spirit Medium, we discover, are male projections. Instead of accepting Zenobia and Priscilla as real human beings, Coverdale sexualizes one woman and etherealizes another. "As we do by this friendless girl, so shall we prosper!" says Hollingsworth when he brings Priscilla to Blithedale. Unwittingly, he pronounces his own judgment. Priscilla is a test case for all major characters in the novel[50] because she has been oppressed and needs help. Hollingsworth will not prosper as long as his admirable goal of rescuing stranded human beings does not also include treating Priscilla as an equal instead of a victim. The masque and veil imagery indicates that Priscilla and Zenobia are both used and abused under various pretenses by Moody-Fauntleroy who regarded his first wife and their daughter as mere decoration pieces (182, 192) and by Westervelt and Hollingsworth who put them in veiled bondage.

Strangely enough, all four main characters have a warped view of women. Coverdale sees Zenobia as the traditional dark lady, gorgeous and dangerous, generous and haughty. In Priscilla he finds "mysterious qualities which make her seem diaphanous with spiritual light" (129), though the story shows her to be a submissive woman of sensitive nerves much more than the spirit medium the world has made her out to be. As the Veiled Lady she may represent "New England's idealized notion of womanhood."[51] Coverdale is horrified at Hollingsworth's male chauvinism, his view that "woman is a monster . . . without man, as her acknowledged principal" (122), but his own idea that woman is a kind of "Sacred Virgin Mother" who refines sensual man through her tenderness is only the opposite absurdity (121). Zenobia's view of women is not as independent as her vitality might suggest. She is unable to free herself from the notion of "a woman's doom" (223), the belief that a woman's virtues are "merely impulsive and intuitive" (217), and the conviction that a woman's life inevitably goes "all astray" once she has swerved a hair's breadth out of the beaten track (242). Priscilla, finally, personifies Hollingsworth's ideal of a woman who feels "a deep, submissive, unquestioning reverence" for the man she loves (242).

It is significant that the vigorous discussions between the main characters of the novel on the topic of women's rights and women's nature take place under "Eliot's Pulpit" (117). When the novel nears its climax, it gains depth through some Puritan and Indian reverberations. How much Hawthorne admired the apostle Eliot becomes clear from one of his children's stories, in the collection "Grandfather's Chair." In this tale the grandfather tells his grandson, "I have sometimes doubted whether there was more then a single man, among our forefathers, who realized that an Indian possesses a mind, and a heart, and an immortal soul. That single man was John Eliot." Here Charley interrupts the grandfather with, "I would have conquered them first and then converted them." "Ah, Charley," replies the grandfather, "there spoke the very spirit of our forefathers! . . . But Mr. Eliot had a better spirit. He looked upon them as his brethren."[52] At Eliot's Pulpit, Hollingsworth preaches in such a convincing way that the skeptical Coverdale feels, "No other speech of man has ever moved me like some of those discourses" (119). And yet this is the man who will soon be exposed as an egotist, who uses women like tools for his own purposes instead of treating them as the Apostle

Eliot treated the Indians. When Hollingsworth declares that a woman acting without man as her "acknowledged principal" is an "almost impossible and hitherto imaginary monster" (122), Zenobia's "humbled" response partly gives in to his "necromancy," partly exposes him ironically: "Let man be but manly and godlike, and woman is only too ready to become to him what you say" (124). Zenobia later feels that Hollingsworth puts her on trial for life, and to Coverdale the scene looks like a Puritan witch trial (214). Under the "grim portrait of a Puritan magistrate," the queenly Zenobia is treated like a primitive witch by the same man who regards Priscilla as a defenseless maiden and collaborates in her victimization by Westervelt.

Zenobia plays the role of the Queen after whom she named herself, "not of a queen triumphant, but dethroned" (213). Zenobia of Palmyra is a splendid exotic image for Zenobia of Blithedale. The proud Arab queen, widow of Odenathus, declared herself Queen of the East in defiance of the Roman Empire. "With masculine energy she pushed forward to the frontiers of her kingdom so as to include Egypt and a large part of Asia Minor. . . . Her victorious troops . . . occupied Alexandria." She was finally defeated by Aurelian. In despair, she fled into the desert, but was . . . taken captive and led in gold chains before the chariot of the victor to grace his triumphal entry into Rome.[53] Zenobia of Blithedale is a true force of nature as well as spirit, as powerful and as defeated as her namesake. She creates herself, so to speak, by naming herself, and destroys herself, like Cleopatra, when she fails to win the love and power she desired. Priscilla, too, combines the strength of nature and spirit, but in a quiet, enduring, tenacious way. Both women are guilty of taking over the roles into which the men have cast them: amoral force of nature versus submissive spirit. The point is not that they are better than the men but that they express the power which the rational men have denied in themselves: the irrational mystery of body and soul.

Hawthorne, to his credit, does not simply take over the old stereotypes of the dark and fair lady, the exotic dangerous temptress and the ethnic spiritual redeemer, both mysterious and therefore "veiled" in different ways. In *The Blithedale Romance* he makes use of these romance elements and yet distances himself from them by various devices: by using a partly satirical, partly unreliable, and yet intelligent narrator; by fusing the allegorical traits of both women and blending the popular gossip about their pasts with their real history and behavior; and by relating their character traits to the male images projected upon them. Hawthorne thereby creates a complex web of characterization which corresponds to his use of folk superstitions and other primitive romance elements in *The Scarlet Letter* and *The House of the Seven Gables* and which invites readers to judge for themselves beyond the opinions of author and narrator. Thus in form and technique, as in narrative and imagery, Hawthorne fuses the irrational and the logical.

In all three of the Hawthorne novels we have discussed, the myth of the American Eve as either light or dark, angelic or satanic, primitively noble or primitively savage, is not discarded but employed consciously in a new way. Hawthorne shows us the dependence of these images on individual and collective prejudices and the creative or destructive power in both light and dark figures. Like the previous novels, *The Blithedale Romance* shows the impossibility of separating personal and social images and conflicts. As long as Hollingsworth is an authoritarian in his relationships with the women he pretends to love, he cannot succeed in establishing a utopian community or reforming criminals. As long as Coverdale does not give up his "Paul Pry" attitude and his aloofness toward women he either fears or adores, his presence at Blithedale cannot improve any human relationship inside or outside the community. Hawthorne expresses in a vignette, so to speak, what Melville describes on an almost cosmic plane in *Mardi:* that idealism without human sympathy and justice can destroy women and primitive people as well as the idealist himself.

Hawthorne failed to see the importance of pioneering efforts in community building, women's rights, prison reform, and other progressive movements prevalent in his time. *The Blithedale Romance* may have contributed to the negative image of "crazy" utopian reformers which the academic world harbors to this day. But his artistic portraits of men and women transcend his private prejudices. He understood on a psychological and personal level what he missed seeing on the wider social and political scene: that rationality without instinct, idealism without compassion, men without equal women (like whites without equal nonwhites) would lead to perversion and destruction. Had he understood this problem fully, he would not have written Franklin Pierce's campaign biography in the same year, 1852. The blithe romance, which Pierce and many other Americans clung to, of preserving peace and harmony without tackling the issue of justice for all did not last for many more years.

A Marble Faun and Marble Women

When in 1858 Hawthorne began to write *The Marble Faun,* he was far removed from American politics and New England reformers. The years of consulship in Liverpool lay behind him, and his residence in Italy had immersed him in the world of art and shadowy Roman ruins. Again, he felt an "enchantment of origins," a fascination with humankind's past and with mythic and instinctual powers almost lost to Western civilized men. It is not by accident that the most memorable characters in *The Marble Faun* are Donatello, a faunlike primitive person, and two women, Miriam and Hilda, very different from each other but each strong in her own way, and both showing similarities to the "faun." Donatello, the Count of Monte Beni, is a precivilized, simple-minded child of nature, surrounded by Umbrian legends, who can appear like a sylvan faun or even "the genial wine-god in his very person" (237). Hawthorne wrote in his notebook after a visit to the villa Borghese, "The faun [is] a natural and delightful link betwixt human and brute life, and with something of a divine character intermingled."[54] "Simplicity is . . . either sub- or superhuman,"[55] and thus a primitive character like Donatello can have much in common with a "divine" woman like Hilda. Before they are transformed by suffering, they are unaware of human complexity.

Kenyon, the American sculptor, is a paler figure reminiscent of Coverdale. He is a "man of marble" (411) who lives a "cold artistic life" (409). In his art he is gifted with "plastic cunning" (392), bringing his statues to life "with a word," while the actual work of chiseling is done by an assistant, "some nameless machine in human shape" (115). Kenyon is the typical American Adam who shapes his images of women and primitive people as he shapes his sculptures: the fierce Cleopatra, the imperfect faun. The point of the story is, however, that his art surpasses what the author repeatedly calls the sculptor's "fancies."[56] In private life Kenyon does not always trust Miriam and prefers not to be bothered with her confession of some dark deed, and he adores the innocent Hilda in her cool reserve; but his Cleopatra statue, the image of a passionate and enchanting woman, surpasses his conceptions of the two friends. While Kenyon lacks some "acuteness and sympathies" (270) to understand the struggle in Donatello's soul and becomes almost frantic over his failure to express in clay the image he had projected on the faunlike Count, he finally succeeds almost against his will in catching an "animal fierceness" and later, unknown to himself, "a higher and sweeter expression" in his bust of Donatello (272–73). The subconscious elements, expressed in his art and ignored in his everyday life, will in the end humanize him. They are the same irrational forces which confront him in the two women and in Donatello.

It is a romantic principle that organic beginnings in the natural world harbor a spark of divinity. Hawthorne locates this phenomenon in the realm of art: "there is an affluence of divinity in the first sketch" of a great artist (138). In the tradition of the Great Chain of Being, women were a step below men in the evolution of humankind. They were therefore in their innocence closer to divine beginnings, as were children and the "lower races." Donatello does not remain an innocent, but together with Miriam he finds, after crime and repentance, a "wayside Paradise" (435); he is guided to a "higher innocence" (283). The circular movement in which he develops is the movement of the whole novel (434). In Emerson's words,

> Line in nature is not found;
> Unit and universe are round.

Hawthorne is not as certain as Emerson that in the end evil will always bless and ice will always burn. In the imagery of *The Marble Faun*, Thorwaldsen's sculptural understanding of the clay model as Life, the plaster cast as Death, and the sculptured marble as

Resurrection (380) shows that the end is not identical with the beginning, but that it can be a transformation of the beginning into new life. Donatello, Miriam, and Hilda suffer this sea change, although in very different ways. Where the original strength of Donatello and Miriam is instinctual, Hilda's is idealistic. But from the beginning Hilda shares with Donatello a strong, childlike spirituality. "The simplest character is ever the soonest to go astray" (240), thinks Kenyon in meditating on Donatello's past. The cultural or religious simplicity of Hilda can make a person stumble as much as natural innocence, and Hilda admits this when she realizes she has failed Miriam in her greatest need (386). But her trust in the unseen makes her own "resurrection" and that of Kenyon possible. If Donatello and Hilda share, then, a certain spirituality and strong simplicity—the one in the realm of nature, the other in the realm of art and culture—there are other primitive powers germane to Donatello and Miriam.

Miriam Schaefer is an assumed name which expresses a complex character. "Miriam" may derive from the Hebrew word for "rebellion" and therefore may point to an Eve figure. But in its derivation from the Greek "Mariam" it is also considered another form of "Mary," the second Eve. This aspect is underlined by the name "Schaefer," in German, "shepherd," stressing her gentle power of commitment and sacrifice. We are introduced to Miriam as a self-assured artist who treats her admirer Donatello in a very condescending way. She regards him as a "simpleton" (7), a "child" or an "unfledged chicken" (14, 25), a perfect image of the Faun of Praxiteles. But she soon realizes that he has some advantage over her: he does not even know his age and seems to live happily outside of time, whereas Miriam is unable to shake off an oppressive past (15). Also, she realizes early a certain "bull-dog" nature in him, and the unexpected savageness in such a gentle creature makes her uneasy. But she has "a faculty of bewitching people," as Kenyon says, and so Donatello as well as the mysterious model keeps haunting her (18). "There was an ambiguity about this young lady. . . . Nobody knew anything about Miriam, either for good or evil" (20). The rumors about her past are in part "wild and romantic fables," reminding us of the dark past of Zenobia. But whether she is the heiress of a Jewish banker, a

German princess, or the offspring of an American planter with a drop of African blood in her veins, she definitely shows "a certain rich Oriental character in her face" (22). "She was a beautiful and attractive woman, but based, as it were, upon a cloud, and all surrounded with misty substance, so that the result was to render her sprite-like. . . ." Miriam's "natural language, her generosity, kindliness, and native truth of character" allow Kenyon and Hilda to receive her as a dear friend (23), but her aura of savage mystery connects her with Donatello.

More mystery surrounds Miriam than any of Hawthorne's other women figures. Whether her life before the murder of the model was innocent or not is unclear, since she is surrounded by "monstrous fictions" (33). Was the model an artist who promised to teach her an invaluable secret of old fresco painting on the condition that she return with him to his "sightless gloom" (34)? Does her artistic preoccupation with murderous Jewish heroines— Jael, Judith, Herodias—suggest a guilty past or simply a fascination with these strong characters because she is named after another Hebrew heroine (43)? Do her idealized pictures of "the bliss and suffering of womanhood" (46) point to her innocence? Why would Miriam give her life to know whether Beatrice Cenci thought herself innocent or not (67)? Why does she ask the model, "Do you imagine me a murderess? . . . You, at least, have no right to think me so!" (97). Why is the secret of her past symbolized by her in a "dark-red carbuncle—red as blood" (130)?

Without answers to these questions we can only look to Miriam's repeated assertion of her innocence before the event at the Tarpeian Rock (128, 431) and to the descriptions of her as a victim. She is compared to the historical Queen Zenobia by Kenyon when he observes her kneeling in desperation before her pursuer: "What a terrible thraldom did it suggest! . . . the nameless vagrant must then be dragging the beautiful Miriam through the streets of Rome, fettered and shackled more cruelly than any captive queen of yore following in an Emperour's triumph" (108). Both the model and Miriam herself see fate operating in their lives more than any specific wrongdoing: "We must submit" (95). "As these busts in the block of marble . . . so does our individual fate exist in the limestone of Time" (116). When Kenyon realizes that

Miriam was involved in a "mysterious and terrible event" which the world heard about, he assures her, "You were innocent. . . . I shudder at the fatality that seems to haunt your footsteps" (430).

The sense of being fated or doomed, of being acted upon instead of acting, is a characteristic trait of many women as well as primitives in fiction. But the strong women in Hawthorne's work vigorously oppose their fates. Hester steps into the market place "as if by her own free will"; she fights for custody of her child; she turns the letter of shame into a mark of triumph. She preserves some of this independent strength until the very end. Hepzibah, pitifully or heroically, fights to hold on to some dignity and love. Phoebe staves off the Pyncheon gloom and doom. Zenobia fights the mistake of her early marriage and chooses her own death rather than a life of humiliation. Priscilla achieves a "veiled happiness" against all the odds of her life. Hilda, though she may show a misguided strength in clinging to her "purity," fights the allega-tion of her involvement in a crime she did not commit.

In all these stories, however, the women first seem to see their lives as determined by fate before they begin to sense their power to shape life. In this regard Miriam and Donatello have much in common. Miriam has tried vigorously, like Zenobia, to put the past behind her. She gives up her real name, her status in society, and her wealth. She has the "freedom of thought" and "force of will" (430) to reject an ill-omened marriage which seems to have been dictated to her. Donatello is only too eager to help her achieve independence and to ignore her past (82). But his fate is determined by his identity as a primitive child of nature in modern nineteenth-century society as much as a woman's is. Donatello "must sin in order to survive,"[57] but that does not mean he cannot be held responsible for the murder of the model. No Hawthorne character can be absolved of accountability, as, for example, Miriam's model (similar to Chillingworth in *The Scarlet Letter*) would like to be. "You mistake your own will for an iron neces-sity," Miriam tells him (96). But there is a "sad fatality" (81) inherent in Donatello's originally happy life. He is an anomaly in his environment. The repeated images of a loyal dog (14, 43, 148) are complemented by those of a "fierce brute" (18), a wolf (12), and a tiger (148). His murderous thoughts before the actual killing of the model are twice articulated (91, 148). While they aggravate his deed, they are merely indicative of a natural "lack of moral severity" and the strong impulsiveness of the "lower orders of creation" to which the faun belongs (9–10). But Donatello, like Miriam, does not remain locked in a fated identity. Their instinctual power in the end is transformed into the power of commitment.

There are other resemblances between Miriam and Donatello. While Donatello is a tiger, Miriam is compared, indirectly, to a "tigress" (126) through Kenyon's magnificent statue of Cleopatra. The statue suggests Miriam's exotic origins as the Faun of Praxiteles does Donatello's. Cleopatra exhibits a "grace and dignity," a "repose of despair," and yet there is "a great smouldering furnace deep down in the woman's heart." She can "kindle a tropic fire." The sculptor has given her "full Nubian lips, and other characteristics of the Egyptian physiognomie," which fit Miriam's legendary ancestry containing "the one burning drop of African blood" (23). Donatello's mythical pedigree similarly reaches back to "the mysterious fountains of the Nile" (231). The woman "apotheosized in an indestructible material" looks "fierce, voluptuous, passionate, tender, wicked, terrible, and full of poisonous and rapturous enchantment" (127). She is "tiger-like" even in her repose, "the fossil woman of an age that produced statelier, stronger, and more passionate creatures than our own" (377). Of course, Miriam is not Cleopatra. But as a nineteenth-century woman she still harbors the passionate natural force of a fossil age or a Roman goddess, just as Donatello embodies the pristine power of the age of fauns or Etruscan knights.

The faunlike Count and Miriam also show similarities in their power of fascination, whether frightening or happy. If Miriam is bewitching (79), so is Donatello. She says, "He perplexes me— yes, and bewitches me" (82, cf. 85). Occasionally they are in dread of each other. Donatello "shudders" when he observes Miriam's paintings of the Hebrew heroines in which a fusion of "perfect womanhood" with the aspect of a "vulgar murderess" seems to be "dashed off with remarkable power" (43). After Donatello's transformation, when Miriam yearns to see him again at Monte Beni, she admits to Kenyon, "I am greatly in dread of

Donatello" (283). Momentarily, Miriam can put on the enchanted Arcadian mood of Donatello before the murder (82); she becomes a graceful nymph dancing with her faun (85).

The powers of natural beauty, mystery, rebellion, enchantment, and Arcadian joy which Donatello shares with Miriam are valued but not glorified in *The Marble Faun*. Hawthorne contemplates the defects as well as the virtues of a Golden Age. In Donatello's ancestry there lurk, besides strength, geniality, and cheerfulness, "deficiencies both of intellect and heart" (235). Donatello's and Miriam's simple passion for life and freedom gives them the joy of a sylvan dance but also brings death and sin into their life. It is the simplicity of the "inferiour tribes of being . . . mingled with . . . human intelligence" which can "partly restore what man has lost of the divine" (71). Through the fusion of intelligence and instinct Donatello and Miriam become stronger human beings.

Deficiencies of innocence and simplicity are also portrayed in Hilda. She is not at all the glorious fair woman whose purity is unequivocally praised by the author and who therefore arouses the ire of some critics. She cannot even be called a "wise" woman in terms of the biblical story of the Wise and Foolish Virgins.[58] She is simply a character limited by idealism, as Donatello is limited by passion and Miriam by a desperate drive for independence. The treatment of Hilda does not necessarily indicate a "divided loyalty" in Hawthorne[59]—the author sees light and darkness in most characters, except Satanic figures—but her strength is more allegorically drawn than Miriam's.

Hilda's initial innocence is not an Arcadian unselfconsciousness. Her "silent sympathy" is not, like Donatello's, with nature but with art. Living in Rome, she has "ceased to consider herself an original artist," (56) which is nothing admirable in Hawthorne's eyes, since he deplores the artists who "linger year after year in Italy, while their originality dies out of them, or is polished away as a barbarism" (132). She becomes a copyist of great pictures in which she unfailingly discerns the "central point" and "that evanescent and ethereal life—that flitting fragrance, as it were" (58). She achieves her acclaimed copies "not by any intellectual effort, but by this strength of heart, and this guiding light of sympathy" (57). Since Hilda is not destined, it seems, to be a

genius, she is admired by Hawthorne for not becoming the equivalent of a "female scribbler" in literature, turning out "pretty
fancies of snow and moonlight" (61), and for instead devotedly
rendering the old masters' pictures. She not only copies angels and
madonnas, however, but reproduces (from memory) the portrait
of Beatrice Cenci with such talent that Miriam calls it a "magical
picture" whose "subtle mystery" of a terrible crime has been seized
perfectly by the "innocent, delicate, white soul" of Hilda (67).

Hilda is in her own way a rather emancipated transcendentalist.
When Kenyon deplores her seeming "utterly sufficient to herself,"
Miriam partly agrees:

> It is a mistaken idea which men generally entertain, that Nature
> has made women especially prone to throw their whole being into
> what is technically called Love. We have, to say the least, no more
> necessity for it than yourselves;—only, we have nothing else to do
> with our hearts. When women have other objects in life, they are
> not apt to fall in love. I can think of many women distinguished in
> art, literature, and science—and multitudes whose hearts and
> minds find good employment, in less ostentatious ways—who lead
> high, lonely lives, and are conscious of no sacrifice, so far as your
> sex is concerned. (121)

The name "Hilda" originally meant "sharp sword" or "battle
maid," and Hilda's greatest shortcoming is her harsh judgment of
sinners. When she declares that Beatrice Cenci's doom is just,
Miriam exclaims, "Your innocence is like a sharp steel sword" (66,
384). Hilda is insensitive to the suffering of others. When Kenyon
observes Miriam's desperate kneeling before her persecutor, Hilda
thinks Miriam is just bathing her hands in the fountain water
(108). Hilda needs a sin to soften her (209), and sin comes to her
in the shape of her friends' failings. She feels implicated by her
knowledge of the crime and guilty of failing Miriam (386). She
also errs in confessing the sins of others to a priest who does not
believe that the confessions of heretics are bound to secrecy. But
Hilda is too ignorant and frightened to think about the complex-
ities of the Roman church, and her actions are not unusual for one
whose friends have committed a murder and are hiding from the
law.[60]

Hilda does change, however, and becomes a stronger, warmer woman, more critical and more understanding. The old masters still hold her attention in the picture gallery, but "they no longer warm [her] with their influence" (334). She almost turns into an "infidel" and sometimes doubts "whether the pictorial art be not altogether a delusion" (336). She no longer surrenders herself to her feelings. "She saw beauty less vividly, but felt truth, or the lack of it, more profoundly" (338). Hilda asks on her desperate pilgrimage among altars and shrines, "Why should not there be a Woman to listen to the prayers of women; a Mother in Heaven for all the motherless girls like me!" (348). Her search for the motherly side of God and for a person to entrust with the secret of her soul proves to be a healthy instinct, a sensitivity to what was lacking in her rational Protestant upbringing. When this "daughter of the Puritans" observes a young man in a church, the narrator seems to express her thoughts as well as his own: "He stood before a shrine, writhing, wringing his hands, contorting his whole frame, in an agony of remorseful recollection, but finally knelt down to weep and pray. If this youth had been a Protestant, he would have kept all that torture pent up in his heart, and let it burn there till it seared him into indifference" (347). When Hilda herself breaks down before an altar and sobs out a passionate prayer (352), a healing process begins, in spite of the foolishness of her following confession to the priest. Her pent-up emotions are released and merge with the power of her religious trust and moral fervor. "Softened out of the chillness of her virgin pride" (370), "bewitching" and "fairy-like" with a "gleam of delicate mirthfulness" (451), she can in turn release suppressed emotions in Kenyon.

Hilda's gentle power of budding life, her "delicate energy" (120), is mirrored in some of the imagery used to depict her. The early images of the tower and the dove are not altogether favorable, since the staircase to her tower reminds the narrator of Jacob's ladder *and* the Tower of Babel (53) and since the doves symbolize gentleness and purity *as well as* elusiveness and a character who has "no need of love" (121). But the latter image is simply Kenyon's projection. Similarly, the opinions connected with the picture done by a painter observing Hilda in a gallery are projections of various male viewers. Some see in her "Innocence, dying of a Bloodstain" (330); others, imagining a lady who stabbed her lover and repented the deed, see the sadness of Beatrice Cenci or "The Signorina's Vengeance" (330–31). At the end of the novel the images of Hilda include a buffalo calf that is "shy and sociable by the self-same impulse" (421), a rosebud (451, 453), and the amazing marble woman whom Kenyon finds before his reunion with Hilda.

The marble statue is a "fragmentary" woman figure, "headless," "slightly corroded," and "earth-stained" (423), a "fallen goddess" (427), an "imperial bride" (424). For Kenyon recovering the statue from the "cellar-like cavity" symbolizes a kind of mythical descent preceding rebirth. His putting the head back on the broken statue (423) is a beautiful image of what happens to him as well as Hilda; their idealism has to undergo the experience of "headlessness" before they can gain a new understanding of life. In re-membering the fossil woman he suddenly understands "Womanhood . . . without prejudice to its divinity" (424), transcending the animal fierceness of a Cleopatra as much as the tame beauty of "Maidenhood, gathering a Snowdrop" (375). The fossil power that had almost been buried under the sculptor's "plastic cunning" surfaces in his experience of "something dearer to him than his art." It is the "greater strength of a human affection" which shatters all images, even those of the "divine statue" that tumbles down before him in a heap of worthless fragments (424). Hilda's power of trust and affection releases in his "deepest consciousness" also a new trust in Miriam's innocence (431). His understanding of Donatello's fortunate fall may still reflect the abstract reasoning of a "speculative sculptor" (460)—Hilda rightly objects to his turning a joyful discovery of grace into a rational concept—but between her shocked religious sensibility and his rationalizing they have gained maturity as witnesses to Donatello's and Miriam's power of commitment.

Donatello's transformation is similar to Hilda's, but he moves in the other direction, starting with "headlessness" and reaching a "higher sense." "[A] soul had been inspired into the young Count's simplicity. . . . He now showed a far deeper sense and an intelligence that began to deal with high subjects, though in a feeble and childish way. He evinced, too, a more definite and nobler individuality" (262, 283). The change in Miriam, finally, gives her the simple loyalty, integrity, and unselfconscious devotion of Donatello's original nature, but the process is gradual. Before the murder, her strength is devoid of a spiritual element. She is a brooding pessimist (162) and a doubter. "I would give all I have or hope—my life, Oh, how freely!—for one instant of your trust in God!" she whispers to Hilda (166). She can even appear to be a cold-blooded proponent of efficiency when she reflects, like other defenders of the death penalty, on the persons thrown from the Traitor's Leap: "Innocent persons were saved by the destruc- tion of a guilty one, who deserved his doom" (170). After the murder she acts at first like a newly liberated Miltonic Eve (or, rather, Miltonic Adam),[61] suggesting that they forget their shame: "Cast it all behind you!" "Surely, it is no crime that we have committed" (175).

Miriam's exhilaration over new freedom soon turns to sober- ness, however. "Mine is the responsibility!" she exclaims in the Medici Gardens. After the crime her drive for independence is transformed into the power of dedication. Her deep commitment to Donatello comes slowly, however, and she loses her pride only gradually. When Kenyon meets her again in the "Marble Saloon" of Monte Beni, there is still a remnant of her former condescen- sion toward Donatello in her repeated declarations that she yearns to make a sacrifice of herself (280, 283), that she who beguiled him into evil "might guide him to a higher innocence," might "educate and elevate him" (286). When Donatello finally speaks her name and asks her forgiveness for his time of "strange horror and gloom" (320), she no longer talks of doing something *for* him, of sacrificing herself or educating him. She is simply human with him: "Two souls were groping for each other in the darkness of guilt and sorrow."

In the end Donatello and Miriam are penitents, but they achieve a natural, peasant-like simplicity in their "wayside Para- dise" (435). Miriam is determined not only to remain loyal to Donatello but also to set Hilda free (456). She has been described as "a high priestess of the carnival," "the mystical controlling force in the lives of all her friends," a "Prospero figure," "pure magician."[62] The comic image of a "plump and comfortable tabby cat" lying on the altar of the Pantheon "in a genial sunbeam," then raising herself and blinking in the sun "with a certain dignity and self-possession, as if conscious of representing a Saint" (458), suggests Miriam's saintly sacrifice; it also indicates her undiminished animal vitality.

The strength of Donatello and of the two women characters is indicated by the many images of marble throughout the novel. Marble can stand for eternal significance or for cold pride; for artistic splendor as well as the sculptor's rough, primordial material. Marble can imprison or petrify life as well as express it. Kenyon's marble sculpture of Hilda's hand conveys Hilda's "delicate energy" and "virgin warmth" (120). The marble Cleopatra exudes "a heat . . . which does not cool down, throughout the centuries" (127). Marble is not quite indestructible, as shown by the corroded woman figure which meant so much to Kenyon and the cracked marble urn held by the forlorn-looking nymph in the fountain at Monte Beni. In the fountain images especially, marble is associated with the natural life-force.

The fountain occurs in three different forms at important points in the narrative, and each form corresponds to a phase of Thorwaldsen's cycle of life, death, and resurrection. The first fountain is located in the court of the palace where Miriam lives, and it seems to be a symbol of her origins; the artist who may have designed it is an "unnatural father," and this could be a hint that Miriam's doom is caused by incestuous circumstances similar to those of Beatrice Cenci (38). But the fountain also symbolizes her outcome. Just as "nature takes the fountain back into her great heart" by letting moss and weeds grow over naiad and monster mouths, so Miriam and Donatello are taken back into nature's heart, Miriam by beginning to love the simplicity and matured singlemindedness of Donatello and Donatello by gaining a painful understanding of nature's dark side. "The fountain is not altogether glad" because the echoes of the forest reverberate through the centuries in its murmur (38). The second fountain is the fountain of Trevi, also "adopted" by nature, which is famous for the "native purity" of its water (145). But Miriam discovers in it her own dark shadow and the shadows of Donatello and the model. The model's mysterious attempts at ablution and Miriam's vain attempts at exorcism turn this fountain into an image of death in life. The third and last fountain is at Monte Beni. In spite of its utterly forlorn-looking nymph with the cracked urn, it is an image of hope and of an indestructible life-force. The mythical lady of the fountain is "somehow interfused throughout the gushing water. She was a fresh, cool, dewy thing, sunny and shadowy, full of pleasant little mischiefs, fitful and changeable with the whim of the moment, but yet as constant as her native stream, which kept the same gush and flow forever, while marble crumbled over and around it" (244). The water, more indestructible than even marble, is an image of the divine spring of primitive life present in the faun and in the women. Hawthorne has returned to his early image of the shattered but gushing fountain in Rappaccini's garden.

The reader who is familiar with Hawthorne's biography and notebooks will certainly wonder whether the author conceived the idea of a highly intelligent woman's relationship with a very primitive man from his knowledge of Margaret Fuller's life story. Shortly before he started working on *The Marble Faun*, the sculptor Joseph Mozier told him of Fuller's last days in Italy and of her (in Mozier's opinion) half-idiotic husband. It was a narrow-minded, mean report which was merged with Hawthorne's own prejudices. His notebook assessment of Fuller was

> the sharpest and most critical judgment he ever made on the human clay. A kind of wrath, a secret animus, surges up in his reflections on a woman who had, at least, passed for a friend and colleague. It was as if his buried animosities, his long-held prejudices against literary women and meddling reformers, and his fears about the seductions of Rome itself had surfaced. . . .
>
> Whatever Hawthorne's own, bitter, masculine prejudices, whatever the truths he managed to incorporate into his extraordinary prose recollection, he had, in spite of himself, sketched out the portrait of a difficult and vital woman—a woman more vivid and unkind, more instinct with life and passion, than he had ever quite created among his fictional heroines.[63]

The portraits of Miriam and Donatello make beautiful sense out of Hawthorne's angry puzzlement over Margaret Fuller and Count Ossoli, whether Hawthorne was conscious of it in his writing or not. Kenyon's sculptures surpassed the "fancies" of his private life; Hawthorne's women characters surpass his grudges against Fuller or any other "scribbling women." In Miriam he had, "in spite of

himself, sketched out the portrait of a difficult and vital woman
. . . instinct with life and passion" and in love with a very simple
man.

The Marble Faun represents Hawthorne's attempt to grasp the
confrontation of America and Europe. Americans always had an
ambiguous attitude toward Rome, because it seemed to corrobo-
rate the old myth of a corrupt Europe pictured in so many gothic
novels, and at the same time it had brought forth the most
astonishing works of art. Democratic Americans in the Puritan
tradition abhorred the religion, politics, and manners of Rome,
and yet they discovered the deficiencies of the New World in
getting to know the old one.[64] Hawthorne points in his novel to
a vitality in the Mediterranean psyche and an emotional power in
the Roman Catholic faith that were underdeveloped in many
Americans, especially in American men. In doing so, he does not
take over the images of the traditional femme fatale and noble-
but-dangerous savage, nor does he always reverse them. Instead,
he starts the reader thinking: Are dark, sensuous, foreign women
always temptresses and fair American ones always virtuous? Are
women in general as childlike as members of other races or ethnic
groups are supposed to be? In fusing realistic and romantic elements he establishes a rich pattern of meaning for each character
but especially for the women and the primitive faun.

Hawthorne's fascination with the "western" and the "savage"
worlds can be traced in all his works. In "The May-Pole of Merry
Mount," for example, there is an "uneasy air of savagery erupting
into civilized conditions." In *The Marble Faun*, the ultimate germ
of Hawthorne's idea may have been "the conventional western
frontier and the literary Indian . . . with whom he had identified
his youthful literary fortunes in 'The Seven Vagabonds.' " The
description of the faun statue "sounds suspiciously like an Indian,
or like an Indian trader, which perhaps explains Hawthorne's
puzzled sense of anachronism [as Kenyon expresses it], for whether
he knew it or not, the frontier disappeared some time between the
. . . writing of *The Scarlet Letter* and *The Marble Faun.* "[65] Similar
to Hawthorne's reflections on a primitive Eden are Thoreau's
argument that mankind needed the Indian and Brownson's argument that mankind needed Christ.

In Hawthorne's fiction, however, the Eden that mankind needs comprises not only American Indians or Etruscan fauns; its most important inhabitants are women. The three fair-haired maidens—Phoebe, Priscilla, and Hilda—are characterized as mediums of spirituality.[66] Personally, Hawthorne saw his wife, Sophia, as his spiritual salvation. In one of his letters he writes to her: "Thou enablest me to interpret the riddle of life, and fillest me with faith in the unseen and better land, because thou leadest me thither continually. . . . God gave you to me to be the salvation of my soul."[67] The cadences of these words are very much those of the Twenty-third Psalm. In sentimental literature women are the spiritual salvation of men, but Hawthorne does not fit into this scheme. His love letters to Sophia, though they are often mannered, self-conscious, and exaggeratedly playful, express not only spirituality but ardent passion. "Hawthorne was unwilling to think even of love in heaven as entirely divorced from physical elements."[68]

Apart from Hawthorne's life, his fictional characters speak for themselves. His dark heroines can be spiritual. Rappaccini's daughter is an image of love and trust in spite of her contamination. Hester Prynne is an angel of mercy as well as a passionate woman. Alice Pyncheon and Zenobia die in bringing about the repentance of Matthew Maule and Hollingsworth, but their passion and beauty are expressions of a spiritual force. Miriam is as much the spiritual salvation of Donatello as he is hers. Thus the dark woman progressively is a symbol of saving grace. Hawthorne's fair maidens are spiritual but not without strength and substance, especially in the later works. Phoebe in her domestic simplicity is not a mediator of religion as much as she *is* a religion. Her sunshine mentality provides security, happiness, and human warmth as ends in themselves. Even Priscilla in her clinging tenacity embodies some transcendental spirituality. Hilda is the strongest religious mediatrix, in spite of the traditional symbols that describe her nature. Rose Garfield in *Septimius Felton* is an ineffective fair heroine, but the strange Sibyl Dacy in the same work is not. She is a kind of Priscilla character in her relationship to the world of spirits and legends and, unlike Priscilla, a powerful femme fatale who can twine her "poison tendrils" (178) around Septimius. But she is also strong and emancipated like Miriam. With almost

Swiftian sarcasm she talks about the future of women (171), and when she and Septimius speculate on how they might want to spend the future centuries if they both become immortal by the elixir, Hawthorne gives us a revealing dialogue. Septimius wants to be a saint in one era and wicked in the next, because too much saintliness is "enervating and sickening." " 'Good,' said Sibyl quietly, 'and I too.' " Then Septimius protests: " 'Not so, Sibyl. I would reserve thee, good and pure, so that there may be to me the means of redemption,—some stable hold in the moral confusion that I will create around myself, whereby I shall by and by get back into order, virtue, and religion. Else all is lost, and I may become a devil, and make my own hell around me; so, Sibyl, do thou be good forever, and not fall or slip a moment. Promise me!' 'We will consider about that in some other century,' replied Sibyl, composedly" (174–75). This passage seems to contain an ironic reflection on the cliché of woman saving her man by virtue and religion so he can be wicked for a while.

Septimius, though part Indian, shares in "the customary American abhorrence for any mixture of blood" (141) and unconsciously seeks to repudiate his taint, "the wild natural blood of the Indian, the instinctive, the animal nature" (188). To this end "he exerts his rational powers excessively in order to master and control nature to achieve immortality and thereby assert the dominance of spirit (white civilized reason) over flesh (red primitive instinct)."

> In Hawthorne's view the two strains of blood represent the spontaneous joy and the restraining guilt or sorrow which characterize the extremes of the human self and in fact define the very dynamics of that self, a mixture of flesh and spirit, emotion and reason, community and isolation. In this sense, Hawthorne seems to suggest, we are all mixed bloods; and rather than attempt to negate one or the other side of our dual heritage, we ought to learn like Hester Prynne in *The Scarlet Letter* . . . , how to live between these extremities of the self, between the red man's wilderness and the white man's Boston.[69]

Wherever "red primitive instinct" is suppressed, woman is suppressed in her right to human wholeness. Septimius tries to live forever by the power of intellectual discovery instead of acknowledging his common mortality. In his Faustian pursuit, he has no room for religion or any kind of Other that he might be responsible to. In casting Sibyl as his redeemer, he deprives her as well as himself of wholeness and integrity.

Hawthorne refrains from portraying women who are strictly redemptive figures or temptresses. Fair and dark lady, sensual and spiritual—these categories cannot be neatly separated in his works. A lovely clinging vine like Priscilla might be choking, and a passionate tigress like Miriam might save a man's soul. The new American Eve in Hawthorne appears outwardly like the old—dark or fair—but the value judgments of these images are relativized and sometimes even reversed. What all his women have in common is aboriginal power.

2
Women and Savages in Melville

Typee: *Types of Savagery and Femininity in a Paradise Lost*

To turn from Hawthorne to Melville is to turn from a world distinguished by impressive, complex women characters to one teeming with an intriguing mixture of races and nations that are foreign to the average American of Western descent. There is a strange relationship between these two worlds. Just as Hawthorne's women share in some of the characteristic traits of primitive people, so Melville's exotic natives show many traits usually considered "feminine."

Black or Indian characters are only incidental to Hawthorne's main plots, and women are virtually absent from several of Melville's works. The latter fact at first sight seems to be easily explained by pointing to the masculine sea world which is Melville's main setting. But at a deeper level this explanation is unsatisfactory.

> In Conrad's similarly restricted world of shipboard, women always figure, if not actually then by inhabiting the memories of the sailors—e.g. in *Typhoon* both officers and men are always thinking what their mothers and wives at home would feel, are writing letters to them, or recalling memories of their homes and shore-leaves, so that their women-folk seem vividly present. This is never so in Melville's ship-worlds.[1]

Within Melville's largely masculine world, the characterizations of women seem disturbingly narrow at first sight. The women whom he does portray in his fiction can be as ridiculously savage as the two native queens mentioned in *Typee,* as arrogant as Mrs. Glendinning in *Pierre,* or as grotesque as Goneril in *The Confidence Man.* The "good" women seem, in contrast, to be too angelic or idealized: Fayaway in *Typee,* Yillah in *Mardi,* Lucy in *Pierre,* or Hunilla in "The Chola Widow."

Critics have been tempted to search Melville's personal life for some explanation for the dearth of women characters in his fiction and the vacillation between extreme images of the feminine. There is no proof for the contention that Melville's "sexual frustrations and religious doubts" were precipitated by his marriage. Until recently, critics saw no reason "to question [the] impression that his marriage was in the long run devoted and affectionate on both sides."[2] It is likely, however, that the marriage was in later years stressed by Melville's deteriorated physical and mental condition, probably caused by severe depression. In 1867 worried friends and relatives who deplored his lack of success and "normality" tried to persuade Lizzie Melville to separate from her "insane" husband.[3] Melville seems to have had a warm relationship with his sisters, and the personality of his somewhat overbearing mother, who had a hard time coping with genteel poverty and widowhood, cannot be the only reason that Melville "could seldom picture a woman without terror."[4] There may have been in Melville a "strain of homosexuality . . . entirely inward and subdued" which led him to see "female beauty—tender, erotic, and joy giving— . . . only in men."[5] One critic has gone so far as to assert that all of Melville's fictional women are, covertly or overtly, "toads and scorpions."[6] Melville's personal experiences on the South Sea islands may also have shaped his views on sexuality and women. He was rumored to have fathered a child during his stay on the island of Typee.[7] Whether this report was based on fact or not, Melville's sexual experiences on the South Sea islands may have made it difficult for him to adjust to the Victorian propriety of his society.

On the whole, the biographical information provides few clues for the interpretation of Melville's women characters. A careful reading of the works themselves reveals that whenever Melville described a predominantly male world, he emphasized its sterility and alienation. Whenever he portrayed something dangerous or terrifying in women, he discovered in them what he found in primitive South Sea islanders: an elusive, enchanting beauty and goodness and an unfathomable potential for cruelty. Yet he knew that these two sides of the primitive were also hidden in Western civilized males: "the primeval savageness . . . ever slumbers in human kind, civilized or uncivilized."[8] In fact, the civilized white man in *Typee* is called "the most ferocious animal on the face of the earth."[9] His savageness, however, is so smothered by civility or ideality that a good, or neutral, primeval urge can turn into a refined or monomaniacal cruelty, as in Pierre or Ahab. The Ishmael figures of Melville's fiction are searching for a lost paradise where this perversion has not taken place. They search among two kinds of human beings: primitive people of other nations and races, and women. At first, exotic women seem to be special incarnations of a paradisal world. But even in *Typee,* the earliest novel, the state of nature evokes admiration as well as horror in the observer, as do most women characters in the four novels to be discussed here. Melville did not necessarily use stereotypes when he portrayed ridiculous, ruthless, or dangerous women and evil natives. He simply knew that women as well as black slaves or South Sea natives are "better and worse than the theory of primitivism."[10] Popular sentimental novels had idealized women and savages as custodians of everything Western man had given up. Melville came closer to truth and justice when he discovered a terrifying potential in these two groups.

Typee has been considered a defense of the Noble Savage in the tradition of Rousseau or, rather, the popularizers of Rousseau. The dark and ambiguous character of the natives and Melville's rejection of primitivism in *Typee* was long overlooked.[11] More recent critics have emphasized the raw edge of horror in the idyllic Typee world, though they were not the first to discover this darker dimension. Sophia Hawthorne, in a discerning comment on the nature of *Typee,* wrote in a letter about "all this golden splendor & enchantment glowing before the dark refrain constantly brought as a background—the fear of being killed & eaten—the cannibalism in the olive tinted Apollos around him—the unfathomable mystery of their treatment of him."[12] Today, *Typee* may be seen primarily as "a rejection of primitivism," or a "testing of a Rousseauistic response to experience and the rejection of that report, not simply on the part of Tommo . . . but because it is inadequate in itself."[13]

The paradox of a modern-day paradise with its delightful and threatening dimensions is reflected in the narrator's, and Melville's, portrayal of women. Fayaway in many readers' minds is the most memorable female character in *Typee*. Though she has been typed as "a cream-puff out of sentimental novels transferred to an exotic setting" and has been considered dispensable for the novel as a whole,[14] she is still a central symbol in the work, if not a full-bodied character. She is a metaphor for the island of Typee, an expression of unspoiled nature, trustingly open to the white invader and despoiler, and cruelly forsaken whenever he has had his fill of paradise and yearns to get back to civilization to save his skin and his identity.

The novel is well under way when we are introduced to "the beauteous nymph Fayaway" (85). Her natural beauty is praised profusely. "Her full lips, when parted with a smile, disclosed teeth of a dazzling whiteness; and when her rosy mouth opened with a burst of merriment, they looked like the milkwhite seeds of the 'arta,' a fruit of the valley, which, when cleft in twain shows them reposing in rows on either side, imbedded in the red and juicy pulp" (85). Though a South Sea native, Fayaway has "strange blue eyes" which "beamed upon the beholder like stars" (86). She displays the "easy unstudied graces of a child of nature . . . breathing from infancy an atmosphere of perpetual summer, and nurtured by the simple fruits of the earth" (86). At times the imagery is sensuous in detail, as when Fayaway's delicate bands of tattooing are compared to "those stripes of gold lace worn by officers in undress," or romantic in intensity, as in the description of the women's floral decorations: "Flora was their jeweller. Sometimes they wore necklaces of small carnation flowers, strung like rubies upon a fibre of tappa, or displayed in their ears a single white bud, the stem thrust backward through the aperture, and showing in front the delicate petals folded together in a beautiful sphere, and looking like the drop of the purest pearl. Chaplets too, resembling in their arrangement the strawberry coronal worn by an English peeress . . . often crowned their temples" (87).

Fayaway is not only physically beautiful; her face is "singularly expressive of intelligence and humanity" (108). There is "tenderness in her manner" and "liveliest sympathy" for the plight of Tommo and Toby. Tommo, like any insensitive Western tourist, is in a rapture of delight when he gets permission to break a Typee taboo that prohibits women from entering canoes. This allows him to contemplate the incomparable loveliness of a Typee nymph in a canoe, smoking fragrant tobacco from a quaintly carved pipe (133). The scene ends with Fayaway shedding and spreading her robe like a sail while she stands upright like an avatar of nature in the wind-driven canoe.

Was Melville in *Typee* teasing his sisters with a story equal to those romantic novels they loved to read? Fayaway may at first seem to be a juvenile invention, but "it is a striking fact that the woman represented by Fayaway is the only woman in whose company the Ishmael-voyager rests easily."[15] Equally striking is the fact that no Fayaway figure can be found in the rest of Melville's novels. There is no other type of woman with whom the Ishmael-voyager rests easily because he does not rest easily with anybody or in anything, not because he needs a submissive Fayaway. For a short while he thinks he can find peace in nature, but soon he discovers that human beings are unable to live with unspoiled nature. Fayaway is left behind "speechless with sorrow" (250) when Tommo makes his escape from a paradise "well lost." "Modern man and Paradise are mutually destructive,"[16] and Tommo cannot escape without becoming a killer. The natural forces, however, which he kills or leaves behind, will haunt him forever.

Besides Fayaway, other women characters are expressive of nature itself, whether warmly active, lusciously beautiful, or demoniacally cruel. Tinor, mother of Kory-Kory, is a "notable house-wife," a "genuine busy-body" (84), kind and motherly. The rest of the native women do not stand out individually. They are repeatedly called "nymphs" (14, 110, 123, 131, 132, 161, 163), "mermaids" (14, 132), and "sylphs" (15); when they swim in a group they are "amphibious young creatures" who swarm around Tommo "like a shoal of dolphins" (132), and when they anoint their bodies with the greenish "tappa" to keep the skin soft and white, they look like "some vegetable in an unripe state" (182). In other words, they are part of nature, and the luscious landscape around them in turn shows feminine traits. Descriptive phrases like "the once-smiling bosom of the valley" (26) blend women and nature even more.

With the exception of the heroic (and minor) character Mrs. Pritchard, the wife of a missionary consul who refuses to let a Frenchman haul down the British flag (18–19), all the women characters in *Typee* exhibit either unabashed sexuality or demonic cruelty. The Queen of Nukuheva is portrayed with a cartoonist's flourish. Interested in the tattooing of an "old *salt*" Her Majesty "hung over the fellow, caressing him, and expressing her delight in a variety of wild exclamations and gestures. The embarrassment of the polite Gauls . . . may be easily imagined; but picture their consternation, when all at once the royal lady, eager to display the hieroglyphics on her own sweet form . . . threw up the skirts of her mantle, and revealed a sight from which the aghast Frenchmen retreated precipitately" (8). The gigantic old dowager queen of the Sandwich Islands, Kaahumanu, a woman "of nearly four hundred pounds," is even more intimidating. She "was accustomed, in some of her terrific gusts of temper, to snatch up an ordinary sized man who had offended her, and snap his spine across her knee" (186). But a Western missionary's wife gets the most sarcastic treatment in the novel. This "very lady-like personage . . . took her regular airings in a little go-cart drawn by two of the islanders, one an old grey-headed man, and the other a roguish stripling." While the old man practically does all the pulling, the lady looks about her "as magnificently as any queen driven in state to her coronation." Whenever the wheels get stuck in the sand she strikes the heavy handle of her huge fan "over the naked skull of the old savage" while the young one dodges her lashes. This "paragon of humility" (197) exemplifies the savagery of civilization.

Besides savage women, *Typee* offers many male savages with feminine traits, and they are as powerful as the women. Fayaway's beauty seems to pale beside "one of the most striking specimens of humanity" (135), a native named Marnoo. The "matchless symmetry of his form" and the "elegant outline of his figure . . . might have entitled him to the distinction of standing for the statue of the Polynesian Apollo" (135).[17] Among the many aspects of Marnoo's beauty is his cheek, which shows "feminine softness."

The narrator is so spellbound by the native's appearance that he feels like a spurned woman when Marnoo for a while does not pay the slightest attention to him. Another native, Kory-Kory, the faithful attendant given to Tommo, is feminine in doing the job of a loyal maid. He brings food and insists upon feeding Tommo "with his own hands" as if he were an infant (88). He carries the ailing Tommo on his back or bathes him, occasionally regarding him "as a froward, inexperienced child" (89). The inversion of traditional images is clear: the natives are not the helpless children which Westerners like to consider them, but, rather, controlling forces—as long as Western cannon power or alcohol has not debilitated them. If there is a weakling among the male natives he is largely a victim of civilization. King Kammehammaha III is "a fat, lazy, negro-looking blockhead, with as little character as power." His royal blood is "an extremely thick, depraved fluid; formed principally of raw fish, bad brandy, and European sweet-meats" (188–89).

The typical Noble Savage Mehevi, however, is a great chief and warrior, a powerful and harmonious combination of masculine and feminine traits. He is a bachelor who carries on various love intrigues in leisure (190, cf. 157–58). A plurality of husbands, instead of wives, is the custom in Typee valley, and "this solitary fact speaks volumes for the gentle disposition of the male population" (191). When a leech tries to heal Tommo's hurting leg, Mehevi plays a mother's role: "[U]pon the same principle which prompts an affectionate mother to hold a struggling child in a dentist's chair, [he] restrained me in his powerful grasp and actually encouraged the wretch in this inflicting of torture" (80). Mehevi's warrior's costume appears feminine from a Western perspective, with its "gaudy plumage," "enormous necklaces," ear decorations shaped like cornucopias "stuffed with freshly plucked leaves," "braided tassels," and "anklets and bracelets of curling human hair" (77–78).

Motherliness is also a trait in the "soldier-priest" Kolory, who carries around a wooden stick that is revered as the god Moa Artua. A priest in Typee shows none of the patriarchal sternness of Western religion. Kolory carries the little god "as if it were a lachrymose infant" (175). He gives it an "affectionate hug," talks to the "baby-god," "alternately fondles and chides it," shuts it up and nurses it again until it finally seems to communicate some divine message (176).

Old Marheyo, father of Kory-Kory, is likened to an English squire in his dotage (96) or to a "valiant Templar" (122). He is an eccentric (151) and a fatherly, not a feminine, type, but he has an understanding of motherhood. His most outstanding trait is his comprehension of the only two English words that Tommo teaches him, "Home" and "Mother" (248). At the moment of Tommo's direst need, just before his escape, Marheyo speaks these two words, expressing an understanding of Tommo's homesickness, and, "whether Melville so intended it or not, this is more than a sop to nineteenth-century sentimentality."[18] Marheyo realizes that Tommo must rediscover his own historical and social identity. Tommo needs primitive roots but not the exotic ones of an alien culture. He had felt the desire "to light out for the territory" (as Huck Finn put it). He had felt the urge of all American Adams to cut the feminine apron strings and to discover another frontier, but he finds out that total escape from "Home" and "Mother" brings with it a loss of power and identity.

The savage women and the feminine savages in *Typee* share a primitive strength. They are beautiful, mysterious, or frighteningly cruel. They are close to nature and therefore uninhibited, but there is something more that unites the two groups. The Typee natives are not ocean people. They hardly ever leave their homes; they do not climb the mountains around their valley; their waters are lakes or inland streams. They prize sea fish, sea salt, and seaweed, but they make only rare excursions to the ocean for these delicacies. They are representatives of land and of land values, of body more than of spirit, of safety more than of adventure. These traits of the *Typee* natives also pertain to various women characters in later Melville works.[19] The Faustian adventurer feels compelled to return to these powerful forces of the land whenever the sea of his ideals threatens to engulf him.

The similarity between primitive natives and women of all cultures is a conscious or unconscious presupposition in the popular literature of the nineteenth century, but Melville portrays both groups in a special way. The story of *Typee* is told through many different voices. "It is . . . the narrator's detached spatial imagination which allows him to see the implications which underlie the confusion of his earlier experiences. The world is seen as inherently 'wolfish' and man as essentially a savage. Civilization has succeeded only in magnifying and developing a basic savagery which is found in a less appalling form in a primitive culture."[20] The young and inexperienced Tommo escapes an unbearable situation aboard ship and tries to find Paradise in the simple, peaceful natives, the lush vegetation, and the starry eyes of Fayaway. The more mature writer, partly inventing and partly recalling Tommo's experiences, sees a deeper reality. Eventually the simple dichtomy between idyllic Typee and evil America is revealed to be as erroneous as the dichotomy between male and female. A woman, Western or Oriental, can be as strong, courageous, or cruel as any man; a man can be as gentle, beautiful, or responsive as any woman.

Melville, like Hawthorne, uses some old stereotypes which he takes over from his sources and from the popular literature of his day, but the fusion of various voices and styles in *Typee*—novel, travel report, autobiography, anthropological essay, and utopian fiction—creates something unique. Melville mingles, for example, the innocent astonishment of Tommo before the childlike worship of the Typees, "like a parcel of children playing with dolls and baby houses" (176), with the acquired knowledge of the travel writer, who can observe that the religion of the Typees, while appearing as decadent as the satirized Christian missions, expresses the same strong conviction of eternal life and temporal accountability. Thus the author rejects the common notions of nineteenth-century primitivism. By juxtaposing a gigantic native queen who beats up her subjects, a symbolic dream figure like Fayaway, a cruel missionary's wife, and a heroic consul's wife, the author asserts that women of various cultures share the same powerful traits which are usually ascribed to white men only. In placing savage culture and religion on the same level as Western civilization, he acknowledges the force and integrity of primitive communities.

Melville's point, however, is not the total relativity of all distinctions based on nation, race, sex, or religion. Rather, "the primitive ascends everlastingly, in Melville's universe."[21] Primitive strength inspires terror in the white man, and guilt over subduing it. Tommo feels this terror when he sees the ferocious expression of the native he may have murdered (252). It is the same terror which Benito Cereno will feel for the rest of his life in remembering "the negro." This terror is present in the hidden aspects of Typee valley, in some scenes of *Mardi,* and in the whale of *Moby-Dick.* But the redeeming aspect of the primitive is just as strong. Billy Budd, in some ways a primitive human being, "ascends" in his good and simple humanity, just as Pip does in *Moby-Dick* or Hunilla in "The Encantadas." There is a "destructive vigor of the primitive," as shown in "Benito Cereno,"[22] and also a mysterious power of innocence, neither of which civilized man can afford to ignore. *Typee* is Melville's first groping attempt to understand this complexity, and he does not discover it in exotic savages alone; he sees it also in women of all cultures.

Omoo: *Lure of Savagery and Return to Motherly Roots*

Before Melville portrayed the mysterious wisdom of savages like Queequeg or Pip and the ideal brightness of women like Yillah and Lucy, he described the alluring power of ignoble, perverted savagery and the hero's last-minute rescue through the forces of motherhood.

Melville's view of the Tahitians is very different from his impression of the Typee natives. Except for the first impression of Tahiti (66), *Omoo* contains none of the idyllic scenes of *Typee.* The tone of the work is one of despair, and the style of *Omoo* is a mixture of satire and comedy. It is a drifting, roving story, presumably the most autobiographical of all of Melville's works, and some critics have praised it as a collection of Dickensian character sketches. The Falstaffian rake, Dr. Long Ghost, who could have stepped right out of Dickens (or even more likely, out of Smollett), is a key to Melville's changed emotional attitude. "Under the influence of this man, the narrator's frail idealism weakens, and his despair slowly grows deeper."[23] But the narrator's temptation of opportunism among pretend-savages or of identity loss among real savages is halted by a rediscovery of human roots and relations. Getting to know a kind Tahitian family with a caring mother reawakens the memory of home and family ties.

There are various reasons for the ignoble savagery described in *Omoo*. Western civilization has so corrupted the savage of Tahiti that there is hardly anything "noble" about him. Melville is not very consistent, however, in defining the reasons behind this corruption. On the one hand, he depicts the Tahitians as totally unsuited to Christianity because they are naturally lazy, lax in principles, and childlike; on the other hand, he attributes their depravity to Western influences and contends that they were originally as good as the Typees. This double-edged point of view expresses his continuing uncertainty about the nature of primitive people, which is symbolized by the crippling disease that befell the islanders, elephantiasis. Although the Western invaders cannot be held responsible for this sickness, its slow, fatal progress and grotesque symptoms symbolize the doom of the natives more effectively than syphilis or smallpox (127–28).

The first individual in *Omoo* to arouse the narrator's horror is not a native but a "renegado from Christendom and humanity—a white man, in the South Sea girdle, and tattooed in the face. A broad blue band stretched across his face from ear to ear, and on his forehead was the taper figure of a blue shark, nothing but fins from head to tail" (27). He is an Englishman called Lem Hardy, and he represents the narrator's initial loathing for a civilized person turned primitive, an instinctive reaction echoing Tommo's horror of being tattooed. In *Typee*, tattoos frequently take the form of trees or vines; here the shark image signifies all-devouring rather than benign nature. "What an impress! Far worse than Cain's" (27), exclaims the narrator. Although the protagonist Tommo initially feels immune to this subhuman aspect of sav-agery, as the story progresses it threatens to swallow him up.

The first true savage introduced to us as a distinct individual is an ignoble primitive. It is Bembo, the harpooneer. He is a Maori, not a Polynesian. "A dark, moody savage, every body but the mate more or less distrusted or feared him. Nor were these feelings unreciprocated. . . . Hard stories too were told about him; some-thing, in particular, concerning an hereditary propensity to kill men and eat them. True, he came from a race of cannibals; but that was all that was known to a certainty" (71). As if to underline for readers of *Typee* that Bembo represents a type of savagery only hinted at but not really portrayed in the outwardly pastoral world

of Typee valley, Melville describes him as "none of your effeminate barbarians" (71). This daredevil seems intent upon destroying the crew in order "to revenge the contumely heaped upon
him" (92). A sailor had cast "some illiberal reflections on [Bem-
bo's] maternal origin" (87), and the disdain had been operating
"upon a heart irreclaimably savage" (93). Again Melville seems
uncertain whether Bembo is corrupt by nature or has been turned
into a fiend by the hate of the fellow sailors. One of Bembo's
exploits concludes with the comment, "Such a man, or devil, if
you will, was Bembo" (72).[24]

"Devils" who are at least outwardly strong can also be found
among the women of *Omoo*. One of the most colorful women is
Queen Pomaree Vahinee I, a historical figure about thirty years
old at the time of Melville's Tahiti visit and a woman famous for
her domestic fighting. In *Omoo*, she is already divorced from her
princely first husband and married to a chief of Imeeo. She is
surrounded by a licentious court. Her conjugal fidelity has been
questioned, and she, and her mother, were for a long time excom-
municated from the church. In the past, she was "always given to
display" (303). Queen Victoria gave her a crown which she wore
constantly and a chariot which was later sold to pay her debts
(303, 174). "The Tahitian princess leads her husband a hard life.
Poor fellow! he not only caught a queen, but a Tartar, when he
married her. . . . If ever there were a henpecked husband, that
man is the prince" (303). Whenever her husband displeases her,
the queen boxes his ears, whereupon he takes to the bottle. In the
vivid description of one of their marital battles, the native chief
acts as savagely as his queenly wife, but his behavior is a reaction to
hers. Other violent, male rulers are mentioned. Tammahamaha
III is an irresponsible king who causes eighteen thousand bullocks
to be slain because roving white hunters pay him a silver dollar for
each hide (211). Pomaree II, father of the wild queen, is known to
have been a debauchee and drunkard, and he is efficient in
slaughtering enemies. But none of the male kings equals in savagery the "vixen queen" (304), Pomaree Vahinee I. She acts
leniently and forbearingly in public but is a "Jezebel" in private life
(305). Her half-barbaric, half-Victorian splendor does not last
long; a pathetic figure in the end, she goes into the laundry
business (306).

As in *Typee,* female savagery is not restricted to South Sea natives. Old Mother Tot is "a shrivelled little fright of an English-woman. From New Zealand to the Sandwich Islands, she had been all over the South Seas; keeping a rude hut of entertainment for mariners, and supplying them with rum and dice" (146). Like Queen Pomaree she has a propensity for ear boxing. "By some wicked spell of hers, a patient, one-eyed little cobbler followed her about, mending shoes for white men, doing the old woman's cooking, and bearing all her abuse without grumbling. Strange to relate, a battered Bible was seldom out of his sight; and whenever he had leisure, and his mistress' back was turned, he was forever poring over it. This pious propensity used to enrage the old crone past belief; and oftentimes she boxed his ears with the book, and tried to burn it" (146–47).

In addition to these especially grotesque figures, *Typee* contains some rather shady male as well as female natives of dubious character. The comely youth Kooloo, for example, "quite a buck in his way" (157), assures the narrator of his "infinitesimally extensive" love only to sponge some clothes from him, which shortly thereafter he proudly displays in the street while not even deigning to greet his "friend." Kooloo is nothing but "sounding brass and a tinkling cymbal" (157). No more appealing than Kooloo is Arheeto, the casuist who is extremely worried about whether to keep the European or the native Sabbath (Sunday or Saturday) but does not mind asking the narrator to forge some papers that would certify him as "one of the best getters up of fine linen in all Polynesia" (165). A young girl of similar moral calibre is Miss Ideea. When asked whether she is "mickonaree" (a Christ-ian), she tells the narrator in exclamations and unmistakable gestures that only certain parts of her person and body are "mick-onaree." "The explanation terminated in a burst of laughter" (178).

While these characters are seen very critically, the narrator, Paul, is not really conscious of the alluring power inherent in their easy-going nature. He alternately criticizes them and condemns the Westerners as the source of their faults. He sees the tendency to be hypocritical as a general trait among the Tahitians. While in Miss Ideea's case it may have been induced by certain deplorable missionary tactics (179), it is also a quality "inherent in Polynesians." "It leads them to assume the most passionate interest, in matters for which they really feel little or none whatever; but in which, those whose power they dread, or whose favor they court, they believe to be at all affected" (175). In many instances the narrator tries to show the incompatibility of the natives and the missionaries. "The Tahitians can hardly ever be said to reflect: they are all impulse" (174). They are characterized by "indolence, bodily and mental," and a "constitutional voluptuousness." These are "fitted for the luxurious state of nature" in the tropics, but "the greatest possible hinderances [sic] to the strict moralities of Christianity" (175). Paul and Dr. Long Ghost, however, roving among the natives, find "the luxurious state of nature" very attractive. They are especially fascinated by the girls of Tamai, a solitary inland village. Since Western influence is hardly noticeable in Tamai, the visitors find there "the most beautiful and unsophisticated women" (234) and they beg for a performance of the Lory-Lory, the "backsliding" dance. "Bosoms heaving, hair streaming, flowers dropping, and every sparkling eye circling in what seemed a line of light," the girls abandon themselves to the spirit of the dance (241). The narrator's ironic report on the "backsliding" girls also reveals his uneasiness over the dancers' licentiousness and puzzlement over their changing moods. When the doctor, in his usual amorous mood, presses one of the girls rather hard and she gives him a sudden box on the ear, Paul reflects, "Though soft as doves in general, the ladies of Tamai are, nevertheless, flavored with a slight tincture of what we queerly enough call 'the devil' " (242).

Sentimental images of the natives are quickly punctured in *Omoo*, partly by rakish good humor and reflective bewilderment, partly by a serious consideration of the islanders' plight. But their natural simplicity remains attractive. On the whole, girls and women are characterized, as in *Typee*, by images from nature, such as "vixen" (304), "gazelles" (279), "a bud" (278), or from fairy tales, such as "nymph" (129, 259, 278), "fairies" (241), "witches" (268). Their beauty is "seducing" because they are "soft, plump, and dreamy-eyed" (129), but they are not comparable to the dream figure Fayaway. At times mischievous, the girls are described as Gypsies (255), "romps," and "wicked hoydens" (268). There is little real feeling in them (129). Some "exceedingly romantic" female figures in the novel are simply satires on popular romantic fiction (256).

The more objective view of the natives, however, does not imply a less critical stance toward Europeans and Americans. On the contrary, throughout the book, Melville considers most of the negative Tahitian attitudes and most of their deplorable condition as having been caused by Western influences. Alcohol, smallpox, and especially venereal disease spell doom for the island (191). The peculiar savagery of Queen Pomaree and her husband is possible only when Western culture is artificially and callously grafted onto the native. Grotesque and comic, they represent a confusion, rather than fusion, of the two cultures. The outlook for the natives is hopeless (192). Despair over the lost natural strength prompts the cynicism, the Swiftian satire, and the Smollettian humor in *Omoo,* and these different voices color the images of the natives and the women.

But toward the end of the novel a more positive note is sounded through the symbol of the cocoa-palm and the three mother images that follow it.[25] Just as "Home" and "Mother" are clues to Tommo's rescue in *Typee,* a sense of his own cultural roots and connection with others, especially women, is important for Paul at the end of *Omoo.* This theme, however, is implied through symbols rather than narrative and action. Although the narrator is horrified at the sight of an alienated and tattooed white man, he is close to being a lost man himself when, after his adventures with the cynical Long Ghost, he considers settling down in Tamai or applying for some office in the service of Queen Pomaree. Foreigners who do so "generally marry well; often . . . into the blood royal" (247). The hero's complacent opportunism is counteracted and subtly censured by Melville through the strong images of women and home at the end of the novel.

The first of these images is Mrs. Bell, the wife of a sugar planter and "the most beautiful white woman [Paul] ever saw in Polynesia." She is a kind of church bell or wedding bell calling the rover home. Melville points to her also as a mother image: "So, merrily may the little bells increase and multiply, and make music in the land of Imeeo" (296).[26] The second image is Arfretee, wife of Po-Po and "a right motherly body" (278). She welcomes the travel-stained strangers warmly by providing delicious food, a bath, sleep, and new (European) sailors' garments; the two are soon refreshed and come forth "like a couple of bridegrooms" (279). The third and last mother image is the whaler "Leviathan," the ship which is to take Paul away from Tahiti. She has "a sort of motherly look:—broad in the beam, flush decks, and four chubby boats hanging at the breast" (290). Paul is finally admitted on the boat as a true Yankee (314) and, with some parting gifts from his substitute mother, the "warm-hearted" Arfretee, he settles down and feels "the sailor's cradle" rocking under him" (316). Melville, of course, never makes a sentimental statement about the importance of "Mother" and "Home," but through these symbols of nurturing and affiliation he indicates the hero's need for social and historical identity and the dangers of rootlessness.

Arfretee and Po-Po together are an important symbol of life and hope in the dark, cynical world of *Omoo*. Po-Po, a positive image of a Tahitian man, is an "aristocratic-looking" islander with a "free frank air" (277), a kind of elder in the church, a man of wealth and "nearly related to a high chief" (280). He is a very generous host who refuses to accept precious foreign coins for his hospitality (315). In the worship service which the rovers attend with their host family, Po-Po is the only speaker who can keep the attention of the natives. He preaches "like the very Angel of Vengeance" (298). The missionaries have given him a ridiculous name. Jeremiah Po-Po means "Jeremiah-in-the-Dark," a substitute for his pagan name, "The Darer-of-Devils by Night" (277), but Po-Po is a prophet in the best sense, a beacon of hope. Arfretee is as noble as Po-Po. With the same generosity with which she welcomes Paul and Long Ghost, she shelters and feeds some old pauper women who seem to be victims of Western rule on the islands (279). Arfretee helps the narrator to regain his identity by giving him a new frock and cloth for a sailor's hat to take the place of his exotic turban (283). She and Po-Po also impress Paul in their role as parents. They have several lovely children, among them the "most cruelly reserved" fourteen-year-old daughter Loo, who ingeniously repulses the amorous Long Ghost with a piercing thorn (294). When Paul has witnessed the household worship in this family, he is convinced that Po-Po and Arfretee are true Christians (280).

Thus, toward the end of *Omoo* natives and women appear in a new light. A native can be trustworthy, warm-hearted, and truly

Christian. A woman can be spirited, sympathetic, generous, and faithful, and not all young girls are flirts or hypocrites like Miss Ideea.

Omoo differs from *Typee* in its preponderance of ignoble savages and a mood of anger or comic despair, instead of mingled delight and terror. The natives of Typee valley are more admirable but also more inscrutable; the natives of Tahiti are objects of anger, humor, and pity. In part, this difference is explained by the two narrators; Paul has arrived at a more objective point of view compared with the adolescent Tommo. The savages in *Omoo* do not show as many feminine traits as those in *Typee*, the New Zealander Bembo being the best example, but the impulsiveness, lack of reliability, and sensuousness in most of them are traits traditionally considered feminine. In *Omoo* many of the impressions and judgments of the two rovers are offset or corrected by other experiences, and through comedy or satire women and natives are seen with more critical distance than in *Typee*. Instead of the youthful, idealized Fayaway, we have the warm-hearted, talented mother figure Arfretee. Violent native queens are portrayed in *Omoo* as well as *Typee*, but Queen Pomaree is a more individualized character who is partly a victim of misguided British missionary zeal and French military power (306, 287). Absurd personal violence is not restricted to natives, as proven by Old Mother Tot, nor is it restricted to women, as shown by figures like Bembo and two native kings (211, 302); and the culturally legitimized violence of the Western invaders is seen as much more devastating. There may indeed be "toads and scorpions" among the women of *Typee* and *Omoo*,[27] but there is as much male viciousness.

Three basic attitudes toward natives and women come under scrutiny in *Omoo*. The first two are those of Doctor Long Ghost and of Lem Hardy, both individualistic Adam figures without social ties and with an obscure past (12, 27). Long Ghost's attitude is based on the principle: sample and enjoy them, then move on. Lem Hardy's stance toward the natives is rather: give up your identity, imitate them, marry them. Like a "Napoleon" he vanquishes some tribes by military power, brings others to his feet, and then accepts "the exquisitely tattooed hand" of a native princess (27–28). The third attitude is that taken by irresponsible representatives of government and church; it is based on the principle:

convert them to your side, fit them into your system, or, in some sad instances, annihilate them (24, 122, 124). This stance applies not only to natives in general but also to women. For example, a military intervention can start simply through "the seizure of a number of women from the shore, by men belonging to one of the French vessels of war" (124), and a religious conversion of native "handmaidens" can quickly lead to immorality among the priests (142). Each of these basic attitudes violates the integrity of persons as well as cultures. As in Hawthorne, the personal and social realms are interrelated. The narrator Paul experiences the fate of the natives himself; he is alienated from his roots, among his shipmates as well as the Tahitians. Under Long Ghost's influence he almost becomes a Lem Hardy, trying together with the Doctor to find employment in the service of the Queen (247–48, 284). This attempt could have led to a marriage "into the blood royal" (247). Many Western men like Lem Hardy have provided a kind of maid service to some "cannibal majesty" (247) and ended up as members of a tribe. Such personal opportunism is as damaging to individual identity and integrity as the governments' and the churches' drive for power.

Jeremiah Po-Po and Arfretee are important reminders of the family ties and social integrity which Paul has neglected. They are the true primitives, in contrast to natives like Pomaree or her debauched father who are more perverted than primitive. Ethnic identity is lacking in the sailors as well as the islanders of *Omoo*. A healthy male-female relationship is also impossible, for loss of roots implies loss of branches, namely, sexual and social ties which have revitalizing power. The savages and the women in *Omoo* teach the narrator about the "primitive and enduring nature" of humankind, and Melville portrays this lost power, "sinking to the most primitive and forgotten, returning to the origin and bringing something back, seeking the beginning and the end."[28]

Mardi: *Whirlpool of the Primitive and Lure of the Ideal*

In *Mardi* the rootless hero who uses women and savages for his own purposes is not allowed to return to some "Home" or "Mother."

He propels himself into the ocean of his ideals, unable to recognize the true powers in his life: savages haunting him as a murderer and two women whose identities confuse him, one appealing to his sensual nature, the other the object of his quest as knightly savior and suitor.

Time would solve the riddle of *Mardi,* Melville predicted when the reviews were not very favorable. Various attempts have been made to unriddle *Mardi.* Merrell Davis sought to decode the flower symbolism. H. Bruce Franklin made use of solar myth and saw Taji as a Whistonian comet. Mildred Travis, employing Greek mythology, saw Yillah and Hautia as two aspects of Venus. Maxine Moore ventured an elaborate interpretation making use of an almanac, astrology, and Tarot cards. Carolyn Karcher and Joyce Sparer Adler contributed important insights into Melville's views on race and war in *Mardi.* [29] The riddle is still partly unsolved, but critics recognize the boldness of the endeavor in spite of its many flaws. Especially in comparison with *Redburn, Mardi* did not strike the readers of Melville's time as a "sensible" book. But in its non-sense lies its very meaning, since it expresses Melville's restlessness and near despair over his impression that "heaven hath no roof," that there is "no humanly available, operative resting place to the absolute, no final cosmic order or Truth."[30] *Mardi* offers some evidence, however, that there is indeed a heaven, even though without roof, and a truth, though one that cannot be formulated but only lived. The extensive social satire in *Mardi* would not be possible without the conviction that ultimate values exist, and the narrative illustrates Melville's belief that man has to merge his primitive drives and instincts with his ideal longings into an active concern for love and justice. Otherwise he will perish heroically like the isolated Taji who considers himself "his own soul's emperor" (654).

According to *Mardi,* the merging of the primitive and the ideal can happen only when the woman and the savage are seen as they are, and cease to be viewed through the prejudices and preconceptions of the white man. Love or fear of the exotic Other can lead to a loss of reality. "Though in your dreams you may hie to the uttermost Orient, yet all the while you abide where you are" (370). Women and savages in *Mardi* are in part male projections of oriental dream figures or nightmare images, and man can come to his senses only when he gives up fantasizing about them and starts opening his heart to justice and reality, like the converted King Media (630, 649, 653).

Mardi consists of three main parts. The first includes the rather factual story of the narrator's clandestine desertion of the ship *Arcturion* with his Viking friend Jarl, their life on the *Chamois*, and their meeting of the Polynesian couple Samoa and Annatoo on the *Parki*. The second part describes the quest of the narrator (who from chapter 54 on calls himself Taji) for the fair maiden Yillah, starting with the murder of Aleema, the old man who held her in bondage, and the story of Taji's haunting by the sensuous Hautia and her heralds and by Aleema's avengers. This part takes place in the symbolic world of Mardi, a group of South Sea islands. The third and longest part (121 chapters compared to 38 and 36 for the two previous parts) is the story of the philosopher Babbalanja and his discussions with the poet Yoomi, the historian Mohi, and King Media, who rules the kingdom of Odo in Mardi. Although the bulk of the book is devoted to the development of the philosopher and king, it is ostensibly Taji's story.[31] Taji's relationships to the primitive people around him and to the two women Yillah and Hautia are just as important as Media's and Babbalanja's opinions on Taji's quest and on the social problems they encounter in travelling through the isles. King Donjalolo's or King Uhia's relationship to women, for example, as well as the oppression of serfs and war captives in Odo or slaves in Southern Vivenza, mirror conditions in civilized countries on which Melville comments satirically. Taji's story in the first two parts and the philosophical and political reflections in the third part are relevant to our consideration of women and exotics.

The first primitive character with whom Taji (not yet having assumed that name) has a close relationship is Jarl, a Scandinavian sailor. He is an old Viking without the piratical tendency of the mythical Norsemen, possibly a "descendant of heroes and kings" (12). He is illiterate but honest, true, and simple in his loving devotion to the narrator (13). Jarl is "a King for a Comrade" (11), and the king imagery from this point on shapes *Mardi* in various ways. Jarl may have taken the narrator "for one of the House of Hanover in disguise; or, haply, for bonneted Charles Edward the Pretender" (14). This imagery ties in with the many descriptions of island kings who are mentioned later in the story. Thus the problem of *Mardi* can be summed up in Blaise Pascal's words: "What it is to be a king and what to be a man."[32] For Melville, very primitive human beings like Jarl can represent the essence of kingship, and a civilized person like Taji, who gets "royal" treatment from Jarl and pretends to be a half-deity expecting worship from superstitious islanders (165), fails the test of true kingship, because he lacks a sense of commitment beyond his rather selfish quest.

Jarl combines male and female characteristics. He is "laundress and tailor" for his friend (14). He always keeps busy "like an old lady knitting," and he keeps track of time "like an experienced old-wife" by carving a notch on one of the oars for every set sun (46, 43). He unravels old hose and darns frocks. He is superstitious (18, 57) and, on account of his taciturnity, inscrutable. But the narrator is certain that he is "nothing of an idealist; an aerial architect; a constructor of flying buttresses." His ruminations cannot possibly be "Manfred-like and exalted" (36). The remark obliquely suggests that the narrator himself carries the germs of a Byronic Manfred in his personality.

Jarl is sober enough not to idolize Yillah, as do both the narrator and Samoa. For the royal Viking, she is just "a sort of intruder, an Amonite Syren" (147). Jarl wears a tattoo on his arm of a crucified Christ figure which Yillah admires intensely (147), and his attitude is often one of "Samaritan charity" (15). On the other hand, Jarl can be "bold as a lion" (66). He is an experienced whale hunter whose favorite weapon is a harpoon (58). His tragic end is foreshadowed in the image of Belshazzar (64)[33] and in the narrator's grimly facetious contemplation of their common future: "I used to look upon the Skyeman with humorous complacency. If we fall in with cannibals, thought I, then, ready-roasted Norseman that thou art, shall I survive to mourn thee; at least, during the period I revolve upon the spit" (34). Though the narrator shows a degree of self-criticism in owning up to his own complacency, he is not self-critical enough to see how much he takes advantage of Jarl's devotion and how he mingles admiration and condescension in his repeated use of the phrase, "my Viking."

Although Taji shows little true appreciation of Jarl's basic humanity, at the one point when he should have been harsh with him, he sees him as a hero. Jarl has a low opinion of Annatoo's capabilities at sea (101), although she has repeatedly proven her courage, determination, and fair ability to steer the boat (71, 78, 101), but mostly he detests her lustfulness, her pilfering, her lack of reliability, and her cooking. In a fit of rage he suggests they dump her into the ocean (115). Of course, the narrator is too civilized for such action. But shortly thereafter when Jarl accidentally kills Annatoo in trying to cut down the mast during a sudden storm, he feels no horror and offers no rebuke. Instead, the narrator comments that the men owe their survival to "my own royal Viking our saviour" (117). Annatoo is swallowed up in a whirlpool unmourned, but in the next chapter the narrator gives us an elaborate account of the death of the *Parki*, because to a seaman a ship is "a creature of thoughts and fancies, instinct with life. . . . I have loved ships, as I have loved men" (120). The reader wonders.

Taji is far along on his quest for Yillah when he hears the news that Aleema's revenge-hungry sons have killed Jarl. "Slain for me! my soul sobbed out," is Taji's immediate reaction (364). But when Media and Babbalanja persuade him to "seek the living, not the dead," he does not even try to recover Jarl's body, nor does he admit that his search for Yillah is hopeless and irresponsible (365). The Neptune image of Jarl (127) is the key to his true nature: "Taji's ambiguous description . . . renders a false image of Jarl, whether we see him as the loyal and sincerely devoted old chummy or as the dull-witted victim of Taji's cleverness. Once recognized as the figure of Neptune . . . Jarl is perceived as deep, subtle, moody, capable of cruelty and violence yet basically without malice, a personification of the ocean itself. Taji fails to recognize the sea god . . . mistaking his chummy for a jovial uncle."[34]

Taji is even more insensitive to the death of the savage Samoa than he is to Jarl's. In his relationship to both men, Taji shows a lack of conscience and fellow feeling. Samoa is another primitive figure, much more savage than Jarl, who commands almost royal attention. He "had long followed the sea and was well versed in the business of oyster diving. . . . The native Lahineese on board were immediately subordinate to him" (68). Samoa greets Taji and Jarl "bravely as the Cid." He is a tall, dark islander with a "clear, firm voice," "a very devil to behold, theatrically arrayed in kilt and turban" (66).

Though manly enough, nay an obelisk in stature, the savage was far from being sentimentally prepossessing. Be not alarmed; but he wore his knife in the lobe of his dexter ear. . . .

The middle cartilage of his nose was slightly pendant, peaked, and Gothic, and perforated with a hole; in which, like a Newfoundland dog carrying a cane, Samoa sported a trinket: a well polished nail. (98)

This description brings to mind a passage from "Benito Cereno," which sums up Captain Delano's ignorant and superficial relationship to black people: "Captain Delano took to negroes, not philanthropically, but genially, just as other men to Newfoundland dogs."[35] The narrator of *Mardi* is not as naive as Delano, but in spite of his sophistication he treats savages with a mixture of admiration and indulgence, as one might treat inferiors in rank or pets. Upon meeting Samoa he comments, "I was pleased with him. Nor could I avoid congratulating myself, upon having fallen in with a hero, who in various ways, could not fail of proving exceedingly useful" (98). Samoa is the quintessential savage, combining angelic and devilish features which are expressed in his grotesque tattooing, "his marks embracing but a vertical half of his person, from crown to sole; the other side being free from the slightest stain. Thus clapped together, as it were, he looked like a union of the unmatched moieties of two distinct beings" (99). Samoa is credited, however, with having "a soul in his eye."

With grotesque humor, we are told how Samoa, with the help of Annatoo, amputates his own wounded arm and then proceeds to hang the dead arm, wrapped well to keep away fowl and fish, from the topmast-stay. The narrator asks himself: "Now, which was Samoa? The dead man swinging high as Haman? Or the living trunk below. . . . For myself, I ever regarded Samoa as but a large fragment of a man, not a man complete" (78). The reference to Haman is derogatory, since the devilish figure of the Book of Esther is unlike Samoa, who is savage by nature and upbringing but without evil intention. The comment on Samoa as a fragment of a man will later prove to be ironic, because it is Taji himself who will end up as a fragment of a whole man, a monomaniac.

The narrator repeatedly uses biblical imagery in a very clumsy way, and by this device Melville depicts Taji's imperceptiveness. When the priest Aleema, on the boat that carries his three sons and Yillah, raises his musket in fear of an attack by the *Chamois*, Taji reports that Aleema menaced them "with the fate of the great braggart of Gath. But I quickly knocked down the muzzle of his musket, and forbade the slightest token of hostility" (128). This reference to the story of David and Goliath is ironic because later the narrator acts like a Goliath in overcoming Aleema through sheer physical force and bragging that he would slay him again if it would bring back the lost Yillah (423). Aleema, on the other hand, becomes a kind of powerful David. His ghost keeps haunting Taji throughout the cosmos, destroying him in a much more ultimate way than Taji destroyed Aleema. In Melville's universe, "the strong arm . . . is no argument, though it overcomes all logic" (319).

Taji is like Aleema in another way, though he is not aware of the likeness. Aleema, in his view, is the benighted, cruel heathen who wants to sacrifice an innocent girl to some imagined god, whereas he considers himself the enlightened, courageous knight who wants to save her. Taji does show a limited self-criticism when he asks himself whether his rash action was actually motivated by the selfish desire for a beautiful young woman. "But throttling the thought," he reports, "I swore to be gay. Am I not rescuing the maiden? Let them go down who withstand me" (135). He does not realize that he, like Aleema, puts Yillah in a kind of bondage. Aleema sacrificed her to a primitive religious principle; Taji sacrifices her to his narrow ideals.

The portrait of Annatoo is likewise colored by the narrator's prejudices. Her story is certainly not the misogynist comic interlude that it appears to be on the surface. Rather, "Samoa's and Annatoo's story is an inverted burlesque of the story of Taji and Yillah, placed on a physical and mundane level which hovers between, and never reaches, either hilarity or pathos."[36] Annatoo, like Yillah, has been kidnapped as a young girl (68, 157). Both die in the sea. Annatoo is a caricature of Yillah. She is dark and bawdy whereas Yillah is fair and chaste. Both women lead their men in a constant chase, and both think of themselves as irresistible (147, 114). The narrator regards these traits as typically female (101, 147). He also reiterates that "tired joke, the Riddle of the Female"[37] in ironic comments like "Marvellous Annatoo! who shall expound thee?" (102). Certainly in Annatoo Melville

also caricatures many traits of Hautia, since Hautia represents
nothing but the dark side of Taji's fixed image of woman. Annatoo
often coils herself away "like a garter-snake under a stone" (102).
She is sexually aggressive (114) and is described mainly in images
from myth and nature; she is called Pandora (91), Cleopatra (69),
a "tragedy queen" (75), a fury (107), a termagant (81), a Tartar
(75), a tigress (90), an inscrutable penguin (102), a "Load-Stone
Rock sailing by which a stout ship fell to pieces" (92).

Though Taji is astonished at Samoa's henpecked condition, he
too is under the sway of a woman, or, rather, two women. In his
quest he acts only under the compulsion of Yillah and Hautia.
Samoa, in contrast, is "not wholly to be enslaved" by Annatoo
(84). Taji makes fun of Samoa and Annatoo for coming to terms
in their stormy married life (84), yet Taji in his relentless quest
sacrifices friends to abstract goals. In facetiously calling Samoa's
marriage to Annatoo a suicide (69), the narrator unwittingly
foreshadows his own suicidal quest for Yillah.

Yillah and Hautia are projections of Taji's mind. His pursuit of
an ideal is embodied in the conventional form of a male pursuing a
female. But the two women are also fictional characters like any
other female figures in Melville's work, and they have concrete as
well as mythical features.

Although the narrator has not even seen Yillah when he decides to rescue her, he has been told that she is beautiful. The idea
of being the saving knight appeals to him. He realizes that virtue
and the selfish desire to possess a beautiful girl are hopelessly
mixed in him (135). Having conquered the maiden by becoming a
killer and an inventor of elaborate lies (140, 142), he makes some
rather racist comments which show that his fixed notions of
women resemble his ideas of savages. He is certain that Aleema's
sons are unable to pursue him on the water because to him all
savages are alike, tied to the land and unacquainted with the sea.
"Let the Oregon Indian through brush, bramble and brier, hunt
his enemy's trail, far over the mountains and down in the vales;
comes he to the water, he snuffs idly in air" (141). When Yillah
keeps inquiring about Aleema, her liberator suggests, "Think not
of him, sweet Yillah. . . . Look on me. Am I not white like
yourself? Behold, though since quitting Oroolia the sun has dyed
my cheek, am I not even as you? Am I brown like the dusky

Aleema?" (142) He then invents the details of a common child-hood with Yillah. The narrator, even before pretending to be Taji, the sun god, is a fake-exotic character who plays the primitive. Confronted with Annatoo's contempt earlier, he had wondered whether "perhaps women are less apt to be impressed by a preten-tious demeanor, than men" (92); but in order to conquer Yillah, who possesses only limited critical faculties (158), he makes use of an enormous pretence. He tells her, falsely, that they are sailing toward Oroolia, while telling his companions that he wants to voyage to the island Tedaides, when in fact he wants to avoid land altogether to enjoy gliding around with Yillah. "Was not Yillah my shore and my grove? my meadow, my mead, my soft shady vine, and my arbor?" (145)

Yillah seems to lack substance. She represents mostly what the men in the story wish her to be. She is an idol for Samoa and the narrator, and a siren to Jarl (147). To Mohi she seems to offer long life, to Media (before his conversion) health and wealth, to Babbalanja the ultimate of beatitude (651). But at the time of their departure from Serenia, Babbalanja tells his friends that Taji is searching for a phantom and should give up the hunt (637–38). Taji sees Yillah strictly in conventional romantic terms: "Of her beauty say I nothing. It was that of a crystal lake in a fathomless wood: all light and shade; full of fleeting revealings; now shadowed in depths; now sunny in dimples; but all sparkling and shifting, and blending together. But her wild beauty was a vail [sic] to things more strange" (152).

The romantic mystery maiden, however, gains reality as a victim of two would-be liberators, one savage and one civilized. Yillah is not a complete dupe. She gradually realizes that her lover and rescuer is not a god, or even a half-deity, but a mortal. This recognition leads her to cling even more closely to him. In the end she knows that the whirlpool of which Aleema spoke remains her destiny (159). For a while, happiness overcomes those forebod-ings: "We lived and we loved." But the whirlpool image keeps haunting Yillah (189), until she disappears.

During the rest of Taji's story, Yillah's powerful influence over Taji is expressed through Hautia. Indeed, the distinction between Hautia and Yillah begins to blur. The fair, victimized maiden corresponds to the dark temptress; the "black damsels," images of sensuality, have something in common with Arabian houris. Hautia's messengers, who pelt Taji with symbolic flowers, correspond to Aleema's avengers who not only serve to underline Taji's criminality but also personify his conscience and guilt and thereby add to his ambiguous humanity.[38] Likewise, Hautia's messengers are an expression of Taji's conscience and consciousness of Yillah's fate. The messengers' flowers are very specific symbols; they describe especially Hautia's alluring nature.[39] But Taji does not yet give in to Hautia's temptations. He abhors her (643). He "vaguely . . . began to fear her" at one of the messengers' early visits, although in the end he insists, "I fear thee not; but instinct makes me hate thee" (640). Only after Hautia persuades Taji that through her Yillah could possibly be found does he give in to her (641). As he enters her "bower," she is more clearly than before a Spenserian Acrasia. Although Taji sees her as a "vipress" and "shining monster" (653), as a lure to find the ideal Yillah, she is irresistible to him. "Thus we stood: snake and victim: life ebbing out from me to her" (652). He plunges for pearls at her behest and turns into his own "spirit's phantom's phantom" (653). His words seem to come from the planets because he is condemned to an eternal circularity of questing without hope.[40]

Woman, then, is not the paradise she was expected to be, the "Last Lost Hope of Man" (651), just as primitive man is not the ideal to whom civilized man can turn to find a remnant of Eden. "In some mysterious way seemed Hautia and Yillah connected" (643), just as noble and evil savage are inseparable. Taji thinks he steers clear of low sensuality when he resists Hautia, not realizing that his sensuality was already involved when he first desired Yillah and slew Aleema to possess her. He is not a man denying experience and sensuality in favor of ideality.[41] His sensuality is involved in his relationship to both women. He persuades himself that only ideal virtue impels him, but he actually uses both women to emphasize his virtue, saving the one and resisting the other, just as he used Jarl and Samoa for his purposes. While adoring one woman and abhorring the other, he only gradually becomes conscious of their real power.

Taji's story is not the whole of *Mardi*. While his heart hardens "like flint" (639), King Media, in the third part of the novel, is softened by his experience in the kingdom of Serenia.

King Media at first has a relationship to primitive natives and women that is similar to Taji's. Media is an interesting variation in Melville's portraits of South Sea islanders. The narrator describes him as a genial Epicurean who is a gracious host, treats his servants and subjects as slaves (173, 191), thinks of himself as a half-deity (176), and acts as authoritarian as Belshazzar when he judges on the bench (182). He overlooks the dire poverty of the common serfs in his kingdom, "war-captives held in bondage" (191), whose dwellings in ravines are hidden from the sight of the more comfortable citizens. In keeping with his complacent attitude toward these poor ethnics is his opinion of women. He compares a good wife to a good pipe, "a friend and companion for life. And whoso weds with a pipe, is no longer a bachelor" (376).

Media, however, becomes more and more sensitive, partly under the influence of Babbalanja's wise babbling but primarily through his wide travels which culminate in his visit to Serenia. What he dreams in a nightmare (565) becomes reality: an insurrection takes place in his kingdom. But he does not flee from his responsibilities. When the raging mob calls upon him to renounce his rule, "through the tumult Media sailed serene," convinced that "among all noble souls, in tempest-time, the headmost man last flies the wreck" (654). Sadly, Media's troubles are caused, like the deaths of Jarl, Samoa, and Aleema, by Taji's irresponsibility; Aleema's sons are in the forefront of the sedition (653). Media's opinion of woman also changes. No longer does he encourage Taji's chase. "Yillah is behind thee, not before. Deep she dwells in blue Serenia's groves, which thou would'st not search. Hautia mocks thee; away!" (649)

Media thus puts Taji in critical perspective. There is, of course, no unqualified acceptance or rejection of any principle or idea in Melville's "ironic diagram."[42] Taji is not merely a fumbling, conceited character without a real understanding of woman or savage. Just as Ahab in *Moby-Dick* is admired in spite of his monomaniacal ambition, Taji's quest commands some respect and sympathy. Especially the chapter "Dreams" brings us close to Taji and gives us an understanding of his inability to drop the quest (366). However, seen in the context of all the island kings he visits and all the wisdom which Babbalanja, Mohi, and Yoomy share with him, limited though their perspective may be, Melville's critical stance toward him is very clear.

The kings, like Taji, are unable to balance the instinctive power of the primitive with the conscious shaping of the mind. Donjalolo, deprived of freedom by his ancestors, becomes effeminate and "self-hugged" in the midst of his thirty wives, who are nothing but pleasure objects to him (217–44). Uhia lives only for ambition and future power and gives up all sensuality for this uncertain goal (275). Jolly old Lord Borabolla lives mostly for food and drink (290). King Abrazza sees only what is pleasant and congenial; so he pities the slaves in his kingdom instead of helping them (589). The Pontiff Hivohitee cultivates "the power of quenching human life with a wish" (334). In Southern Vivenza, generations of slaves are having their souls bred out of them "as the instinct of scent is killed in pointers" (532). The tribe of Hamo is denied the freedom that other citizens enjoy (513). The imperialistic King Bello loves to take control of faraway people, whom he considers barbarous. The natives of these countries, for example, in Vivenza, in turn oppress the aboriginal people still living in their midst and push them off their land remorselessly (468). The similarities to the treatment of blacks and Indians in the United States and to England's treatment of its colonies are obvious in these examples. None of these individuals or groups knows how to merge primitive instinct and moral sense to achieve a state of personal wholeness and social responsibility.

Mardi is unified by images of fratricide and war. Taji is associated with Cain. Wars are always fought for the benefit of "kings."[43] In this male world of subjugation and exploitation might makes right in sexual as in social relations. The failures in the world of *Mardi* lie not only in the individual and the societal realm but also in the link between the two realms, namely, marriage. Critics have often been puzzled by Melville's broad mockery of marriage and praise of bachelorhood in *Mardi*,[44] especially since the author was newly married when he wrote the book. But Melville's view of women (and of marriage and bachelorhood) cannot be understood without discerning the various voices of his narrators and the degree of ironic distancing achieved by them. There are obvious caricatures of marriage in *Mardi*: the stormy married life of Samoa and Annatoo; the wedding ceremony in Mondoldo in which the groom gets a flowery cord with a great stone attached to it around his neck, and the connection of this wedding with a funeral (320–21); the testament of old Bardianna

in which he bequeathes to the woman Pesti, who used to pester
him with her wish to marry him, only his blessing and to a spinster,
who seems to have respected his bachelorhood, his possessions
(583). Media, Babbalanja, Yoomi, Mohi, and Jarl are bachelors,
and there are occasional comments on the advantages of this
status (376, 585, 607), but none of these figures expresses Melville's opinion simply. In fact, throughout Melville's work, the
bachelor is seen with a very critical eye because he often "shuns
real commitment" or "shuts his eyes to evil and pain."[45] Possibly
Melville knew the extremely popular book by Donald Grant
Mitchell, *Reveries of a Bachelor* (1850) and was partly imitating,
partly parodying his sentimentalities in *Mardi* and especially in "I
and my Chimney."[46] The jolly bachelors in *Mardi* who eat, drink,
smoke, travel, and philosophize at leisure are on a life voyage as
chartless and senseless as Taji's. Only Media comes to recognize
their predicament. When he tells Taji that Yillah can only be
found in Serenia (649), he implies that love and marriage cannot
be separated from the loving commitment of all to all which finds
expression in Serenia. Even the primitive Samoa is wiser in
matters of marriage than the sophisticated Taji, for he not only
manages to live with the "Tartar" Annatoo but defends her
bravely before those who hate her (115). Thus the caricature of a
primitive marriage is a truer picture of marriage than the sentimental romance of the fake sun-god, Taji, and his kidnap victim, Yillah.

The many South Sea natives described in *Mardi* are no representatives of a remnant paradise. They imitate or mirror the vices
of civilized people. These savages are not likely to fall into Taji's
error, to extol the subjective, abstract ideal over the primitive
power of social relations, to search for Eden among exotic people
and in unreal women. Many of the exotic primitive people in
Mardi, just like the women, remain shadowy figures, but their
shadows still express the unquenchable, haunting power of nature.

Pierre: *The Good and the Bad Angel Exchange Roles*

In *Typee*, Melville describes an exotic paradise inhabited by a
lovely, innocent Eve figure. The hero does not quite fit into this

world; he has to leave it to save his life. Woman and country are too primitive for the Western sailor. In *Omoo*, the narrator gets to know male and female savages so well that he realizes they are as ambiguous as civilized characters. He is no longer awed by the primitive world, especially primitive women. He feels neither admiration nor fear in it, but he does not feel at home either. From the real South Sea world Melville shifts to the exotic world of the mind in *Mardi*. The women Yillah and Hautia, both primitive in different ways, are creations of the narrator's subconscious, yet they are still projected into the real exotic world. In *Moby-Dick,* Melville shows that the primitive exists in the heart and mind of Western man as well as the savage, but his setting is still the exotic ocean world, and women hardly appear on the scene. In *Pierre,* however, he locates the primitive in the mind of the hero and the two women with whom his destiny is interwoven while staying within the civilized American world, first rural and then urban. In both women, Lucy and Isabel, Pierre finds a primitive strength— Isabel has it by nature, Lucy acquires it by faith—but their power turns out to be his damnation instead of his salvation. Since he is unable to see either Lucy or Isabel as what they really are, and they are unable to see themselves, the three characters ruin each other. Lucy, the conventional bride, turns into a Christ figure, but her powerful presence drives Pierre to murder his cousin. Isabel, the angelic, victimized sister, becomes the jealous temptress when she is treated more like a wife than a sister, and provides the poison for their joint suicide.

In *Pierre* Melville no longer seeks to show that the exotic noble savage is no more noble or more savage than the civilized person. Instead he shows that the civilized man who believes in an exotic nobleness within himself or within women is bound to find only ambiguity in both. There is something exotically idyllic about the world of Saddle Meadows in which Pierre grows up and something exotically indigent about the bohemian world of the Apostles in which he dies. Both, however, are part of the Western civilized world which Melville wants to strip of its cultural veneer to expose "the primitive and enduring nature of man."[47] He locates primitive nature primarily in women, and if it appears frightening in them, it is because women usually have been considered primitive only in the sense of being more passive, more emotional, and less intelligent than men.

Melville, like Hawthorne, starts out with conventional stereotypes, the angelic fair lady and the dark temptress; the bad foreign, "French" spirit (exemplified by Isabel's mother, the French influence on Pierre's and Isabel's father as well as later on Glen Stanly) and the orderly, "natural" world of Saddle Meadows. The mock-romantic and mock-heroic tone of the first chapters, however, immediately indicates that traditional values are being devalued and finally "transmogrified," as are their opposites, Pierre's subjective counter-values of rebellion and bohemian chivalry.[48]

Pierre has grown up with all the clichés of a superficially pastoral world. "Love is profane" in young men, he tells his "angel" Lucy, "since it mortally reaches toward the heaven in ye" (4). Pierre's cultural notions are mostly derived from his queenly mother, a widow who is affluent, haughty, kept beautiful by "unfluctuating rank, health, and wealth," and "never worn by sordid cares." A true storybook character, she is an "unattainable being" to her suitors and appears "pedestalled" to her admiring son (5). But an inkling of her demonic character is contained in the statement, "litheness had not yet completely uncoiled itself from her waist" (3). Later snake imagery is connected with Isabel and Pierre. That mother and son feel as close to each other as sister and brother is a fact that foreshadows Pierre's tragedy of substituting a "sister-wife" for the "mother-sister." Their closeness also precludes a healthy relationship between Pierre and Lucy since Lucy accommodates herself to the conventions in which his mother trained him and according to which she tolerates her. Lucy is no rival of the mother but a lovely submissive addition to the family, "beautiful, and reverential, and most docile" (20).

When Lucy is first introduced, mainly through the eyes of Pierre and Mrs. Glendinning, she is depicted as a simple fair maid. As Pierre's bride-to-be she is the blue-eyed girl with cheeks "tinted with the most delicate white and red, the white predominating," blue eyes which "some god brought down from heaven," hair like Danae's "spangled with Jove's shower," her teeth "dived for in the Persian Sea" (24). "Her own natural angelhood" (26) is described in mock-romantic tones satirizing the sentimental novels of Melville's day.[49] She is a "sweet linnet," born and raised in the city but each springtime ildly longing for the verdure of the countryside

(26). Her simplicity, however, does not preclude her partaking of that "veil of mystery" attributed to most sentimental heroines, that "infinite starry nebulousness" (36). The mention of this trait anticipates Lucy's later transformation from a figure of primitive pastoralism to one of primitive Christianity.

Neither Mrs. Glendinning nor Pierre really knows Lucy at the beginning of the story. Mrs. Glendinning ranges her and Pierre among the healthy, animal-like beings whom Pierre's father saw as his ideal: "as the noblest colts, in three points—abundant hair, swelling chest, and sweet docility—should resemble a fine woman, so should a noble youth" (20). Comparing herself to "a quart decanter of . . . potent Port," she patronizingly describes "The Little Lucy" as "a very pretty little Pale Sherry pint-decanter of a girl" (60). The imagery surrounding Lucy in the early chapters serves two purposes. She is the proverbial beautiful girl whose virgin purity is reflected in a "spotless bed" with a "snow-white, ruffled roll" (39), skin like "rosy snow," and a "white, blue-ribboned dress" (58). Her characterization as a "heavenly fleece"—"fleecy Lucy" is fleecily invested in her flowing white dress (58–59)—points ahead to her role as a sacrificial victim. In fact, Pierre cruelly puns on her being "fitted for the altar" when he reveals to her that he is "married" (183). Whiteness is, of course, freighted with symbolic meaning in Melville's work. White and red are the only colors that appear in each of the works, but white is used much more frequently than red.[50] Lucy's whiteness on the surface represents proverbial purity and is seen ironically; on the symbolic level it points to divine mystery.

When Pierre receives the fateful letter from Isabel, he thinks that a good angel bids him read the note whatever may be the consequence and that a bad angel tells him to destroy it and be happy (63). Although he does not indicate whether these angels are only the voices of his conscience or stand for real people, Isabel, who wrote the letter, could only be on the side of the good angel, and Lucy, as Pierre perceives her, would stand for the bad one. Their roles will be startlingly reversed later when Isabel declares herself to be Pierre's dark angel and Lucy, who appears to Isabel in a dream, to be—at least for a time—his good one (314). When Pierre casts his lot with Isabel, he is ignorant of Lucy's deeper nature. He does not consider sharing his dilemma with her because a traditional goddess seems ill-fitted to advise him in his crisis of discovering a neglected, illegitimate stepsister. "Like an algebraist, for the real Lucy he, in his scheming thoughts, had substituted but a sign—some empty x" (181).

If Lucy appears to Pierre like a virgin goddess or an algebraic sign, Isabel's primitive nature arouses the deepest longings in him. She embodies the fulfillment of his heroic ideal to "engage in a mortal combat on a sweet sister's behalf" (7). Her mournful face reminds him of the lonely "primeval pine-tree" (40) which he passes by at the river bank, and it makes him aware of having been shielded from all deeper grief by his pastoral surroundings. "Ever hovering between Tartarean misery and Paradisaic beauty; such faces, compounded so of hell and heaven, overthrow in us all foregone persuasions, and make us wondering children in this world again" (43).

Pierre falls in love with an idea and a face, not with a real human being. He is pierced as by a "Delphic shriek" (48) when Isabel sees him for the first time. Something that is savage and primordial in his being had gone untapped in his upbringing and is aroused by the primitive mysteriousness of Isabel's face and voice. Isabel stands for the heart; " 'tis God's anointed" (91). Mrs. Glendinning and Lucy, the latter at least before her crisis of losing Pierre to Isabel, do not like a mystery or a secret (47, 37), and they stand for the head. What appears to Pierre as an ideal Madonna's face (48), haunts Lucy as a "fixed basilisk" (37). The snake images connected with Mrs. Glendinning extend to Isabel and eventually to Pierre by the time he and Isabel have "coiled together, and entangledly stood mute" (192). Martha, Lucy's maid, calls Pierre a "reptile" when he causes Lucy to swoon (200).[51]

As a primitive character Isabel is distinguished by a preference for silence. The whole novel is filled with references to silence as a kind of primeval ground of being. "All profound things . . . are preceded and attended by silence" (204). Isabel is almost an incarnation of this silence in the eyes of Pierre, but, oddly, she has to tell her own story and can do so only with repeated silences, incoherences, and dreamlike phantasies. "She is drowning . . . in her unconscious."[52] "So mysterious [am I to] myself," she tells Pierre, "the air and the earth are unutterable to me; no word have I to express them" (273–74). She is primitive in her passivity and malleability. "Thy hand is the caster's ladle, Pierre, which holds me entirely fluid. Into thy forms and slightest moods of thought, thou pourest me; and I there solidify to that form . . . till once more thou moldest me anew" (324). She is childlike and describes herself as a child: "I have always been, and feel that I must always continue to be a child, though I should grow to three score years and ten" (148). She speaks a childlike language, occasionally without using a personal pronoun for herself: "If thou hast lost aught for me; then eternally is Isabel lost to Isabel" (190). Like a primitive pagan, she dares the sun to prove the truth: "Bleach these locks snow-white, thou sun! if I have any thought to re-proach thee, Pierre" (190). Isabel does not have much individual identity and she does not want any, either. "I pray for peace—for motionlessness—for the feeling of myself, as of some plant, absorbing life without seeking it, and existing without individual sensation. I feel that there can be no perfect peace in individual-ness" (119). She has not been taught about God and does not know the difference between vice and virtue (123, 274). The utter mystery of her life is expressed in the symbol of her mother's guitar, a womb image. It is her only mark of identity because she discovers her name engraved inside it. The sounds of the guitar cast a spell upon Pierre, but they express only "Isabel and Mystery!" (126, 150). They veil the person of Isabel as her ebon hair veils her body (324, 145). She is "hair-shrouded" (126), an image that antici-pates her and Pierre's death when she falls upon his heart; "her long hair ran over him, and arbored him in ebon vines" (362). Her character changes, however, in the course of the novel. As soon as Lucy appears at the Apostles, Isabel feels jealousy. She becomes less the mysterious heroine of romance and more the simple-minded girl with a need for emotional security.

Two other women play a role in the lives of Pierre, Lucy and Isabel: proud Mrs. Glendinning and Delly, the simple farmer's daughter who bears a child out of wedlock and is cast off from society. The dignity of Mrs. Glendinning lacks a genuine basis. She assumes the mien of an ancient queen or goddess, but her seemingly primitive strength is actually a pretension and perver-sion. Various queen mother and divinity images are used in Books i–iv. Mrs. Glendinning gives an "Assyrian toss" to her head (15); she exhibits the "Semiramian pride of woman" (89); the "heavenly evanescence" of her motherly love is "further etherealized in the filial breast" (16); and yet "her stately beauty had ever somewhat martial in it" (20). Even the land which she owns is described as a queen attended by her lady's maids, the seasons (13). She is also associated with the Queen of Heaven. Mrs. Glendinning's name is Mary, and she is the "lovely, immaculate mother" (88), not only a "beautiful saint," but a "gentle lady-counsellor and confessor" (89). Pierre calls her "Sister Mary," and he can celebrate an almost sacramental breakfast with her or lavish loving attention on her ritual of dressing up. The image of a divine and virtuous queen is thoroughly shattered and supplanted by the reality of a narrow-minded, selfish woman whose aristocratic pretensions blind her to the needs of an outcast like Delly Ulver. In revulsion at her pride Pierre resolves to be "impious," to tear all veils from all idols (66). Mrs. Glendinning is driven mad by her son's rebellion and makes sure that Pierre's whole inheritance goes to his cousin Glen Stanly. As if exhausted from this violent act of vengeance, she dies (285).

Delly Ulver, by contrast, is a genuinely primitive woman. Poor, uneducated, helpless, rejected, she gives birth to a child and sees it die soon after. The victim of a heartless society, she inspires Pierre to come to the rescue of her unprotected girlhood. In her passive loyalty she is a shadow image of Isabel's sensuous nature. Her muteness (315, 361) corresponds to Isabel's silences. In her unpretentious humanity she is more likeable than Isabel (315, 321). She fears that she will end up in the hands of villains if Isabel and Pierre are not really man and wife (321). Presumably she becomes another victim of Pierre's idealism.

Pierre's image of Isabel changes gradually. After he has lived with her for a while, she is no longer all in all for him. He is engrossed in writing and brooding. He loses interest in her intellectually because of her inarticulateness. He finally realizes that the ungraspable phantom of life is not in Isabel but in himself. "He is Narcissus plunging to embrace his own image."[53] Isabel is a symbol for Pierre's creativity, first his inspiration and then his despair, and he finds his relationship to his own creativity to be incestuous, sterile, destructive—fiction, not truth. Isabel's silence is therefore a fitting expression for his inability to become a creative writer.[54]

When Lucy re-enters the scene as a potential savior, she is changed in herself and she will change Isabel even before the two have met. Both Pierre and Isabel are struck with fear when Lucy's letter arrives (312). Isabel's jealousy is aroused instantly. Now she is the woman who seems concerned about the world's opinion: "Doth not the world know me for thy wife? She shall not come! 'Twere a foul blot on thee and me. . . . One look from me shall murder her, Pierre!" (313). Ironically, at this point Isabel becomes as violent in her thoughts against Lucy as Mrs. Glendinning was in her rage against Pierre's liaison with Isabel: "Oh, viper! had I thee now in me, I would be a suicide and a murderer with one blow!" (194). In contrast to Isabel, who is concerned with appearances, the formerly conventional Lucy is now the one to defy public and private opinion. She declares, "I must come! God himself can not stay me, for it is He that commands me.—I know that all will follow my flight to thee; my amazed mother, my enraged brothers, the whole taunting and despising world" (311).

At least one critic has pointed to the influence of the Apocalypse and the Gospels on *Pierre;* by this interpretation Lucy is the New Jerusalem, Isabel is Babylon, and Pierre is the Christ of the Gospels and of the Apocalypse.[55] While these identifications are too narrow, Lucy's emphatic "I am coming to thee, Pierre, and quickly" is in its context reminiscent of the Apocalypse, and various other phrases she uses suggest her role as a Jesus figure: "Thou art my mother and my brothers." "Thou *art* my Pierre." "[I am] vowed to dwell with thee forever."[56] While early in the story Isabel had told Pierre, "Thy catching nobleness unsexes me" (160), so Lucy now is sure she can serve Pierre as his mystery "wife" without sexual involvement, with "nun-like" devotion, because she believes in his "own calm, sublime heaven of heroism" (310). Lucy fits in well with the idealistic Apostles. Her primitive romanticism gives way to a peculiar notion of primitive Christianity. While the Apostles are as childlike as Charlie Millthorpe or as coldly relativistic as Plotinus Plinlimmon, Lucy is utterly committed, although her commitment may be based on the desire to control Pierre.

Isabel has no choice; she has to let Lucy come. She has dreamt of her as Pierre's good angel and feels herself to be "thy other angel, Pierre. Look: see these eyes,—this hair—nay, this cheek;

all dark, dark, dark,—and she—the blue-eyed—the fair-haired—oh, once the red-cheeked!" (314). Isabel becomes conventionally primitive in typing herself as the bad dark heroine, invested with "funerealness." "Oh, God! that I had been born with blue eyes and fair hair! Those make the livery of heaven!" (314). But she wants to outdo Lucy in her altruism: "The Bad angel shall tend the Good . . . her considerateness to me shall be outdone by mine to her" (315).

Lucy shows an inflexible resolve and quiet wisdom in her attitude toward her mother. Mrs. Tartan is simply a Mrs. Glendinning in a narrower, more bourgeois way. When Lucy insists on living with Pierre and Isabel in their bohemian abode, she confronts her mother with such fortitude that Pierre as well as Isabel stand in awe of her. She even seems to command the sounds of Isabel's guitar, and Isabel is so overwhelmed that she falls on her knees before Lucy "without evidence of voluntary will" (328). This experience does not keep her, however, from petty jealousies later (333–34).

While Lucy can at times be the truly good angel—her nearness once again inspires in Pierre faith in the presence of a God (317)—she also finally resembles Pierre in her primitive absolutism. Isabel had helped Pierre escape the shackling illusions of the life at Saddle Meadows, an artificial Typee world in which he existed as a kind of well-bred, magnificent, tame horse (20, 22, 31), but she becomes the insecure, immature, jealous sister-wife. Although Lucy has the potential to save Pierre after loss and illness have matured her, under the circumstances of her life with Pierre as well as Isabel her actions are necessarily doomed. She is another Fool of Virtue, like Pierre. She resembles a marble statue "as if her body indeed were the temple of God, and marble indeed were the only fit material for so holy a shrine" (328). The "supernatural whiteness" of this marble temple is as ambiguous as the white and marble images surrounding Hawthorne's Hilda.

Thus to Pierre both Isabel and Lucy become "pale ghosts," "for Pierre is neuter now" (360). Neither the catnip (Lucy) nor the amaranth (Isabel), neither "man's earthly household peace" nor "the ever-encroaching appetite for God" (345), neither land woman nor sea woman, can save the titan from himself. Lucy becomes too ethereal to physically withstand the shock of learning the truth about Pierre and Isabel. Isabel, whose face for Pierre had been one that "might turn white marble into mother's milk" (189), turns out to be a deadly presence: "Wife or sister, saint or fiend! . . . in thy breasts, life for infants lodgeth not, but death-milk for thee and me!" (360).

The simplistic types of the dark lady and fair lady in *Pierre*, which have their origin in Pierre's narcissistic mind,[57] reveal the primitive core of man as well as woman. If the female seems more primitive, more mysterious, more childlike, and more passive than the male, then these traits simply reflect man's own hidden primitive nature, a savageness which civilization and titanic endeavor have polished or buried alive. Because woman's domestic role has kept her away from many processes of civilization, her primitive origin is easier to discover. Melville realized that it takes a narcissistic male mind like Pierre's to project man's heavenly aspirations and hellish desires on woman. But he also knew that behind the sentimental illusions of Good Angel and Bad Angel there lurked a primeval reality that had to be unearthed and revealed as neither male nor female but human.

Throughout the novel, Melville uses images of the American Indian to suggest Pierre's own primitiveness. His great-grandfather was mortally wounded and "unhorsed" in an Indian battle (5). His grandfather, the famous general, killed Indians "by making reciprocal bludgeons of their heads" (30). Pierre is often reminded of this grandfather and his battles; even at the Apostles he sleeps in the general's camp-bedstead and wears his military cloak (301). As Pierre sinks more and more into poverty and despair, the author compares him to a "Texas Camanche" [sic], who "goes crashing like a wild deer through the green underbrush. I hear his glorious whoop of savage and untamable health; and then I look in at Pierre. If physical, practical unreason make the savage, which is he?" (302). Pierre wears Indian moccasins at the Apostles (303). The probing of his mind is compared to "following the Indian trail from the open plain into the dark thickets" (84). He is also compared to a frontiersman seized by wild Indians (307).

Pierre is primitive in other ways. In his darkest hours he is described as a baby toddler (305). In moments of confidence he wants to "gospelize the world anew" (273). He has even been compared to "a sophomoric Ahab" or, when he becomes the murderer of his cousin, to the Indian-hater in *The Confidence Man*.[58] Pierre is also given exotic traits. He inherited his father's exotic interest in a "dangerous" French (or part French) woman. Among the bohemian Apostles he appears as "a strange exotic" (271). He "mines" into his savage nature. The cruelness of "some dark hope forlorn . . . makes a savage of a man" (20), and what absorbs Pierre's time and effort at the Apostles is not so much his book but "the primitive elementalizing of the strange stuff, which . . . has upheaved and upgushed in his soul" (304). For Pierre, as for Taji, Ahab, and the Indian-hater, there is no Emersonian way out; evil will not always bless, and ice will not always burn.[59] Pierre tries to solve the mystery of iniquity by turning to the primitive forces of his own being and by drawing on those of Isabel and Lucy. He does not solve the mystery but experiences its silent terror.

By laying bare the primitive impulses of a man like Pierre, Melville shows the primitiveness ascribed to women to be an underlying universal potential in all human beings. "That irrespective, darting majesty of humanity . . . can be majestical and menacing in woman as in man" (160). To Melville, in times as dark as those in which he wrote *Pierre*, even God may appear as a savage, as he did to Fred Tartan at the sight of his sister's dead body: "Oh, my God, my God! Thou scalpest me with this sight" (362). Savageness need not be satanic; it may reveal divine power, inscrutable and irresistible.[60] In Pierre, however, it is perverted into wrongheaded idealism, incestuous desire, and murder.

The Tales: Eloquent Silences Among the Voiceless

A better understanding of Melville's female characters, and their relative scarcity and inarticulateness, can be gained by considering his treatment of blacks. This issue has been discussed with special intensity in reference to "Benito Cereno."

"Benito Cereno" has often proved embarrassing to critics. Traditionally, the apparent embodiment of good in the Spanish captain and evil in the African crew and its leader Babo has been called "unfortunate."[61] Recent critics, however, have read the story in totally different ways. They emphasize that Melville did not pretend to speak for the blacks but dramatized the fact that their voice had not been heard.[62] They point to Melville's portrayal of the damage which oppression inflicts on the oppressor and the merging of the identities of victim and oppressor. Delano, for example, grinds his foot into the prostrate Babo. The court impersonally sanctions the original enslavement of the blacks, seeing only the whites as victims.[63] "Benito Cereno," to many readers in our day, is not primarily the story of a slave revolt but the story of a white racist mind.[64]

We are given only "edited" versions of black characters in the story, the impressions of Delano or Benito Cereno or the court. Even when the legal records state repeatedly that "the negroes have said it" and therefore Don Benito cannot be wrong (346),[65] we do not know with what pride or defiance or under what pressure an individual black may have made certain statements. "The negroes" do not count individually, and their collective witness is important only insofar as it corroborates the statements of a white person.

Captain Delano's racial prejudices are the expressions of a "long-benighted mind" (328). In Babo he sees a "rude face," reminding him of "a shepherd's dog" (261), a "pleasing body servant" of "steady good conduct" (263). Some of the blacks, who actually play their parts with tremendous sophistication, look to him like "organ-grinders . . . stupidly intent on their work" (273). For those who get into little hassles he recommends the Protestant work ethic: "keep all your blacks employed . . . no matter at what useless task" (273). He offers Benito fifty doubloons for Babo, as though he were a commodity. Now and then he speaks "a blithe word to the negroes" (290). To him, whites "by nature" are "the shrewder race." The blacks would be "too stupid" to plot a rebellion with Benito, and besides, "who ever heard of a white so far a renegade as to apostatize from his very species almost, by leaguing in against it with negroes?" (295). Of his provisions, he would like to give soft bread, sugar, and bottled cider to whites only (302). His mind employs all the typical stereotypes. Blacks are "sight-loving" (302), fitted "for avocations about one's person," "natural valets and hair-dressers; taking to the comb and brush congenially as to the castanets". They are of an "easy cheerfulness . . . as though God had set the whole negro to some pleasant tune" (306). Babo's shrewd use of a Spanish flag as a shaving apron is taken by Delano as a sign of "the African love of bright colors and fine shows" (307). Though Delano has a "long-benighted mind" (328), he thinks himself very open-minded. Observing the steward Francesco (an ingenious plotter, as it turns out later) he thinks that mulattoes with European features are wrongly considered as devilish, that the addition of white blood cannot have a bad effect on character (314).

Don Benito's image of the blacks is less naive than Captain Delano's but no more accurate. While horror and suffering have taught him all about the abyss of evil in human beings, his court deposition and his later conversations with Delano show that he is unable to discern the cause of the blacks' ferocity. While he reports that the slaves wanted nothing more than to be transported to some African country to gain their freedom, he does not say a word about the evil of slavery which is perpetuated by the court with the implied consent of both captains. Benito's frequent references to "Providence" (351), to "God and his angels" (344), and to prayers and votive offerings (338, 348), and also the imagery that connects him with the Emperor Charles V,[66] indicate that for church, state, court, and gentleman captain the black is equally an "invisible man," without legal identity, voice, or support. A pregnant image at the climax of the narrative is that of Don Benito holding on to Captain Delano's hand "across the black's body" (325).

Another side of Delano's "long-benighted mind" is revealed in his view of black women. As he leers through the ship's rigging at a slumbering negress "with youthful limbs carelessly disposed," he likens her to a doe with a "wide-awake fawn" at her "lapped breasts" and meditates with satisfaction: "There's naked nature, now; pure tenderness and love." As he observes other negresses, he feels "gratified" that they appear "unsophisticated as leopardesses; loving as doves," and even capable of making "capital soldiers" (318). These are the same women who are later described as hardly restrainable in their readiness to have the whites tortured and murdered while they solemnly dance and sing highly inflammatory songs (346).

Thus Delano projects his own naiveté and his animal drives

onto the blacks. The slaves are physically the losers in the story, but their elemental power and instinctual drive for freedom are contrasted with the pale weakness of Benito Cereno and the moral obtuseness of Delano. The black women, even more than the men, represent the unquenchable force of nature, but not the idyllic nature that Delano takes refuge in, a serene, charming sunset scene behind the "chained figure of the black" (324).

The silent, "unabashed" look of Babo's impaled head ends the story. Don Alexandro's skeleton is considered to be proof of barbarism, but the impaling of Babo's head is supposed to be part of "civilization."[67] Don Benito refuses to see Babo in court, and the slave is an invisible and inaudible man to those who are not acquainted with the "recesses" of such a person's mind (351). But Melville pays tribute to the superior brain in his small, insignificant body, just as he pays tribute to the "royal spirit" of the silent Atufal (277). There are innumerable references to silence in the story, but Babo's final silence is the most powerful: "Since I cannot do deeds, I will not speak words" (352).

As a figure of strength, Babo can be seen as a kind of Malcolm X or Nat Turner with all the attributes of a tragic hero. "But he could not be cast in such a role from a New World or an Old World perspective, and in Melville's time the Third World lacked an adequate voice or a significant vote."[68] In the 1850s, the world not only lacked an adequate voice for blacks and other nonwhite groups; it also lacked a voice for women. It was heard in public debates on women's rights, but rarely did it take shape in a fictional character that transcended stereotypes. Hawthorne's women are an exception, and Melville's strength lay more in the description of ethnic and exotic characters than of women. Yet the many silences of Isabel and the "mute wooing" of Lucy speak as eloquently as Babo's or Atufal's silence or the ritual dancing and chanting of the slave women on the San Dominick.

In "The Tartarus of Maids," the ominous silence belongs to an entire group of victims, the exploited women workers in a paper mill. "Not a syllable was breathed. Nothing was heard but the low, steady overruling hum of the iron animals. The human voice was banished from the spot. Machinery—that vaunted slave of humanity—here stood menially served by human beings, who served mutely and cringingly as the slave serves the Sultan" (202).

"The Tartarus of Maids" was written in 1851 when Melville's wife was pregnant with their second child. The story's pervasive allusions to sexual organs, gestation, and birth in a world of icy storms, steaming chimneys, and colossal wheels driven by a "Blood River" create a grotesque atmosphere. It is the one story by Melville in which the characterization of women at first sight seems to lack any image of power. Like none of the other stories, it points to the doom of a technological world in which men, having lost their vital powers, no longer search for those powers in women or other "underdeveloped" people. The loss seems total for both sexes. The countryside around the Devil's Dungeon paper mill looks "like one petrifaction" (197). The cause of doom is not the machine itself; it is a man, "Old Bach," a dark-complexioned bachelor who employs only unmarried women—married ones "are apt to be off-and-on too much" (210)—and exploits them twelve hours every day. "Rude, manger-like receptacles" are arranged around the room, "and up to these mangers, like so many mares haltered to the rack, stood rows of girls. . . . The air swam with the fine, poisonous particles, which from all sides darted, subtile-ly, as motes in sunbeams, into the lungs" (203–4).[69] The seeds-man-narrator and the factory guide "Cupid" have to cough in the stifling air, but the "girls," as the women workers are pointedly called, "are used to it." "So, through consumptive pallors of this blank, raggy life, go these white girls to death" (205).

The women, however, are never totally lifeless. "Slowly, mournfully, beseechingly, yet unresistingly, they gleamed along, their agony dimly outlined on the imperfect paper, like the print of the tormented face on the handkerchief of Saint Veronica" (209). The "girls" are not automatons but human beings reminding the narrator of the sufferings of Christ. "Agony" and a "tormented face" suggest an intense struggle and, hence, life. The women are part of the "inscrutable nature" to which the seedsman rushes back after he narrowly escapes deadly frostbite and the "metallic ne-cessity" of precision machines (211).

Melville the artist scatters in this story the seeds of his message very directly. He implies in the last sentence that a Tartarus of Maids is directly related to a Paradise of Bachelors. The bachelors' discarded London shirts may provide the rags for the pale girls in the factory (204). Melville foresaw the interdependence of rich and poor people on a shrinking globe, and he realized in this story that sexual issues are significantly involved in the global intercourse of exploitation. What he objects to in the Paradise of Bachelors is not the unmarried status of the men but the mindless Epicureanism that refuses to recognize suffering and need, and instead seeks enjoyment at the expense of some "natives" or some women. The bachelor was a convenient metaphor because the sentimental literature of Melville's time abounded in romantic reveries of pipe-smoking bachelors at comfortable hearthsides. They were "vampires of sensibility, lacking vitality of their own and especially equipped to tap that of others." Melville may have had in mind not only such bachelors but their male sentimental authors as well when he has his seedsman write "Cupid" on a piece of paper and then watch the word emerge half-faded from the girl-tended machine. "The sentimental author was dependent on female suffering for his material just as he was dependent on female readers for his livelihood, but he resented and subtly tried to reverse this subjugation."[70] "The Paradise" and "The Tartarus" appeared in the year before the publication of *Pierre,* the work in which Melville would try to write "Cupid" on paper, imitating as well as satirizing male writers who exploit female readers and portraying a "bachelor" who drives two women to madness and death.

The grim picture which Melville drew of factory life was true to the conditions of the day. Between 1830 and 1860 innumerable young women were employed in the mill towns of New England. The women left their families in order to gain financial independence, get their parents out of debt, or send a brother to college. They frequently lived in substandard boarding houses built by the company. There was a turnover rate of 40 percent of the labor force at some mills, and reformers charged that the women often went home to die. In the 1830s women went on strike in large numbers to protest wage cuts. In 1845 the women dominated the Ten-Hour-Movement that demanded shorter working hours. After 1845 the mills attracted increasing numbers of Irish immigrants. Whether Melville had ethnic, foreign women or Yankee women in mind, his nightmarish tale of a paper mill contained such realistic details as the seventy-two-hour work week, the sexual division of labor (men holding all supervisory positions and women tending the machines), and the health hazards of lint-polluted air. Ten years after "The Tartarus of Maids," Rachel Harding Davis was to write *Life in the Iron Mills,* but few writers before her thought of portraying the life of women working in factories. Melville as a common sailor had seen "the world of nineteenth-century American society and its commercial empire through the eyes of its victims."[71] Therefore he was able to create an image of "the girls" in the Devil's Dungeon paper mill, silent victims whose suffering was proof of their strength.

Various kinds of silences can be found in Melville's primitive characters and his women. "There are Melville's wonderful primitives: Queequeg, Tashtego, Daggoo, whose silence is the silence of strength, of the repose of elemental power, of indifference to the trappings of civilization. But the most silent of all are Hunilla and Bartleby. . . . In [Hunilla] is the stubbornness of life itself."[72] Life itself, "inscrutable nature," is what keeps Hunilla, the patient Chola widow of "The Encantadas," and Bartleby, the stubborn scrivener, from giving in. The silent victims of individual and collective blindness are the images of strength in Melville's universe. He marvels at Hunilla: "Humanity, thou strong thing, I worship thee, not in the laureled victor, but in this vanquished one" (94).

"Inscrutable nature" is what Melville found more visible in women and savages than in civilized men, because imperialistic, economic, and technological powers that denied the mysterious wholeness of human beings had located "naked nature" in women and primitive people only. Delano, Cereno, and the bachelors in their paradise deny "naked nature" in themselves and thus do not recognize their own civil cruelty toward other human beings. Melville wrote his stories during the years of legalism in American politics. He knew that the 1850 Missouri Compromise and the 1854 Kansas-Nebraska Act were civil legitimizations of naked nature's cruelty because they favored the continuation and spread of slavery. A denial of "naked nature" as it is civilly incorporated into legal sanctions causes Captain Vere to sacrifice Billy Budd. Vere's agony over the decision proves him to be more human, however, than Delano and Cereno.

The apparent dearth of women characters in many of Melville's works does not prove that women are unimportant in Melville's world. Though silent and scarce, they provide a forceful counter-part to the male world, which is judged deficient. Melville's portraits of women reveal unusual strength. The women also have so many traits in common with ethnic or exotic characters that these could often take their place. This substitution may have been a means for avoiding the pitfalls of the popular sentimental novels. Melville's personal experience of savage humanity over-shadowed his experience of women, yet it taught him all about masculinity and femininity.

3

Harriet Beecher Stowe's *Uncle Tom's Cabin:* Women and Blacks Revolutionizing Society

A well-known social history of the nineteenth-century South features a chapter entitled "Women and Negroes: One and Inseparable."[1] Certainly women and blacks in the Old South shared an inferior social status. Both groups, along with whites of ethnic descent, were subservient to an empowered group of cavalier gentlemen of English ancestry and unmixed blood. But women and blacks were also believed to have an affinity of character: "Let women and negroes alone, and instead of quacking with them [by giving them education] physic your own diseases. Leave them in their humility, their grateful affection, their self-renouncing loyalty, their subordination of the heart."[2] In Harriet Beecher Stowe's fiction blacks and women are almost interchangeable in the hierarchy of values. Both "achieve moral triumphs in spite of or perhaps because of the oppressions of a predominantly masculine and commercial world."[3]

How does the constellation of blacks and women in the woman's world of Stowe relate to the very different world of Hawthorne and Melville? The two great representatives of the American Renaissance rediscovered the power of the primitive human impulse which in women, as well as in ethnic and exotic characters, had not been as suppressed by the processes of civilization as it had in most Western males. Hawthorne's women and

Melville's primitives represent demonic impulses as well as vital innocence. Harriet Beecher Stowe is more directly interested in the "primitive Christian" values of women and blacks than in their primitive human qualities. For Stowe these two groups embody Christian faith more convincingly than authoritarian white males do and therefore they have the potential to revitalize society. Although critics have frequently assumed that she finds only submissive innocence in blacks and women and that she glorifies black accommodation and female devotion to home and hearth, recent scholarship has corrected this view.

Stowe's shortcomings are obvious. Not only did she occasionally use the same clichés in style, plot, and setting as most of the historical romancers in the first half of the nineteenth century, but she reacted against the popular version of a terrifying Puritan God by proclaiming a God of love whose image often verged on the sentimental.

Stowe's weaknesses as a writer, however, partly due to her family's Puritan prejudices against the arts and partly to her burdens as a wife and a mother of seven children, were also her strengths. She was, and still is, able to affect an immensely diversified spectrum of readers in every corner of the globe through *Uncle Tom's Cabin*. The almost incredible publication history of this novel is well known. The book was such a literary freak that Henry James called it "a wonderful 'leaping fish.' " One hundred thousand books were sold in less than two months after publication in March 1852. By November, twenty different editions could be found in English bookstores. Before the decade was over, innumerable translations had appeared around the world.[4]

As a woman, Stowe provided a "feminine" point of view which in most of the less intelligent "scribbling women" despised by Hawthorne degenerated into a flood of clichés. As a person "unrefined" by the literary circles of her time, she stands out as the only important writer of the mid-nineteenth-century to address openly and critically the "peculiar institution" of slavery. "Stowe turns a handicap into an asset. Lowly feminine feeling can revolutionize man's world."[5] Although Stowe's insistence on feeling reflected an intriguing feminism, she has been accused of vindicating women in a costly way. "She had to debase all that was best in her religious heritage, repress all that was strongest in her own creativity—and then, boast of it."[6] The question is whether Stowe's "feminization" of religion is a sentimental dilution or a true transformation. Are blacks in *Uncle Tom's Cabin* shown as "feminine" in a negative sense and women as glorious domestic priestesses or angels? And how are both supposed to reform society?

Women and blacks are shown in astonishing diversity in *Uncle Tom's Cabin*. This lively variety of characters surprises many readers who associate the book with the character types derived from the minstrel Tom plays or who know the novel only through the sentimental excerpts which are frequently anthologized. "Those critics who label *Uncle Tom's Cabin* good propaganda but bad art cannot have given sufficient time to the novel to meet its inhabitants. If they should ever linger over it long enough to take in the shrewdness, the energy, the truly Balzacian variousness of Mrs. Stowe's characterizations, they would surely cease to perpetuate one of the most unjust clichés of American criticism."[7] "In *Uncle Tom's Cabin* (and even more in *Dred*, her second slavery novel) Mrs. Stowe provides extremely interesting material about the regional laws and customs, about the differing skills and trades and occupations, about the African tribal origins and American family trees that made one black American different from another in the midcentury."[8] Edmund Wilson found a startling "eruptive force" in the work: "Out of the background of undistinguished narrative, inelegantly and carelessly written, the characters leap into being with a vitality that is all the more striking for the ineptitude of the prose that presents them."[9] Although Wilson mentions her inept style, another critic maintains that "from the merely artistic point of view, *Uncle Tom's Cabin* is an achievement of great subtlety and originality."[10] And Ellen Moers, seeking to put an end to the idea that the novel belongs only to American history, vigorously declared, "My intention is to put *Uncle Tom's Cabin* back in American literature where it belongs, for I think it is a great novel."

Harriet Beecher Stowe was different because she was a woman writer, not a man writer. As a woman writer she was obsessed with money and work because . . . she had to earn a living for her large family. As a woman, she was concerned with "Life among the

Lowly," the subtitle of *Uncle Tom's Cabin,* because she was used to hard manual labor, and she had no property rights. As a woman she was a disruptive radical, because she had nothing to gain from political patronage. As a woman she felt close ties to the literature of England and Europe, because prominent women writers of the nineteenth century made her feel at least as much at home there as here. As a woman she had no control over her place of residence. . . . But when young, as a spinster daughter, she was picked up and moved . . . out West to the frontier city of Cincinnati. . . . Harriet Beecher Stowe was thus the only writer of the American Renaissance really to encounter the fugitive slave. . . . No wonder *Uncle Tom's Cabin* was different.[11]

Although in the popular imagination Uncle Tom is taken to be sickeningly submissive, Stowe's actual characterization of Tom surpasses her stereotypical generalizations about the "African race." Uncle Tom is a man of "truly African features," a "large, broad-chested, powerfully made man," self-respecting, dignified, expressing "grave and steady good sense," and "humble simplicity" (26). He is a loving family father, "a sort of patriarch in religious matters" (33), a slave so loyal that he "would lay down his life" for his master (37). He excuses his master, Mr. Shelby, for selling him because "Mas'r couldn't help hisself" (60). He has the "gentle domestic heart, which . . . has been a peculiar characteristic of his unhappy race" (98), and he is "African" also in being "naturally patient, timid and unenterprising"; yet he shows "heroic courage" when faced with the prospect of being sold down the river (100). His little weakness consists in being "rather proud of his honesty," since he does not have much else to be proud of compared with people of the higher walks of society (123). Having read only the New Testament, "he had not learned to generalize and to take enlarged views", that is, he had not been instructed by Christian ministers who regard the buying and selling of slaves as nothing but a lawful trade (135). The remark about Tom's learning is biting in its irony, one of many which serve to offset the sentimental episodes.

Under his easy-going master St. Clare, a mixture of Byronic aristocrat and Hamlet, Tom is "ever quiet and obliging," showing "apparent contentment" (149). Since his "kindly race" is "ever yearning toward the simple and childlike," little Eva appears to

Tom as "almost divine"; "he half believed that he saw one of the angels stepped out of his New Testament" (152). For the kindly St. Clare, as earlier for Mr. Shelby, Tom would lay down his life, not only to protect the physical life of his master but "to see Mas'r a Christian" (308). In contrast to the slave Tom in William Gilmore Simms's *Woodcraft*,[12] Uncle Tom wants his legal freedom desperately (313), even though he has an unusually kind master and a comfortable life. Under the vicious Legree and his henchmen, Tom acts at first "submissively" (354), but in helping a slave woman fill her basket with cotton, even though he risks brutal punishment by the overseer, and in refusing to beat other slaves or to reveal Cassy's and Emmeline's hiding place, he is a strong and courageous man, an extremely virtuous but not an impossible character. He is more a type than an individual, but so are characters in Cooper, Scott, or Dickens. If he is something of a stereotype, so are the white Yankee Legree, the white Marie St. Clare, and the angelic Eva. Moreover, he is intended to be a type or symbol, for Stowe expresses through him, as through other black characters, her Christian conviction that God lives "among the lowly." "He hides from the wise and prudent, and reveals unto babes" (309).

The modern reader who resents *Uncle Tom's Cabin* "has small reason to resent Tom specifically. He was dutiful to his master and forgiving unto seventy times seven, not becaue of truckling instincts but because he was a true Christian. Present-day Negro distaste for him means only current lack of sympathy with Christian values."[13] In spite of voicing some of the racial prejudices of her day in describing the "African race," Stowe is aware of the rich cultural heritage of Africa. "Tom looked respectable enough to be a Bishop of Carthage, as men of his color were, in other ages" (185). He is no self-conscious martyr, and his acceptance of torture and death does not show that he lacks a desire for freedom. He keeps hoping "that some way of escape might yet be opened to him" (359), but he feels a commitment to those around him. Legree resents Tom's "commiseration for his fellow-sufferers" (359). When Cassy begs him to help her kill Legree he refuses. He also does not want to join in Cassy's and Emmeline's escape because he feels "the Lord's given me a work among these yer poor souls" (408). He advises the two, however, to flee because "it's more'n you can stand,—and you'd better go, if you can." His refusal to flee has been viewed as a resignation to his condition:

> Tom's refusal to obey his master in obedience to a higher law was a truly revolutionary position in the midcentury America of Thoreau and John Brown, as it has been in Jefferson's time, and is in our own. . . . But the way in which Tom acts out his refusal has in recent years turned his name into a curse. While the mulatto fugitives and their white abolitionist allies portrayed in the novel practice resistance, both passive and active, black Uncle Tom practices Christian resignation.[14]

Tom's nonviolent resistance for the purpose of arousing a tyrant's conscience should not be viewed as resignation. Rather, Uncle Tom is a person "who refuses to acknowledge that he is a thing and who maintains his integrity as a human being against every assault of uninhibited perverse power."[15]

Stowe has been accused of other stereotypes in her characterization of blacks. Did she really, unlike the writers of slave narratives and unlike Richard Hildreth in *Archy Moore*, show only submissive blacks and resisting mulattoes? Do the black people in *Uncle Tom's Cabin* always show their true faces to their masters? Is there "no irony" in the black characters of the novel because they are all "static and straightforward"?[16] A look at a wide range of Stowe's black characters will help to answer these questions, and it will also show the "feminine" nature of these figures.

The most outstanding male black character in *Uncle Tom's Cabin* besides Tom himself is George Harris. He expresses more doubt than Christian faith (120); he resents the patience and obedience toward his master which his wife, Eliza, considers necessary (20), and he would rather be killed than remain a slave (117). He and his companion Jim do not hesitate to carry pistols (199) and, after George's "declaration of independence" (203), to shoot anybody who fires at them and their family. George is thus a complete contrast to Tom. In fact, in many of his words and actions he seems almost like a twentieth-century Black Power advocate or Pan-Africanist (444–46). Although other abolitionist authors suggest that mulattoes excel and rebel only because of their white heritage of pride and intellect, nowhere does Harriet

Beecher Stowe rate white blood higher than black. She lets St.
Clare speak of "all our haughty feelings" which burn in the veins of
white fathers' sons (274); and George Harris declares, "If I wished
anything, I would wish myself two shades darker, rather than one
lighter" (444). She shows the conceitedness of Rosa and Jane, the
mulatto chambermaids, who feel far above "low niggers" like
Topsy (245), and many of her all-black characters have much
more integrity and strength than the effete, servile, and arrogant
mulatto Adolph (169, 182, 210, 220), although the author evokes
sympathy for him also (336).

George Harris may be modelled after Frederick Douglass, who
was also of mixed heritage, and to whom Harriet Beecher Stowe
wrote for guidance while composing *Uncle Tom's Cabin*, probably
after having read his autobiography.[17] That the fugitives in her
novel are mostly mulattoes can be explained by the large per-
centage of successful fugitives from slavery whose escape through
the Southern states was possible only because of their light skin.
Moreover, in *Uncle Tom's Cabin* as well as in *Dred*, Stowe illustrates "the enormous importance of nurture in shaping the individual. Although she does not ignore the relevance of hereditary
factors, she states unequivocally that training will determine the
direction in which an individual's talents will develop."[18] When
she describes George Harris as beautiful and daring, she takes over
the stereotype used by other abolitionists who portrayed persons of
mixed blood favorably; but whereas they usually imagined the
heroic mulatto's beauty and intelligence to be in constant conflict
with the savage primitivism inherited from his or her black ancestors, George Harris proudly identifies himself with Africans (444).

The character of Sam, like Tom and George, disproves the
premise that the all-black characters of the novel are submissive,
that they always show their true faces to their masters, and that
they are portrayed without irony. On one level Sam is a stereotype
from the minstrel tradition. To please "Missis" he tricks the slave
trader Haley by causing repeated delays and frustrations, thereby
allowing Eliza to escape. But much more is involved in this comic
interlude. "No American author before Mrs. Stowe had realized
that the comic inefficiency of a Black Sam could constitute a
studied insult to the white man's intelligence."[19] The images used
to describe Sam suggest a defiant hero. His palm-leaf hat is his

special symbol; its braids are coming apart and the strands are standing upright, giving it "a blazing air of freedom and defiance, quite equal to that of any Fejee chief" (51). He pretends eager attempts to catch Haley's horse so the chase can begin but actually drives the animal crazy by hiding a sharp little nut under the saddle and brushing the palm-leaf "inadvertently" in its face (49, 51). "Like the sword of Coeur de Lion, which always blazed in the front and thickest of the battle, Sam's palm-leaf was to be seen everywhere when there was the least danger that a horse could be caught" (52). The imagery is mock-heroic, and yet Sam's ability to talk Haley into taking the wrong route is so cunning that the white trader is made fun of, not the slave (62–64). Sam is ridiculed for his vanity as a self-styled politician and orator and his insistence on "principles" because he actually considers only which side his bread is buttered on. But Sam is seen more seriously in his likeness to Senator Bird, who "liked the idea of considering himself a sacrifice to his country" (82). Although the senator helped to pass the Fugitive Slave Law, he shows a kind heart and a helping hand when he is confronted with the fugitive Eliza. In the case of both the black slave and the white senator, their concrete actions are better, more ingenious, and more courageous than their shallow principles.

Sam is not the only black character who puts on a mask before a white master and who is treated ironically by the author. Aunt Chloe supports Sam's game by delaying the dinner for Haley in any way possible. She "warn't a going to have raw gravy on the table, to help nobody's catchings" (58). She also cannot agree with some of Tom's piety. When Tom suggests they should pray even for mean slave catchers, she decides, "Lor, it's too tough! I can't pray for 'em" (59).

Other portrayals of all-black characters are extremely sober. The tragic Prue is driven to despair and alcohol because she is abused as a breeder. Dreams of angelic realms do not sustain her as they do Eva and Tom. Prue does not want to go to heaven because she expects to find white people there (223). No tearful death scene is painted for her. The brutality of her life and death is consummated in a sentence: "[F]lies had got her,—and she's dead!" (224).

The slave Topsy has been called Stowe's "most brilliant original creation."[20] The famous catechism scene (which possibly owes something to the similar scene with Pearl in *The Scarlet Letter*) is an ingenious exposure of the lack of understanding of middle-class society and the church for the realities of slave life. "I spect I grow'd. Don't think nobody never made me," declares Topsy in answer to the question of who made her (247). There is no sentimental fluff in Topsy, at least not until Eva's death. Topsy represents the nihilistic consequences of slavery as much as "the indomitable free spirit of the mischievous, deceitful, troublesome, eternal American child."[21] In a bright touch by the author, the black child exposes the theological absurdity of an absolute pre-destination for either heaven or hell. "I's so awful wicked there can't nobody do nothin' with me" (255). There is much irony and "masking" in Topsy's behavior. That she ends up as missionary to Africa appears to be a pious cliché, but Stowe makes a good point in a heavy-handed way: there is no racial trait that cannot be changed by environment.

The variety of black characters that surround the famous Uncle Tom put him in perspective. Many of the strong characters in *Uncle Tom's Cabin*, and in *Dred*, are all-black. Tom's choice of patient suffering is one among many other desperate answers to a desperate situation. His serious treatment stands in contrast to the comedy, irony, and masking in other characters. His "feminine" traits are not meant to illustrate weakness but uncommon strength. This point is also made in St. Clare's story of the slave Scipio. "A powerful, gigantic fellow" and "a native-born Afri-can," Scipio has "the rude instinct of freedom in him to an uncommon degree." This "regular African lion" knocked down an overseer, escaped into the swamps, gallantly fought the dogs that hunted him down and finally fell to a gun shot. St. Clare, having laid a wager that he could "break" the man, claimed the wounded slave, nursed him in his own room, set him legally free, and told him he could go wherever he liked. Scipio stayed with him, became a Christian and "gentle as a child," and finally died of cholera after having worked "like a giant" to nurse the cholera-stricken St. Clare back to health (239–40). Scipio shows that Stowe's concept of "gentle" Christianity does not connote weak-ness.

In addition to the wide array of male black images *Uncle Tom's*

Cabin offers some outstanding women. Lucy, the suicide, has "grit" (131); Dinah, the cook, is disorderly but talented and common-sensical; and the mulatto women, Eliza, Cassy, and Emmeline, are especially powerful. These women prove, like the men, that Stowe's portraits of black characters by far transcend her general theoretical statements about racial traits.[22]

The slave Eliza shows strength and daring in her escape from slavery. Her feat of leaping over the icy river seems "impossible to anything but madness and despair" (64). In her later escape to Canada, she dresses up like a man. "Whether Mrs. Stowe was aware of the implications of her decision to put Eliza in the disguise of a man. . . , the implications for the meaning of what the woman stands for in *Uncle Tom's Cabin* are immense. The patient, submissive character, ennobled by feeling and symbolized most by the good woman, is simply ineffective."[23]

A much more complex character is Cassy, the quadroon mistress of Legree who later turns out to be Eliza's mother. Whereas mulattoes were invisible in plantation fiction, the abolitionists elevated them to the special role of heroic victim. Their beauty and intelligence were supposed to elicit sympathy from white readers. Stowe alters the stereotype of the beautiful victim in several ways. When the reader meets Cassy, she is no longer beautiful. "Her face was deeply wrinkled with lines of pain" (360). She is not submissive but "blazing with rage and scorn" (362). Showing none of the proverbial piety and patience of so many tragic mulattoes, she is convinced that "the Lord never visits these parts" (362) and that all of Legree's slaves have become cruel to each other beyond redemption. As she relates her painful history to Tom, all the while nursing his wounds, the separation from her children stands out as her most unbearable experience, and she is filled with the desire for revenge. Legree, meanwhile, has come to prefer the newly arrived Emmeline to Cassy, and Cassy knows he will soon ruin the lovely fifteen-year-old girl. "I'll send him where he belongs,—a short way, too—one of these nights, if they burn me alive for it!" (376). She finally begs Tom to help her kill Legree, and when he refuses she insists on doing it on her own (406). He persuades her to flee instead with Emmeline, and she manages to fool the superstitious Legree with tremendous ingenuity.

The white women of *Uncle Tom's Cabin* are almost as varied as
the black. Marie St. Clare appears mostly as the stereotype of the
spoiled Southern belle who turns into a sickly and finally vicious
planter's wife. Her character is sometimes tiresome, but her exasperating ways make St. Clare's cynicism more plausible. She
foreshadows Faulkner's Mrs. Compson, and her inefficiency
makes the "Mammy" of the house stand out as forcefully and nobly
as the Compsons' Dilsey. Ironically, Marie St. Clare draws a
comparison between her lot and that of the slaves, which was not
uncommon in the mid-nineteenth-century South but sounds
absurd coming from the mouth of the pampered Marie: "It's we
mistresses that are the slaves, down here" (174).[24]

A striking contrast to Marie is Miss Ophelia, St. Clare's New
England cousin who comes to take care of everything which is left
undone by the genteel Marie St. Clare. Ophelia's portrait is an
important one in the novel. Her exasperating efficiency points up
what she considers to be Southern shiftlessness, and she is a parody
of the cold correctness and narrow-mindedness of the New Englander who would rather send missionaries to Africa than touch a
black child. In the character of Ophelia, as well as Marie St.
Clare, Stowe satirizes those who concentrate only on what slavery
does to the soul.[25] Marie admits that black people have immortal
souls, but for her that belief does not mean they are equal to whites
(180); and Ophelia for a long time cannot bear the touch of
Topsy, but she works on her soul from the first moment of meeting
her. Ophelia can look "like one of the Fates" (226). Her manage-
ment of the house is a "regency" (212). Her progressive attempts
at systematic order are doomed by Dinah's clinging to old-
fashioned inconveniences and time-honored clutter, out of which
she creates "glorious dinners" (218). Miss Ophelia's "labors in all
departments that depended on the cooperation of servants were
like those of Sisyphus or the Danaides" (217). When Marie St.
Clare, "in a faint and lady-like voice, like the last dying breath of
an Arabian jessamine," begins to complain about her husband,
Ophelia knits energetically and looks "about as sympathizing as a
stone lion" (179). Stowe's images for women are varied; there is
nothing like a general femininity in her female characters.

Mrs. Shelby, Eliza's beloved mistress, and Mrs. Bird, the Senator's wife, are also individualized. Both are sensitive, kind, trap-

ped by the evils of slavery, and eager to alleviate at least its worst abuses. Eliza calls Mrs. Shelby "a Christian and an angel" (42). Mr. Shelby thinks that his wife suddenly has turned into an abolitionist because Eliza's and Tom's fate has opened her eyes to the fact that slavery cannot be gilded over by pious sermons and kind deeds (38–39). She secretly supports Eliza's escape and later manages through Chloe to raise money to buy Tom back. Mr. Shelby thinks that women, including his wife, "don't understand business . . . never do, and never can" (259), but he himself goes into heavy debt, and he keeps his wife from earning money by giving music lessons, an occupation he considers degrading for a lady (260).

Mrs. Bird is also a woman thought by her husband to undergo a change in attitude. He sees her turning into a politician because she gives a spirited interpretation of the cruelties and absurdities inherent in the Fugitive Slave Law. She is a "timid, blushing little woman . . . with mild blue eyes . . . ; as for courage, a moderate-sized cock turkey had been known to put her to rout at the very first gobble. . . . There was only one thing capable of arousing her . . . ; anything in the shape of cruelty would throw her into a passion" (83). She is determined to break the new law "the first time I get a chance" (84). Soon afterwards when the Senator ignores the law he helped to pass in order to assist Eliza, the author gives us an insight into Mrs. Bird's wifely wisdom: "Now, little Mrs. Bird was a discreet woman,—a woman who never in her life said, 'I told you so!' and, on the present occasion, though pretty well aware of the shape her husband's meditations were taking, she very prudently forbore to meddle with them, only sat very quietly in her chair, and looked quite ready to hear her liege lord's intentions, when he should think proper to utter them" (91). Clearly the woman and the slave are confronted with the same problem: how to circumvent an abstract, inhuman form of government which the "patriarchal institution" of slavery (so called by its supporters) is based on; how to break out of the stifling cash nexus and the pretensions of social class. Women and slaves historically were often united in the same cause. Many planters' wives felt a special resentment for the system of slavery because they were forced to tolerate their husbands' black mistresses and mulatto children. Stowe did not dare to touch on this issue although she herself had an aunt (Mary Foote) who married a West Indian planter and was greeted at his island home by a horde of her husband's mulatto children. From then on she was unhappy, became ill, returned home, and wasted away until her death in the Beecher home when Harriet was two years old.[26]

The white woman whose image touches upon the leitmotif of the novel is Rachel Halliday. Her "face and form . . . made 'mother' seem the most natural word in the world" (140). A Quaker woman, Rachel is motherhood personified. On her "high, placid forehead . . . time had written no inscription, except peace on earth, good will to men, and beneath shone a large pair of clear, honest, loving brown eyes. . . . So much has been said and sung of beautiful young girls, why don't somebody wake up to the beauty of old women?" (140). All the boys and girls of the Quaker settlement "moved obediently to Rachel's gentle 'Thee had better,' or more gentle 'Hadn't thee better?' "

Motherhood of this kind is "the still point of the turning world" of Harriet Beecher Stowe. The religion of love was best expressed in the life of the home and in the mother-child relationship. The authors of the sentimental domestic novels had painted idyllic home scenes or the tragic effects of intemperance on the home, but none had dared to describe the anarchy of the slave's home life. The separation of mother and child, expressed both by the physical separation of slave families at the auction block and by spiritual alienation of white people like St. Clare and Legree, became the central topic of Stowe's novel. Loving relationships are at the heart of the story. The family, especially, is the core of the social community. The focus on "love" often strikes us as sentimental, especially in Eva's pious words. Dying children, however, were not only a staple in nineteenth-century fiction; they were also a heartbreaking reality for mothers in an age that did not have inoculations, antiseptic hospital rooms, and modern medical techniques.[27] (Stowe herself had lost her baby Charles to cholera in 1849.) Moreover, "love" is for Stowe as much a quality of the mind as an emotion. In a letter she writes, "I check myself when expressing feelings like this, so much has been said of it by the sentimental. . . . Love after all is the life blood, the existence, the all in all of mind."[28]

The cult of motherhood was almost sacred in mid-nineteenth-

century America: "Books on mothers of famous men, especially
Mary Washington . . . poured from the presses in the 1840s and
1850s; their message was that men achieved greatness because of
the instruction and inspiration they received from their
mothers."[29] In Harriet Beecher, the daughter of the minister
Lyman Beecher, the importance of motherhood and women's
guiding role receives an added twist. She later wrote in *Oldtown
Folks:*

> Woman's nature has never been consulted in theology. Theologic
> systems, as to the expression of their great body of ideas, have, as
> yet, been the work of man alone. They have had their origin, as in
> St. Augustine, with men who were utterly ignorant of moral and
> intellectual companionship with woman, looking on her only in
> her animal nature as a temptation and a snare. . . .
>   Plato says somewhere that the only perfect human thinker and
> philosopher who will ever arise will be the MAN-WOMAN, or a
> human being who unites perfectly the nature of the two sexes.[30]

Stowe believes that woman's nature can be an influence in theological matters and thereby in the reordering of society. As Christian mothers are the true spiritual guides, so God is seen as a loving
parent. "We must see what generosity, what tenderness, what
magnanimity can be in man and woman, and believe all that and
more in God. All that there is in the best fathers and best mothers
must be in him."[31] In Harriet Beecher Stowe's works "women are
the true spiritual guides." "She never bowed down to the clergy.
She was the daughter, the wife, the mother of a clergyman, and
the sister of seven clergymen—she understood that breed only too
well. But the insight of a Christian mother—ah! that is the norm
by which she tests everything."[32]

Women, however, are not the only group which can save
society from patriarchy, commercialism, and injustice. Many
black people have the same spiritual superiority as women in
Stowe's world. This view has been called "romantic racialism." It
is based partly on German romanticism and partly on the teaching
of Alexander Kinmont, a leading Midwestern exponent of
Swedenborgianism, who delivered a series of lectures in Cincinnati in 1837–38 which Stowe may have attended. (Stowe also may
have read his works.) The German philosopher Johann Gottfried

von Herder emphasized the value and uniqueness of a wide variety of cultural groups, not just four or five biological races. Romantic racialists following Herder saw the black person's innocence and childlike nature as different and beautiful. "To attribute to someone the simplicity of a child . . . especially in the middle of the nineteenth century, was a compliment of the first order."[33] The virtues of black people were then further identified with true Christianity. Especially in Stowe's novel *The Minister's Wooing* "women and Negroes are almost interchangeable when it comes to their natural virtues."[34]

Since women and blacks both suffered similar social constraints, feminism and abolitionism were closely allied. While Harriet Beecher Stowe had many reservations about the leading white feminists of her time, she greatly admired the black feminist Sojourner Truth.[35] It is not surprising, then, that the slave Milly in *Dred* and the black Candace in *The Minister's Wooing* are the greatest redemptive characters in her novels. What is surprising is that Uncle Tom is a man. In a letter of 1853 Stowe says of the baby boy she lost through cholera, "It was at his dying bed and at his grave that I learned what a poor slave mother may feel when her child is torn away from her."[36] "Stowe's insistence on maternal experience as the generative principle of *Uncle Tom's Cabin* identifies the ethical center of the novel, and helps explain the unusual, and often misunderstood, characterization of Tom."[37] Tom has the traditional virtues of a heroine, of an American Eve, not an American Adam, and he is linked to the girl Eva as well as to a variety of black and white mothers. Everything that is good and true in St. Clare is grounded in the memory of his mother. "Mother" is his last word before his death (325). Cassy can deceive Legree because she plays the haunting ghost of his mother whose guidance he did not follow. Tom, before he is sold away from the Shelbys, advises young George Shelby, "Al'ays keep close to yer mother. . . . The Lord gives good many things twice over; but he don't give ye a mother but once" (105). Rachel Halliday's motherliness provides George Harris with the first real "home" in his lifetime (146). Even the rough slave catcher Tom Loker, wounded and abandoned by his fickle friends, remembers the warnings of his mother (206). But these mothers are not the decorative figures that women usually are in antebellum fiction.[38]

They are not pleasing and accommodating but guiding and goad-ing. Although women's virtues are the stereotypical ones of piety, purity, noncompetitiveness, and unselfishness, Stowe's novel "proposes as the foundation for a new democratic era, in place of masculine authority, feminine nurture." There is an "obvious contradiction of gender in the Eva/Christ and Tom/heroine asso-ciations. . . . The Redeemer from the sins of the fathers in the novel is not, as traditional theology puts it, a second Adam (an emblem utterly familiar of course to anyone who was the daughter, sister, and wife of ministers), but . . . a second Eve."[39]

The traditional understanding of feminine spirituality is sati-rized through the character of Mr. Shelby. "He really seemed somehow or other to fancy that his wife had piety and benevolence enough for two—to indulge a shadowy expectation of getting into heaven through her superabundance of qualities to which he made no particular pretention" (14). Stowe paints in these lines the picture of the popular "gentleman" of nineteenth-century fiction, but the important question in *Uncle Tom's Cabin* is, "Who can be a *gentle* man in a system where human beings are only things?"[40] The values of maternal nurturing and "feminine" sensitivity to injustice are not, in *Uncle Tom's Cabin*, relegated to the domestic realm of women. In fact, Stowe suggests that if they are—for example, if men like Senator Bird do not practice in politics what they practice under the influence of their wives at home,—then some day "the masses are to rise," as St. Clare puts it (274). The novelist Lydia Maria Child writes in her *Letters from New York* in 1843:

> When Christ said, "Blessed are the meek," did he preach to women only?
> Whatsoever can be named as loveliest, best, and most graceful in woman, would likewise be good and graceful in man. You will perhaps remind me of courage. If you use the word in its highest signification . . . woman, above others, has abundant need of it in her pilgrimage. . . . If you mean mere animal courage, *that* is not mentioned in the Sermon on the Mount.[41]

For Melville neither nonwhites nor women had a specific voice. He represented the injustice done to them mostly by pointing to their silence. Harriet Beecher Stowe indicates in *Uncle Tom's Cabin* that these masses, female and black, are rising, apocalyptically if not democratically, and that the values usually demanded of blacks and women will be healing and saving if all human beings make them their own. "There is a mustering among the masses, the world over; and there is a *dies irae* coming on, sooner or later" (238). "And this, oh Afrika! latest called of nations,—called to the crown of thorns, the scourge, the bloody sweat, the cross of agony,—this is to be thy victory; by this shalt thou reign with Christ when his kingdom shall come on earth" (407).

When Harriet Beecher Stowe was seven years old, her father proudly declared she was a genius, but he immediately qualified the statement by saying that he wished she had been a boy—he would give a hundred dollars if she could be a boy. "The highest compliment which Lyman paid to his daughters was to tell them they were like boys."[42] She grew up to be a woman and an artist "whose achievement was to beat daddy at his own game, and, more importantly, to realize far more fully than he the meaning of the religious vocabulary they both employed."[43] The "feminization" of Beecher Calvinism, though often sentimental in vocabulary and imagery, can be understood as a radical reordering of values in which primitive Christianity is rediscovered in those to whom male politicians, church leaders, and "cavaliers" had relegated it: women and blacks. If these two groups are considered primitive, Stowe seems to say, let them show what strength they possess in their powerlessness. A similar point can be made about feminine religion in the nineteenth century in general:

> The giving over of religion to women, in its content and in its membership, provided a repository for these female values during the period when the business of building the nation did not immediately require them. . . . The family, popular culture, and religion were the vehicles by which feminine virtues were translated into values.
>
> The constant identification of woman with virtue and with religion reenforced her own belief in her power to overcome obstacles. . . . Religion in its emphasis on the brotherhood of man developed in women a conscious sense of sisterhood, a quality absolutely essential for any kind of meaningful woman's movement.[44]

In some respects, the saving of the world in *Uncle Tom's Cabin* depends on the individualistic, emotional principle of "feeling right" (457): "If the mothers of the free states had all felt as they should, in times past, the sons of the free states would not have been the holders, and, proverbially, the hardest masters of slaves" (456). Yet the new world which the values of the heart would usher in can only be achieved by legal and political means. "One man can do nothing, against the whole action of a community. Education, to do anything, must be a state education; or there must be enough agreed in it to make a current" (275). George Harris knows he cannot change society on his own; therefore he chooses to go to Liberia. "Do you say that I am deserting my enslaved brethren? I think not. If I forget them one hour, one moment of my life, so may God forget me. But, what can I do for them, here? Can I break their chains? No, not as an individual; but let me go and form part of a nation, which shall have a voice in the Councils of nations, and then we can speak" (445). Stowe could never talk about "feeling right" without emphasizing its radical social and political implications. Her very conservatism is a revolutionary force. *Uncle Tom's Cabin* is "the *summa theologica* of nineteenth-century America's religion of domesticity, a brilliant redaction of the culture's favorite story about itself—the story of salvation through motherly love. Out of the ideological materials they had at their disposal, the sentimental novelists elaborated a myth that gave women the central position of power and authority in the culture, and of these efforts *Uncle Tom's Cabin* is the most dazzling exemplar."[45] Stowe showed that not only women but also blacks embodied a power that could transform society. Those who were excluded from decision making, the "lowly" of her subtitle, had the greatest understanding of the primitive Christian insight that the meek will inherit the earth, not the submissive meek but the tough meek who, like Uncle Tom, refuse to submit.

Stowe was a democrat. She considered certain Calvinistic tendencies to be simply religious versions of patriarchal order and antiquated royal absolutism claiming "divine right."[46] But another strand of New England Calvinism emphasized the virtues of the heart, the simplicity of the saints, and the genuinely Protestant idea that the most uneducated believer might interpret the Scriptures more accurately than state and church authorities. This conviction led Stowe to celebrate the intuitive strengths and communal instincts of women and slaves who expressed the "sympathies of Christ" as opposed to the "sophistries of worldly policy" (457). It was from the lowly of her society that she expected a new religious and political order to emerge.

4

William Wells Brown's *Clotel:*
From Victimization
to Vision and Action

*By and large, we are still acting as though American literature were a mere
colonial implantation, no doubt modified by local conditions but in essence an
offshoot of European literature.
But insofar as American literature is a unique body of creative work, what
defines its identity most unequivocally is the historical and cultural experience
of the Afro-American people. At long last we have come to understand that
this is obviously true for American music and dance. . . . When we grasp the
significance of this truth for American literature . . . we will be forced
radically to change our critical methodologies, our criteria for literary excellence, and our canon of great literature—or perhaps even the entire notion of
a canon.* [1]

Reading the early fiction by black Americans after having been
immersed in the study of "great" writers like Hawthorne and
Melville, or a "minor" but seemingly "all-American" writer like
Harriet Beecher Stowe, is like wandering into foreign territory.
Literary criticism of nineteenth-century black authors is still far
from being merged with the discussion of what we could call the
canon of classic American works.[2] Yet in some respects the black
experience on this continent is more inherently American than
the white. The Negroes were among the first Americans, having
been brought to the Virginia shores as early as 1619.[3] There were,
of course, American Indian poets and narrators before the arrival

of either blacks or whites, but in the mid-nineteenth-century literary scene, the interaction between white and black literature, scanty as it was, is more discernible than that of white and Native American narratives. Unlike later white immigrants, the black slaves were systematically stripped of their tribal and familial ties. They were not only unable to speak the language of their masters but often did not even know the language of other African slaves. "Undoubtedly [the Negro] is the only American who has had to rely so exclusively on the American environment in order to recreate his identity. This almost unadulterated Americanness of the Negro is, of course, reflected in his literature—the Negro author in his quest for expression stands as an intensified image of the total American search for self. Alienation, terror and violence have been his premises, as they have been for other American writers from Poe to Norman Mailer."[4]

The two first black American novels published in the United States, William Wells Brown's *Clotel* (1853) and Martin R. Delany's *Blake* (1859) owe much to the slave narratives which preceded them.[5] During the past two decades, scholars have rediscovered the slave narratives of the nineteenth century and have found them to be an influential contribution to the cultural history of black as well as white Americans. Although there are many "as told to" slave narratives written and heavily influenced by white writers, and many strongly fictionalized versions, the unique value of the genre is represented in the authentic autobiographical reports of slaves, describing the hell of slavery, the trials of escape, and the new life of freedom. White readers found in them, as they did later in Western fiction, a portrayal of the human condition in bondage and freedom. By the 1850s the number of narratives published may have run into the hundreds. "Had it not been for the early slave narratives and their influence, Harriet Beecher Stowe would not have had a ready-made audience for *Uncle Tom's Cabin.*"[6]

The most famous example of these narratives is the *Narrative of the Life of Frederick Douglass, An American Slave, Written by Himself* (1845). As mentioned before, it was one of the narratives which influenced Harriet Beecher Stowe. The detached voice of the narrator, the imagery, and the ironic inversion of some all-American themes and dreams make this work an outstanding

American autobiography. Another very popular narrative was written by William Wells Brown. First published in 1847, it went through four editions in its first year and was translated into several languages. Brown published a second revision of his narrative in 1849, less than a year after the fascinating story of William and Ellen Craft aroused astonishment at home and abroad. In a very daring way, they had escaped slavery in Macon, Georgia, during the Christmas holidays of 1848, and Ellen became "for a few short years . . . the best known black woman in the United States." Her imagination and courage in disguising herself as a sickly young planter (so nearly white that "he" looked Spanish), and travelling by coach with her husband, who played her servant, impressed many Northerners who had probably never even seen a slave woman.[7] Brown was among the Crafts' first visitors after they gained their freedom, and their experiences had a lasting effect on his work. Their own narrative, *Running a Thousand Miles for Freedom*, was not published until 1860, since the Fugitive Slave Law forced them to flee to England.

The slave narratives have been variously evaluated. On the one hand, they "served as the mid-nineteenth-century's horror literature."

> The message of paternalism could not be missed: the Fugitive Negro, America's own *beau sauvage*, would be lifted to equality through the efforts of white humanitarians. . . .
> . . . The fugitive slave narratives were the pious pornography of their day, replete with horrific tales of whippings, sexual assaults, and explicit brutality . . . fit for Nice Nellies to read precisely because they dealt with black, not white, men.[8]

On the other hand, disregarding these "gothic" traits, the slave narratives could be read as a primitive American form of the *Bildungsroman*. They usually describe a slave's experiences from birth to maturity; they are concerned with the problem of finding an identity; their protagonists are totally bereft of social and family ties; and they describe American Adams (and some American Eves) who are, true to R.W.B. Lewis's definition, without known fathers or grandfathers. The father is only "some amorphic, distant figure" serving as "a peripheral target of moral reproach."[9]

The early and brutal separation from the mother is often a lasting trauma. The black American Adam in slavery does not even know his age, since any inquiry about it might be considered by the slave holder as "improper and impertinent, and evidence of a restless spirit."[10]

What makes the slave narratives unique is their combination of multiple motifs. They emphasize personal and political freedom and probe the psychological toll of slavery upon the human mind; they feature elements of sentimental and adventure stories as well as melodramatic scenes typical of some late nineteenth-century fiction. The romantic tradition in America had emphasized personal liberty and adventure, and the slave narratives demonstrated these ideals in addition to Emerson's self-reliance, Thoreau's following of a "different drummer," and Hawthorne's power of the heart.[11]

Most fugitive slaves were mulattoes. Because of their lighter skin color their escape was easier. Mulattoes also were more likely to have received some education, whereas the majority of slaves were kept in such utter ignorance that they did not always know the North Star, which could guide them in their flight, or even the name of the state they lived in or the nearest railroad terminus; and, of course, most did not know who the abolitionists were.[12] All slave narratives demonstrate that the slaves showed intelligence and a keen sense of irony in their attempts to mask their true selves in front of their masters. The narratives are "works of the art of concealment."[13]

The mulatto slave did not necessarily have a favored position compared with all-black slaves. On the contrary, he or she suffered the envy of black brothers and sisters and the jealousy of white masters and mistresses. Female slaves were physically more grossly exploited than men. Because their sexual victimization made them sharper examples of the abuses of slavery, the male mulatto author often projected his own experiences onto his female counterpart. In William Wells Brown's case, the injury done to his mother and the helplessness he felt when she and his sister were sold down South were traumatic.[14] But there is another reason why the first black authors chose the mulatto woman as heroine. Literacy among blacks was not yet sufficiently widespread to provide a reading audience, and white readers were reluctant to accept books by black writers on the same terms as those by white authors. Black writers also lacked a genre that fitted their unique experiences. "Like his housing, [the Negro writer] inherited his literary forms at second hand, after the white folks had moved out. Not only did the early novelist write exclusively within the Romantic tradition, but he chose melodrama—the very caricature of that tradition—as his principal literary vehicle."[15] Since the death of a beautiful woman was a very compelling motif not only in the melodramatic tradition but even among writers as great as Poe, it is not surprising that the first black novelist concentrates on the tragic mulatto woman, combining his experiences with the dictates of the literary market.[16]

Brown's fervent abolitionism, however, is the most important reason behind his choice of tragic mulatto heroines. The use of the tragic octoroon as a protagonist in pre–Civil War fiction was not necessarily based on the racist view that a person with white blood is better and that his or her sufferings are more tragic than those of an all-black character. Abolitionist writers simply knew how to impress their Northern audience. Octoroons were living proof of generations of sexual misconduct in the South. They inspired white guilt more effectively than poor black field hands. Also, the motif of a sudden reversal of fate appealed to a middle-class audience whose future was uncertain because of constant immigrations and migrations. That a pampered octoroon heiress could by a legal point (for example, after the death of her master) suddenly be sold down South as a field hand reminded readers of sudden bankruptcy experiences or other changes in fortune common in an industrialized society. The relationship of slave holder and slave could even be seen as similar to that of parvenu and aristocrat, commoner and landed gentleman.[17]

How much Brown's main fictional topic resembles Harriet Beecher Stowe's concerns becomes clear from a passage in Brown's lecture before the Female Anti-Slavery Society of Salem, November 14, 1847, in which he explains "the influence which slavery has over the morals of the people of the South. . . . Three millions of slaves unprotected! A million of females that have no right to marriage! Among the three millions of slaves upon the Southern plantations, not a single lawful marriage can be found!"[18] This was exactly what Northerners were concerned

about. While Southerners feared intermarriage, Northern abolitionists preached against illicit intercourse between the races and
saw the South as a society where no check was put on man's sexual
nature.[19]

Thus William Wells Brown made strategic use of certain themes
that were close to his heart and, at the same time, in keeping with
the white tradition and appealing to his white Northern audience.
In terms of character portrayal, the early black novelists inherited
a solid set of popular stereotypes from white fiction writers: the
Contented Slave, the Wretched Freeman, the Comic Negro, the
Brute Negro, the Tragic Mulatto, the Local Color Negro, and the
Exotic Primitive.[20] Some of these types developed only gradually
in the second half of the nineteenth century, but William Wells
Brown must have been familiar with several of them even though
he did not have a day of schooling in his life and was a slave until
his twentieth year. A tradition of black stereotypes poses difficulties for the black writer.

> The Negro writer hesitates, perhaps unconsciously, to temper the
> goodness of his Negro characters with the dialectical "evil." Fear-
> ful of reinforcing stereotypes in the white reader's mind, he often
> goes to the other extreme, idealizing his characters, making them
> flat rather than many-sided. Or, conscious of the pitfalls listed
> above, and anxious to prove that he is not idealizing his Negro
> characters, the writer goes to the other extreme—in the name of
> naturalism—and paints the American Negro as an exaggerated
> Bigger Thomas. . . . To strike a compromise—and, incidentally,
> the truth—is possibly the most difficult feat for a Negro writer.[21]

Brown may not have reflected exactly on these problems, but they
did exist for him nevertheless. He simply made use of the sources
and models available to him: the slave narratives, anti-slavery
lectures and literature, newspaper accounts, popular fiction, and
his own experiences. In all these, he seems to have had a special
interest in the fate and the characteristic traits of the tragic
mulatto woman or "white slave," as victim and as an imaginative,
courageous heroine. Woman and Noble Savage are merged in this
figure.

The novel *Clotel* is closely related to Brown's own *Narrative*.
When Brown published a revised version of the *Narrative* in one

volume with *Clotel,* he showed considerable sophistication in comparison with authors of other slave narratives. The *Narrative* and the novel authenticate each other. Brown prefaces them with effective documents and uses the objective attitude of an editor more than an author.[22]

Brown, like many slaves, did not know his exact age. He was probably born in 1814. When he died at about age seventy in 1884, he had become "one of the most remarkable men of letters produced by nineteenth-century America."[23] From a fugitive slave, he had developed into novelist, playwright, historian, travel writer, essayist, lecturer, and physician. He advocated prison reform, temperance, and equal rights for women. He was a leading abolitionist in two continents, and was greeted by such notables as Victor Hugo and Alexis de Tocqueville when he was a delegate to the Paris Peace Conference in 1849. He lectured extensively in England before audiences that included Dickens, Milnes, Macaulay, and Tennyson. He is credited not only with being the first black novelist, but also the first black playwright, anthologist, and travel writer.[24]

Brown was born near Lexington, Kentucky. His father was probably a cousin of his master, Dr. Young. His mother was "of mixed blood", and in one of several descriptions of his life he remarks that his mother's father was, according to legend, "the noted Daniel Boone."[25] While a field hand his mother bore seven children by seven different men, and "there was evidence of her strength of mind in her motherly love and her abiding interest in her children even though slavery permitted her to do but little for them."[26] One of Brown's early childhood traumas was hearing his mother's groans and cries when the overseer whipped her severely for being slightly late in starting her work. Brown became a house servant and was later hired out to a tavern keeper, an inveterate drunkard and a cruel master. The fourteen- or fifteen-year-old boy beame so desperate that he fled to the woods, where he was captured by bloodhounds. He was punished by being "smoked" in the smoke-house until he almost suffocated.

More important was his further employment on a Mississippi steamboat and thereafter in a hotel. At this time his family began to disintegrate. Two brothers had died, and Dr. Young sold his mother, sister, and three surviving brothers because of financial difficulties. He hesitated to sell Brown because he was a close relative. The "best" period of slavery for Brown began when he became employed in the printing office of Elijah P. Lovejoy, the abolitionist publisher and editor of the *Saint Louis Times,* who ultimately lost his life at the hands of a mob for defending his anti-slavery editorials. But after only half a year with Mr. Lovejoy, where the illiterate Brown for the first time got acquainted with the world of letters, he was so severely beaten by some sons of slave holders that he had to be sent home to recuperate for weeks and therefore lost his job.

After working again on a Mississippi steamboat, Brown returned to his master, Dr. Young, as a house servant who was also required to perform minor medical care for slaves. This experience was followed by an unusually difficult year (1832/33) in which Brown again worked on the Mississippi, hired out to the cruel slave trader Walker. The steamboat race, the gambling scenes, and the explosion incident in *Clotel* derived from his life with Walker. In his *Narrative,* he describes another aspect of his steamboat job that may have prepared him for turning facts into fiction. With a keen sense for "black humor" he records that he was ordered to rejuvenate the older slaves, in order to improve their market value, by blackening their grey hair with shoe polish, greasing their aged bodies, and coaching them to lie about their age to prospective buyers.

Working on the steamboat, Brown's desire to escape slavery grew so strong that he persuaded his mother to flee with him. They travelled for eight days before they were caught and jailed. His mother was then sold down South as a punishment, and Brown blamed himself for causing his mother's misfortune by asking her to flee with him. He never saw her again. After various short-term occupations, Brown was finally sold to a steamboat owner for whom he became a coachman in Cincinnati in 1834, and from there he tried to escape again, this time successfully.

One of his first problems on his way to freedom was his lack of a proper name, and the story he tells about his childhood names throws some light on the identity problems of mulatto slaves described in *Clotel.* As a boy Brown was first called "William," without any family name. When Dr. Young took into his household a nephew whose name was also William, Brown's mother was ordered to change her son's name to "Sandford." Brown was whipped repeatedly for refusing to answer to his new name. Moreover, as Brown remarks in a later memoir of his life: "My fair complexion was a great obstacle to my happiness, both with whites and blacks, in and about the great house. Often mistaken by strangers for a white boy, it annoyed my mistress very much." When a stranger thought him to be Dr. Young's son, the boy was whipped for this embarrassment.[27] No wonder, then, that the fugitive slave who was neither white nor black, neither William nor Sandford, reports of himself, "I was not only hunting for my liberty, but also hunting for a name."[28] "From William Wells Brown to Cecil Brown the primary unifying metaphor in the Afro-American novel is the quest for identity as free men."[29] Fortunately, the first person who seriously helped the fugitive slave William, alias Sandford, was a kind Quaker who gave him more than food, clothing, and medical care. He offered him his own name, Wells Brown, to be added to the name William, which the former slave did not want to lose again.

From then on, William Wells Brown started his life of independence and self-education. He held various jobs in Cleveland and on a steamboat. In 1834 he married a free black woman, and with two daughters they had several happy years together. The Browns moved to Buffalo, where they opened their home to the Underground Railroad. Gradually Brown became known as a lecturer for the Anti-Slavery Society. He also organized a temperance group. In 1840 he visited Haiti and Cuba. While attending anti-slavery conventions he met Frederick Douglass, William Lloyd Garrison, and Wendell Phillips between 1843 and 1844 and became a disciple of Garrison.

When the Browns' marriage began to disintegrate, they moved to Farmington, New York, to try to make a new beginning. Despite that effort the marriage collapsed in 1847, and Brown took his two daughters to Boston, where he stayed for the rest of his life except for five years in Great Britain. The Browns never divorced, nor did they become reconciled. Mrs. Brown died in 1851 or 1852. Brown remarried in 1860. In 1847 he wrote his *Narrative*, which soon became a best seller. It is unique in comparison with other slave narratives for its realistic scenes, such as Brown's experiences with the slave trader Walker, and its dramatic movement and effective plot. Edmund Quincy, abolitionist editor and son of Harvard's president, found "simplicity and calmness" in this narrative.[30] While Brown's autobiography suffers in comparison with Douglass's *Narrative*, it is still one of the best examples of this genre.

In 1848 Brown's publication of *The Anti-Slavery Harp: A Collection of Songs* anticipates a motif of *Clotel*. The song "Jefferson's Daughter," a satire based on a newspaper notice, tells of the sale of a slave daughter of Jefferson at an auction in New Orleans for $1,000. The year 1849 was marked by the flight of the Crafts and Brown's repeated travelling and lecturing together with them. It was also the year of the Paris Peace Congress, and Brown was sent to Paris as one of twenty delegates from the United States. Thereafter, Brown spent five years in England, giving innumerable lectures for the Anti-Slavery Society and commissioning paintings which depicted realistic scenes from American slavery to be exhibited as a "Panoramic View" of slave life. One of the pictures was of a girl crossing the icy Ohio River with a child in her arms. A report of such an incident had appeared several times in the anti-slavery press of 1848/49, and in retelling the story in the catalogue for his exhibition, Brown publicized it one year before *Uncle Tom's Cabin.*[31] After the Crafts fled to England to avoid recapture, he again travelled and lectured with them. His daughters received good schooling in England as well as in France and became teachers. Brown continued to educate himself, learning French, Latin, and German. He did some travelling in Germany and Italy and wrote for London newspapers.

Since *Uncle Tom's Cabin* had paved the way for a popular reception of anti-slavery fiction, Brown attempted his first anti-slavery romance in 1853. In December 1852 he had published a story similar to one of the plots of *Clotel* in the *Anti-Slavery Advocate*, but it ended happily and therefore did not arouse enough anti-slavery sentiment in Brown's opinion. Thus in *Clotel* he replaced the real Mr. Carter of the earlier story with President Jefferson. "He did not worry, then, about whether the reports concerning Jefferson were literally true in every detail; he merely used them for their sensational value to illustrate the ironical inconsistencies that existed between the theories and the practices of soi-disant democratic American slaveholders."[32]

Moreover, no comprehensive biography of Jefferson was available until 1858, when Henry S. Randall's *The Life of Thomas Jefferson* appeared. Several anachronisms in *Clotel* show that the story does not fit the facts of Jefferson's life.

> Jefferson resided in Washington during a part of his fourth year as vice-president and during his eight years as president—from June, 1800, when Washington became the nation's capital, until March, 1809. If his alleged affair with Currer [the mother of Clotel] preceded his removal to Washington [as the novel suggests], Althesa's age dates the beginning of the action in the novel not later than about 1814. This date is inconsistent, however, with others found in the work—dates which make it impossible to fit the story chronologically into the history of Jefferson's life.[33]

For example, Brown uses an article from the *Natchez Free Trader* of 1842 and thereby gives the impression that the action in his novel started in 1841 or 1842. This date is not consistent with the impression given that Jefferson had fathered Clotel and Althesa before he became president or vice-president. In short, Brown was not interested in asserting the historical accuracy of Jefferson's alleged affair with Sally Hemings. In subsequent versions of the novel he softened or eliminated the Jefferson connection.

Brown's most important source for the main plot of *Clotel* was Lydia Maria Child's story, "The Quadroons," published in 1846.[34] Brown shifted the setting from the vicinity of Augusta, Georgia, to Richmond, Virginia, and changed the names. Another source provided Brown with a climactic scene. Two years before the publication of *Clotel,* Grace Greenwood included in her *Poems* six eight-line stanzas with the title "The Leap from the Long Bridge: An Incident at Washington," with an introductory note about a woman who escaped from the slave prison between the Capitol and the President's house.

For the last three chapters, Brown retold the story he had used in his travel book *Three Years in Europe.* The heroic George, slave-son of a Congressman, sentenced to death for participating in the Nat Turner insurrection, escapes from prison by disguising himself as Mary, the light-skinned slave girl he loves, who impersonates him and remains in his cell.

In all these stories, the heroine is a tragic mulatto, quadroon, or octoroon. Brown's stories were certainly more vivid than his various written sources for this topic because they were based on his own experiences as well as the Crafts' reports of their ordeals and those of some of Ellen Craft's cousins.

The mulatto woman in *Clotel* is a combination of traditional sentimental traits and a bold new kind of heroism. In fact, she undergoes a transformation from victim to heroine. A comment by Thomas Wentworth Higginson, Unitarian minister, reformer, and man of letters, may illustrate that a new consciousness of a hidden potential in women and black people was emerging in the society at large in the mid-nineteenth century. In November 1858, he wrote in the *Atlantic Monthly* an essay on "Physical Courage" in which he suggested that in desperate emergencies the black slave "seems to pass at one bound, *as women do,* from cowering pusillanimity to the topmost height of daring. The giddy laugh vanishes, the idle chatter is hushed, and the buffoon becomes a hero. Nothing in history surpasses the bravery of the Maroons of Surinam, . . . or those of Jamaica. . . . Agents of the Underground Railroad report that the incidents which daily come to their knowledge are beyond all Greek, all Roman fame."[35] Higginson's phrasing ("cowering pusillanimity," "giddy laugh") still reveals much prejudice, since he thinks of women and slaves only in extremes, as buffoons or heroes. Nevertheless, the statement at least shows a tendency to get away from the image of submissive slaves and submissive women, and it is this tendency that also prevails in William Wells Brown's *Clotel.* Brown's black and white women have more courage and imagination than the women in the average sentimental novel, and his male black characters in many instances also grow from buffoonery to heroism, from victimization to vision and action.

A closer look at Brown's women will show how far he goes along with the sentimental novelists' imagery and where he parts company with them. The main women of mixed blood in *Clotel* are Currer, her daughters Clotel and Althesa, and Althesa's children Ellen and Jane. Currer, many years earlier the mistress of Jefferson, is set up for sale in Richmond with her two daughters. She is introduced to us as a "bright mulatto . . . of prepossessing appearance, though then nearly forty years of age" (40). Currer is more than a helpless beautiful woman put up for auction. Brown's women, like his black male characters, aspire to a higher status in society. They want to prove that they can succeed beyond the limits which society decrees for them. Thus Currer, who is known as a first-class laundress, has middle-class aspirations for her daughters. She "early resolved to bring up her daughters as ladies, as she termed it, and therefore imposed little or no work upon them" (41). At a "negro ball," a polite gathering of white men of all classes and quadroon and mulatto girls she is delighted when the son of a wealthy gentleman takes an interest in Clotel, who is sixteen years old and of special beauty. Currer dies early, of yellow fever, but her high aspirations for her daughters determine the unusual "white slave" characters of two more generations.

Clotel when we first see her is the beautiful mulatto par excellence. When she is left alone on the auction block, after Currer and Althesa are sold, her exposure before a rude crowd is reminiscent of Hester Prynne's exposure at the scaffold: "The appearence of Clotel on the auction block created a deep sensation amongst the crowd. There she stood, with a complexion as white as most of those who were waiting with a wish to become her purchasers; her features as finely defined as any of her sex of pure Anglo-Saxon; her long black wavy hair done up in the neatest manner; her form tall and graceful, and her whole appearance indicating one superior to her position" (42). Clotel, like Hester, is elevated in character and attitude. In both instances, the young woman's beauty "shone out, and made a halo of the misfortune and ignominy in which she was enveloped," as Hawthorne describes Hester (53).

Brown, however, quickly turns the description into an indictment of society. He describes how the auctioneer lets the price go up as every new quality of the girl is mentioned, and how the audience enjoys his pausing for rough anecdotes between the biddings. The feelings of the girl are contrasted with the money-oriented coarseness of the auctioneer and the audience. "At this juncture the scene was indeed strange. Laughter, joking, swearing, smoking, spitting, and talking kept up a continual hum and noise amongst the crowd; while the slave girl stood with tears in her eyes" (43). The auctioneer's emphasis on her chastity finally brings the price up to fifteen hundred dollars, and at this point

Brown turns the characterization of the girl into an image of white society and pseudo-Christianity. "The maiden was struck for that sum. This was a Southern auction, at which the bones, muscles, sinews, blood, and nerves of a young lady of sixteen years were sold for five hundred dollars; her moral character for two hundred; her improved intellect for one hundred; her Christianity for three hundred; and her chastity and virtue for four hundred dollars more. And this, too, in a city thronged with churches . . . whose ministers preach that slavery is a God-ordained institution!" (43).

Brown does not prolong the satire. The tears on Clotel's face, unlike Hester's "glance that would not be abashed" (52) mark her as the typical victim of a popular novel. The tone is totally different from that of *The Scarlet Letter,* but Clotel, like Hester, is contrasted with an audience nominally Christian and lacking in basic human integrity. The Puritan women believe Hester should die for her trespass; the slave buyers treat Clotel like a piece of merchandise. In both instances, "the Scripture and the statute-book," as Hawthorne phrases it (52), are used to dehumanize woman.

In the later description of Clotel's fate, Brown sometimes follows Lydia Maria Child's "The Quadroons" so literally that his story reads like any sentimental antebellum romance. He takes over whole passages and very specific images from Child. Thus Brown sometimes does not speak in his own voice, at other times he is innovative in portraying his heroines. The cottage which her lover, Horatio, selects as Clotel's home is surrounded by clematis, passion flower, pride of china, and magnolias, just like the cottage of Child's quadroon Rosalie, and these images create an atmosphere of gentility. In both stories the quadroon's "high poetic nature" requires an outward form of marriage, though the bond, not legally acknowledged, is only "a marriage sanctioned by heaven." In both instances, the first-born child is even more light-skinned than the mother. In describing Clotel, Brown takes over a sentence characteristic of Child which is reminiscent of Stowe's generalizations about the "African race," though more flowery in style: "The iris of her large dark eye had the melting mezzotinto, which remains the last vestige of African ancestry, and gives that plaintive expression, so often observed, and so appropriate to that docile and injured race" (58).[36] Although it is ironic that Brown talks about his own race in the exact words of the female white romancer, especially since he portrays many characters of African ancestry in *Clotel* who are not "docile" at all, popular fiction dictated such imagery. When Clotel hears about Horatio's impending marriage with a white woman, her "pure mind" (81) determines that she will no longer be Horatio's mistress. As in Child's story, the farewell in the moonlight is heartrending. "The moon looked down upon [the lover] mild, but very sorrowfully; as the Madonna seems to gaze upon her worshipping children, bowed down with consciousness of sin" (82). Again, it seems unlikely that the black male writer would have used the image of the Madonna for this type of scene had it not been handed down to him by a popular white female story writer in exactly those words. From here on Child's and Brown's heroines go different ways. Both overcome the temptations of suicide by thinking of their children, but while Child's Rosalie dies of the "conflicts of her spirit," Clotel is kept alive for more dramatic undertakings.

After being sold to a slave trader, Clotel is once more shown as a victim, but now she is despised by blacks and whites alike. Thus her situation becomes more complex than that of Child's Rosalie. Clotel's new mistress, a merchant's wife in Vicksburg, Mississippi, is immediately jealous of the quadroon since "every married woman in the far South looks upon her husband as unfaithful, and regards every quadroon as a rival" (114). Clotel is ordered to cut her hair as short as the "full-blooded negroes in the dwelling" were required to wear it, and Brown takes this occasion to comment on the stratification among blacks of different shades.[37] "At her short hair, the other servants laughed, 'Miss Clo needn't strut round so big, she got short nappy har wel as I,' said Nell, with a broad grin. . . . The fairness of Clotel's complexion was regarded with envy as well by the other servants as by the mistress herself" (114).

The change in Clotel from victim to heroic figure occurs quickly, but it is presaged in the narrative by various stories about the heroism, skill, and imagination of slaves who have escaped to freedom. Clotel finds herself in a Pamela-like situation. Her new master tries to win her by flattery and expensive presents, but she stoutly maintains her virtue. At this point the story of the victimized Rosalie of Child's fiction becomes the story of the real

Ellen Craft, transformed into Brown's active, imaginative, and courageous fictional heroine.

Clotel's intelligence, in disguising herself, matches that of Ellen Craft. "Besides being attired in a neat suit of black, she had a white silk handkerchief tied round her chin, as if she was an invalid. A pair of green glasses covered her eyes; and fearing that she would be talked to too much . . . she assumed to be very ill" (134–35). The servant William with whom Clotel wants to escape slavery is "a tall, full-bodied negro, whose very countenance beamed with intelligence" (133). After many trials and near detections the two slaves arrive on free soil in Cincinnati. Brown does not take the occasion to develop a love story between them, a choice which shows that he has freed himself to some extent from the popular fictional obsessions. Clotel and William part without ceremony; he wants to go on to Canada, and she intends to rescue her child in Virginia. In her search for the child she distinguishes herself once more by courage and imagination. "She again resumed men's apparel" (154); she wears dark, false whiskers, a curling moustache, and high-heeled boots. She can hold her own in a stagecoach conversation on politics and temperance. Since she looks like a Spanish or Italian gentleman, two young ladies fall in love with her. The victim has turned out to be every inch a heroine.

When Clotel finally arrives in Richmond and her identity is detected, the author prefigures her dramatic end in a portrait of Nat Turner. Nothing could be further removed from the sentimental romances than a comparison of a deserted quadroon mistress with a male black insurrectionist like Nat Turner. Even the location of the prison, "midway between the capital [sic] at Washington and the President's house," contributes to the heroic climax. "The inconquerable love of liberty" causes her to jump into the Potomac when slave catchers want to arrest her again on the Long Bridge. "Had Clotel escaped from oppression in any other land, . . . and reached the United States, no honour within the gift of the American people would have been too good to have been heaped upon the heroic woman. But she was a slave, and therefore out of the pale of the sympathy" (177).

Not satisfied with a single heroine, one that had to die in order to be free, Brown reiterates the pattern of womanly ingenuity and daring in the person of Clotel's daughter Mary. She is in love with the mulatto George, who has taken part in the Nat Turner rebellion and is waiting for his death sentence, and selflessly suggests that they exchange clothes so that he can escape while she stays in his cell. In this part of the narrative Brown combines the daring of a new type of heroine with the traditional selflessness of woman's love as it is familiar from the sentimental novels. Clotel, "true to woman's nature, . . . had risked her own liberty for another" (170). Mary's story ends with the reflection that woman "embarks her whole soul in the traffic of affection; and, if shipwrecked, her case is hopeless, for it is a bankruptcy of the heart." This quotation from "a celebrated writer" (199) has only a decorative function, however, because Brown has portrayed more than the "traffic of affection" in the characters of Clotel and Mary. At the end of the experiences of three generations of "white slaves," woman is no longer only victimized, sold, betrayed, and raped, suffering it all helplessly. Clotel and Mary have visions of more than romantic love. Society's stigma has given them a vision of freedom that is the special gift of scapegoats, and they find their identity in acting upon that vision.[38] The mother achieves this only in death, the daughter in her daring attempt to rescue her mulatto rebel, who will be turned into a radical black rebel in the following versions of *Clotel.* The change in the women is possible only because they take over male roles, symbolically, by wearing male attire, and because they hide their true identities.

In contrast to these forward-looking heroines, Althesa's children, Ellen and Jane, end up like the typical sentimental heroines of mixed blood. Ellen commits suicide by poison to avoid abuse from a cruel master (167), and her younger sister, Jane, dies of a broken heart when her lover is shot and killed by Jane's master. The story of Jane mirrors the last part of Child's "The Quadroons," in which Xarifa, the daughter of Rosalie, goes mad when her master shoots her lover in his attempt to free her, and is abused by her master when she does not give in to his will. She finally dies in her insanity. Ellen and Jane, however, are minor characters who let the more active heroines stand out more clearly. The minor figures also include some stereotypical white women—the cold-hearted wife of Clotel's love, Horatio, and the cruel mistress of Clotel in Vicksburg—as well as the black cook Dinah who despises "dees mularter niggers" who "always want to set dey sef up for something big" (121). These figures simply give color to the novel and orchestrate the action of the main heroines.

Surprisingly, Brown also portrays an unusual white heroine who is neither the weak, sickly planter's wife nor a devil who outdoes the cruelties of her husband. Georgiana Peck, later Mrs. Carlton, shows some similarities to Stowe's Eva, but she is older, more mature, and more sober. She is the daughter of the slave-holding Reverend Peck in whom Brown depicted a real person by that name who argued, like his fictional counterpart, for slavery and against natural, inalienable rights.[39] This background gives to the portrait of Georgiana a measure of realism. Educated in the North, she "learned to feel deeply for the injured negro" (67). She, like little Eva in *Uncle Tom's Cabin*, is a perfect preacher, trying to convert her father away from slave holding and the family friend Carlton away from scepticism to a true faith. She persuades her father at least to stop justifying slavery with the Bible, and "whether it was admitted by the father, or not, she was his superior and his teacher" (92). She is also intelligent enough not to emphasize this fact in her outward behavior, being instead "modest and self-possessed, with a voice of great sweetness" (93).

In her serious conversations with Carlton, Brown "transferred to her much of his own passion."[40] Harriet Beecher Stowe likewise transferred some of her passion to her male black characters, Uncle Tom and George. Black as well as white abolitionists must have felt the desire not only to abolish slavery but to merge the traditionally prescribed traits of male and female, black and white, master and slave. Speaking for the author, Georgiana explains to Carlton that the seemingly happy attitude of the slaves, so much extolled by the pro-slavery writers, has a deeper meaning. "You may place the slave where you please; you may dry up to your utmost the fountains of his feelings, the springs of his thought; you may yoke him to your labour, as an ox which liveth only to work, and worketh only to live; you may put him under any process which, without destroying his value as a slave, will debase and crush him as a rational being; you may do this, and *the idea that he was born free will survive it all*" (119–20). Georgiana also explains why the slaves use deception and put on a mask before their masters, causing them to be known as dishonest: "If we would have them more honest, we should give them their liberty, and then the inducement to be dishonest would be gone" (120). Just as she is superior to her father, Georgiana is actually more perceptive and more determined than Carlton, who is a good student of hers. When Carlton cannot bring himself to propose to her, she takes the initiative, a step certainly unusual for a mid-nineteenth-century lady. "Love and duty triumphed over the woman's timid nature, and that day Georgiana informed Carlton that she was ready to become his wife" (125). When the couple plans a gradual emancipation of their slaves, Georgiana argues persuasively against sending them to Africa. "Is not this their native land? What right have we, more than the negro, to the soil here, or to style ourselves native Americans? Indeed it is as much their homes as it is ours, and I have sometimes thought it was more theirs. The negro has cleared up the lands, built towns, and enriched the soil with his blood and tears; and in return, he is to be sent to a country of which he knows nothing" (126).[41] When Georgiana develops consumption and is close to death, she is called a "liberator" as she gathers the slaves around her, preaching to them as little Eva did. She even becomes a savior figure when the author reflects on Carlton's loss of "her who had been a lamp to his feet, and a light to his path" (151). She is no sentimental child, however, but a very determined, practical woman who develops a realistic program for her slaves to earn their own money gradually and learn to live independently (128–29). If her complete virtue is as unrealistic as that of the mulatto women, she also transcends, like them, the image of the helpless, submissive women of popular fiction.

Brown's portrayal of black men is similar to his depiction of women. Some appear as stereotypes, but others are developed as more individualized characters who show strength and ingenuity.

An interesting creation, for example, is the character of Sam. He is "one of the blackest of his race" (99), and he considers himself the most important slave of the Reverend Peck. In his self-importance, his wish to imitate his master, and his attention to fancy clothes he is reminiscent of Adolph in *Uncle Tom's Cabin*, but he is much more intelligent than most all-black slaves in the fiction of the mid-nineteenth century. On one level he represents a comic stereotype. He greases his hair with fresh butter, over-dresses, and gives himself airs as the "Black Doctor." He also brags among the ladies that a fortuneteller told him he would "hab the prettiest yaller gal in town" and become a free man (100). On another level, however, Brown uses his ironic humor "not only as a weapon against the white master, but also against black accept-ance of the doctrine of white supremacy. Black Sam is comical when he judges mulattoes handsomer than blacks and lies about the color of his mother's skin. . . . In contrast to the plantation novels, which find comedy in the crudeness of the slaves' imita-tions of their masters, what is here seen as ludicrous is the black man's acceptance of white standards, his rejection of his blackness."[42] Seen more directly, Sam is an impressive figure in spite of being conceited. When the slaves sing secretly after Reverend Peck's death, Sam is the song leader and gives an impromptu pungent satire on the deceased slave holder (118); only a short while later he appears as the dignified house servant waiting kindly on "Miss Georgy." When Georgiana and Carlton start their program of gradual emancipation, Sam is made the head of the slaves on account of his "general intelligence" (128).

Another strong character is Picquilo, one of the runaway slaves hiding out in the swamps, who joins the insurgents gathering around Nat Turner.

> He was a large, tall, full-blooded negro, with a stern and savage countenance; the marks on his face showed that he was from one of the barbarous tribes in Africa . . . ; his only covering was a girdle around his loins, made of skins of wild beasts which he had killed. . . . Brought from the coast of Africa when only fifteen years of age to the island of Cuba, he was smuggled from thence into Virginia. He had been two years in the swamps and considered it his future home. . . . He moved about with the activity of a cat. . . . He was a bold, turbulent spirit; and from revenge im-brued his hands in the blood of all the whites he could meet. (172)

One of the archetypes of black portraiture is the "natural primi-tive," the symbol of freedom from cultural taboo, and Picquilo definitely fits this pattern.[43]

Brown's realism is especially vivid and harsh in the description of the slave hunt that ends with the burning of a slave tied to a stake. This slave is an example of "the intractable, the ironic, the abused Negro" who is missing in plantation fiction.[44] If Sam represents, at least in part, the ironic slave, the man burned at the stake is the abused Negro. Very skillfully Brown uses a newspaper report to give the details of the man's death. The report ironically reflects not only the slave's dignity in his last moments but also the reporter's prejudice or ambiguity: "Faggots were then collected and piled around him, to which he appeared quite indifferent. When the work was completed, he was asked what he had to say. He then warned all to take example by him, and asked the prayers of all around; he then called for a drink of water, which was handed to him; he drank it and said, 'Now set fire—I am ready to go in peace!' " (55). That the slave "warned all to take example by him" is probably meant by the reporter and understood by the average Mississippi newspaper reader as a warning to other slaves not to run away. In the context of Brown's work it could have a second meaning, as a warning to other slaves to resist oppression to the last breath the way he did. The passage is a good example of the ubiquitous irony in black fiction—so ubiquitous that it has given rise to the popular notion that black characters are never sophisticated enough to be ironic. In fact, however, the ogre of color caste is the one irony that "seems to be every Negro's *vade mecum* and [is] so gross in its proportions that, in strong contradiction to the inherent logic of ironic perception, no exquisiteness of sensibility is required to feel the dry mock of its incongruity."[45]

In *Clotel* many black slaves outwit white masters or slave catchers and show heroism in managing their escapes. "No country has produced so much heroism in so short a time, connected with escapes from peril and oppression, as has occurred in the United States among fugitive slaves, many of whom show great shrewdness in their endeavours to escape from this land of bondage" (131). The heroism is expressed in serious as well as comic scenes. Early black novelists used humor for various purposes: as a relief from grim episodes, as a weapon against bigotry, and as an answer to the stereotypes of the comic Negro created by white authors.[46] The slave who escapes unnoticed because he travels more than fifty miles with a fat pig and the one who leads another fugitive on a long rope, pretending he is a loyal servant bringing back an escaped slave, these are figures who mock the obtuseness of white people. Another means of emphasizing the shrewdness of black slaves is to show their superiority to poor whites in a humorous way. The overseer Huckelby on Reverend Peck's farm, for example, can neither read nor write and is ridiculously pretentious (79). The missionary whom Peck employs to make the slaves more docile finds the poor whites "ignorant as horses" and relates some hilarious stories about their lack of common sense (77).

Even a kind and sophisticated white man like Carlton can be mocked, along with Peck's missionary, by the ambiguously funny remark of a simple slave. When Carlton gives a kind of Sunday school lesson to the slaves and asks them simple questions to see whether the missionary's catechizing has done the slaves any good, he asks a field hand sitting near him, " 'Of course you know who made you?' The man put his hand to his head and began to scratch his wool; and, after a little hesitation, answered, 'De overseer told us last night who made us, but indeed I forgot the gentmun's name' " (105).[47]

Beside the quiet outwitting of whites and the comic heroism of escapees, appears the serious, and sometimes tragic, heroism of slaves. George, the rebel lover and future husband of Mary, is the best example. "He had heard his master and visitors speak of the down-trodden and oppressed Poles; he heard them talk of going to Greece to fight for Grecian liberty. . . . George, fired with the love of freedom and zeal for the cause of his enslaved countrymen, joined the insurgents, and with them had been defeated and captured" (181). He proves his heroism by saving some valuable papers from a burning courthouse, and yet he is to be hanged for treason. When he is asked to speak in his own defense, he delivers an eloquent oratory on his right to do what the American patriots of the Revolutionary War did, namely, fight for freedom. While he does not become a savior figure like Georgiana, he evokes the "genius of a true humanity" before his judges in rephrasing the words of Jesus: "O land of Washington, how often would I have gathered thy children together, as a hen does gather her brood under her wings, and ye would not" (183).[48]

Commonly Brown's women figures as well as his male black heroes acquire some refinement and culture. Just as Currer felt proud bringing up her daughters as ladies to have them rise above her own station, so George, after he settles in England, takes private lessons at night, becomes a partner in the firm that employed him, and is finally "on the road to wealth" (189). These aspirations of a coming black middle class are one of the main trends of black literature.[49] Brown has been viewed as a "conscious or unconscious propagator of assimilationism" and "the first novelist of the black bourgeoisie,"[50] but the genteel tendencies of Brown's characters do not make them any less heroic in overcoming their victimization, and Brown was far more radical than he was bourgeois.

The great variety of blacks and women shows that *Clotel* is not without artistic merit. Except for some pure stereotypes, most characters show, besides stock traits, some features which transcend the stereotype or make creative use of it. If the cook Dinah resents "dees mularter niggers" (121), she is made fun of, but her ignorance is put into perspective by more subtle characters like Sam, who shares her prejudice yet shows intelligence and integrity in other ways. If Ellen Morton commits suicide by poison like so many pathetic heroines in sentimental fiction, she is only one link in the chain of generations of "white slaves," many of whom react much more imaginatively and forcefully to their dire predicaments.

At least one of the stereotypical elements, the rebelling mulatto hero who passes for white, was avoided by Brown in some later editions of *Clotel*. In *Miralda; or, The Beautiful Quadroon*, published in *The Weekly Anglo-African* of 1860/61, Mary, now called Miralda, is not in love with a rebelling mulatto who can "pass" but with a black slave rebel, Jerome, a heroic African who defies his oppressors. However, in *Miralda* as well as in the 1864 edition, *Clotelle: A Tale of the Southern States*, Brown softens the tone and makes the novel more genteel by leaving out, for example, the forceful satirical sermon which Peck's missionary preaches to the slaves. The last edition, *Clotelle; or, The Colored Heroine* (1867), brings the novel up to date after the Civil War and the Emancipation. This version tells of Jerome and Clotelle (formerly Mary-Miralda) returning to America to aid the Union. Jerome is killed in an attempt to recover the body of his white commander. Clotelle becomes a nurse, aids in the escape of Union prisoners and black slaves, and returns to Mississippi to open a school for the freedmen. She has become an "Angel of Mercy."[51] The ending of this version is typically middle-class. Jerome during his time in England develops Horatio Alger–style success values. "Not only is Jerome hard-working, thrifty, loyal, and cultured—he is celibate as well,"[52] at least until he rediscovers his former love. Also, the humanitarian concern at the end of the novel is a middle-class issue.

Clotel, though the most uneven, is yet the most forceful version of the novel. Women and blacks in this work have much in common. They are not as ignorant, passive, or submissive as much popular fiction described them. Some of them show unexpected imagination, daring, and endurance in their desire for freedom and justice. The white Georgiana is as independent in her judgment as the mulatto women Clotel and Mary. The simple black slave Sam is as shrewd as the educated mulatto George. Of course, Brown in 1853 was still influenced by much race, class, and sex prejudice. "Except the pronounced black type, all Brown's women conform to the character pattern set by Charles Brockden Brown and the ancestral pattern established by Fenimore Cooper's Cora Munro. . . . His women are beautiful and charming, finely mannered, appealing."[53] Even the male hero George is almost white. In their beauty and fine manners, however, most of them succeed in turning their victimization into a scapegoat vision of individual and collective freedom and to act on it at all cost. Brown was able to portray blacks in this way because he expressed in them his own outsider's existence, his vision, and his concrete engagement. He later became a fervent supporter of racial identity, as exemplified in the figure of Jerome and especially in Brown's historical works.[54] He also became a defender of women's rights.[55] The seeds for a new beginning in black literature are discernible in *Clotel.*

5
Martin R. Delany's *Blake:* Resistance and Aggression in Women and Slaves

Violence is purgative in . . . books by Negro writers; it releases hostility and announces the black man's existence in a convulsive, unpredictable manner. . . . Violence is a natural and unexpected feature of Negro writing, for in the absence of a coherent and usable literary tradition, the Negro author has remained very close to fact—his first significant artistic achievement was in the form of autobiography—and he has recorded his despair directly.[1]

Martin R. Delany's single fictional attempt has been so much overshadowed by his other achievements that in 1868 his first biographer, Frances Rollin, did not even mention *Blake.* The work has been ignored frequently even in the twentieth century. Lorenzo Dow Turner's careful study of *Anti-Slavery Sentiment in American Literature Prior to 1865,* first published in 1929, does not mention Delany; neither does Darwin T. Turner's *Goldentree Bibliography of Afro-American Writers,* published in 1970. Neither *Blake* nor the better known *Clotel* appears in the *Literary History of the United States* by Spiller, Thorp, and others, revised in 1974. One reason that *Blake* has been overlooked is its form of publication. It did not appear as a book until 1970 and is even in this version still incomplete. Its definite artistic limitations (stilted dialogue, lack of cohesion between its two parts, too many plot elements) are not more severe than William Wells Brown's shortcomings, but they are different. Whereas Brown has a greater gift for storytelling, Delany gives us a wider perspective, a broad cultural panorama which turns his work into "the first picaresque novel by a black writer" or a black epic with an Odysseus-type hero. Even more than Brown's work, Delany's novel is based on oratory, and its seemingly structureless design can be described as rhetorical.[2] Delany, like Brown, was an accomplished abolitionist lecturer, in Pittsburgh.[3] Oratory was one of the arts that were common to both the Emersonian tradition and the early black American literature. Young Emerson's "passionate love for the strains of eloquence . . . was never to desert him; it wooed him under many guises, and invariably wove itself into his conception of the highest art." Whitman likewise was devoted to "the most popular art form of his day," an art "pre-eminently fitted for democracies."[4] The speeches of Henry Holland in *Blake* are the speeches of Martin Delany, the fervent orator, and the story contains many autobiographical elements.

Delany probably began the novel as an answer to *Uncle Tom's Cabin* because he thought that Harriet Beecher Stowe knew nothing about black people. He found value, however, in Stowe's use of the slave narrative material. He resented her use in fiction of a mulatto hero instead of an all-black protagonist and her colonizationist sentiments, but he may have revised his attitude toward her later, since he used two of her poems as epigraphs for the two parts of his novel. The "huts" in his subtitle seem to be equivalent to the "cabins" in Stowe's novel; the rough, dark, roach-infested hut of Daddy Joe in *Blake* stands in contrast to the more idyllic cabin of Uncle Tom.[5] Delany uses many of the incidents and devices which are basic ingredients in an abolitionist novel: "The separation of husbands from their wives and parents from their children, sometimes because of the financial ruin of their master, but more often for less justifiable reasons; the cruelty of overseers; the hair-breadth escapes of fugitives from their wicked pursuers; the insincerity of pro-slavery clergymen; the demoralizing influence of the slave system."[6] There is even an angelic mulatto child in the novel, a girl properly called Angelina, who brings to mind Uncle Tom's Eva. She swoons and almost dies when she witnesses the whipping and burning of slaves and revives instantly when her father, a Portuguese slave trader, promises "never again to traffic in human beings" (220). These concessions to popular taste, however, are secondary to the main tenor of the novel, the militancy of Henricus Blacus and the defiant mood of most black characters, even the women. In his militancy Delany differs strongly from most abolitionist writers, black or white.

Just as in William Wells Brown's case, a long list of designations describes Delany's achievements. He was a physician, editor, lecturer, author, explorer, ethnologist, inventor, politician, and the first black major in the United States army. Most decisive for his life was his ancestry. Frederick Douglass said of Delany, "I thank God for making me a man; Martin thanks God for making him a black man."[7] Delany was born in 1812 in Charles Town, Virginia (now West Virginia). His mother, Pati, was the daughter of an African princess who had been engaged to a Prince Shango when the couple was captured by men from Central Africa and sold to slave traders. Martin grew up with Grandmother Graci's songs and stories from Africa, and his mother must have inherited the proud blood of a Mandingo princess. She was like "a tigress with five cubs."[8] Pati committed the crime of teaching her children to read and write from a New York primer which a Yankee peddler had secretly sold her. She was summoned to court, and only through the intercession of a village banker was she able to escape punishment by fleeing to Chambersburg, Pennsylvania, a free state in which Martin was permitted to go to school. His father, Samuel, was the son of an African chieftain, but whereas Pati was a free woman, Samuel was a slave until 1823. Pati helped him to buy his freedom and in that year, when Martin was eleven, he finally joined the family.

At age fifteen Martin, forced to quit school to bring in money, worked at various odd jobs and read avidly in his spare time. When he was nineteen, he settled in Pittsburgh, where he worked as a barber and continued his education in a school run by a black minister. Delany stayed in Pittsburgh for twenty-five years, dividing his work between moral reform (temperance, self-help programs), abolitionism, and newspaper editing. From 1843 to 1847 he edited *The Mystery*, one of the very few black newspapers of the period[9] and gained a strong reputation for responsible editorship. After meeting Frederick Douglass, he co-edited *The North Star* with him. In 1852 he published a significant book, *The Condition, Elevation, Emigration, and Destiny of the Colored People of the United*

States, in which he advocated black emigration to Central and South America, while maintaining the anti-Liberian position of most abolitionists.

Early in his adult life, Delany began to practice medicine, first as a "cupper, leecher, and bleeder" and then studying with individual doctors to upgrade his profession. This training, combined with the hard work of an editor and family obligations, demanded unusual stamina. In 1843 Delany married Catherine Richards, daughter of a black father and an Irish mother, who would eventually bear him eleven children.[10] The year 1850 was marked not only by the Fugitive Slave Law and Delany's famous, defiant speech against the law in Allegheny but also by his decision to apply to medical school. Only a few black men had been permitted to study medicine in the United States by 1849, and these mainly because they promised to emigrate to Liberia. After being refused admission at several schools, Delany was finally admitted to Harvard Medical School, supported by many white doctors who had written letters of recommendation for him. But the experience lasted only one term. He had been admitted with two other black students, and their white classmates adopted a protest resolution ending with the statement that "we have no objection to the education and elevation of blacks, but do decidedly remonstrate against their presence in College with us." At this time the Dean of the Medical School was Oliver Wendell Holmes, a man who would not fight for a cause. Embarrassed, he decided that "this Faculty deem it inexpedient . . . to admit colored students on the medical lectures." Delany was allowed to finish the term and then was forced to leave.

Another incident in Delany's life also illuminates his rage over the constant degradation and limitation of blacks. In 1851/52 when he tried to secure a patent for an invention designed to help locomotives travel over mountainous terrain, the Patent Office in Washington had a policy of issuing patents only to "citizens," not black people.[11]

Meanwhile, Delany took up the study of phrenology and travelled West to give lectures disproving the notion of blacks' physical and intellectual inferiority. What concerned him most urgently, however, was the question of whether blacks should stay in the United States and fight for freedom or should emigrate and found a separate state. In 1839 he had travelled to Arkansas and Texas to study the possibility of settlements in Texas. Some of the experiences of this trip, including his visit with the Indians, are told twenty years later in *Blake*.

Delany emerged as a forceful leader of the emigrationist movement. In 1854 he chaired the National Emigration Convention in Cleveland which drew over one hundred men and women from ten states and Canada. He managed to include twenty-nine fully accredited and voting women in the membership of the conference, his wife, Catherine, being one of them. As early as 1848 at the National Negro Convention Delany introduced a resolution stating that women have a right to vote and hold office, but the convention allowed women only to attend, not to vote. Thus the Emigration Convention was the first national conference at which black women were fully accredited members.

In 1856 Delany finally decided to emigrate to Chatham, in western Canada. The debate about new laws pressing for the deportation of free blacks had contributed to his despair over the lack of full citizenship in the United States. He now regarded Canada as a temporary refuge for his people. In Chatham he continued to practice medicine while working on further emigration plans and various abolitionist issues. In 1848 John Brown knocked at his door. Delany seems to have approved Brown's plan to bring escaped slaves to Kansas and have them build an independent community, similar to the Cherokee nation or the Mormon settlement, but he probably knew nothing of the Harper's Ferry plan.[12] He was in Africa by the time the raid occurred.

It was the atmosphere of the Provisional Constitutional Convention at Chatham with Brown, however, which determined the tenor of *Blake*, because at this meeting in May 1858 some kind of raid upon the slave states was contemplated, and Delany finished the first chapters of his novel before the end of 1858. The work shows he probably knew more about slave uprisings than John Brown. From January to July 1859, *Blake* was serialized in the *Anglo-African Magazine*. Publication was halted after thirty chapters while Delany went to Africa, and in 1861–63 nearly fifty more chapters were published in *The Weekly Anglo-African*.[13] When the ominous final words of *Blake* in its present form were written— "Woe be unto those devils of whites, I say!"—Delany had been in

Africa and "had led the first party of scientific exploration to Africa from the American continent, all black manned and black financed."[14]

The rest of Delany's life and work is not as important for an understanding of *Blake*. Delany and his Jamaican friend Robert Campbell planned the "select emigration" of blacks from Canada and the United States to establish a settlement in the Niger Valley area, but various events conspired against their dream. The Civil War, especially, turned Delany's attention to other matters. By 1863 he was recruiting black soldiers, and in 1865 he became the first black major in the United States army. President Lincoln, after an interview with Delany on the recruitment of black slaves for the Union, recommended to Secretary of War Edwin Stanton "this most extraordinary and intelligent black man."[15] As a recruiter and later as an agent of the Freedmen's Bureau, Delany lived in South Carolina. In these years his career was "not one of consistent radicalism. . . . He was, after all, committed to nineteenth-century capitalism."[16] He continually espoused "self-help views," anticipating along with Douglass and others the thoughts of Booker T. Washington. In his African plans he had proposed the triad of cotton, Christianity, and civilization to strengthen the culture of an African state founded by American blacks, and his political aspirations during his time in South Carolina were not radical. In 1879 Delany published an ethnological work in which he reversed the arguments of racist theorists. In 1885 he died in Xenia, Ohio, at the age of seventy-two.

Blake represents Delany's prewar thinking. It was begun probably in 1852 or 1853, but most of it seems to have been written in Canada from 1856 to 1859. "Probably his desire for funds to finance his expedition to Africa motivated his interest in publishing *Blake*."[17] The novel was meant to provide the reader with a new set of images for black people, because Delany knew that "to control the image was not only to be where the action was but also to determine the fate of a people."[18] The foremost new image was the all-black West Indian hero, Henricus Blacus, later called Blake, who is pirated away from home to be sold as a slave to Louisiana. He is renamed Henry Holland and marries a mulatto slave, Maggie, daughter of her owner Colonel Franks and a slave

woman, Mammy Judy. When Maggie is sold away from her husband to Cuba and Henry is also to be sold, he escapes and travels
throughout the South, spreading his plan of a unified slave rebellion. He helps several slaves to escape with him to Canada. In
chapter 34 the plot changes completely as Henry sails to Cuba in
order to find his wife. Chapters 35–74 are set in Cuba, and it is
especially this second part of the novel which distinguishes it from
other abolitionist fiction. Six more chapters were published in the
Weekly Anglo-African of May 1862, which have so far not been
uncovered.[19]

The unique combination of settings—Louisiana, various other
Southern states, Canada, and Cuba—is matched by a unique
variety of characters. Beside the pure black Blake stands his
beautiful mulatto wife; the traditional Christian slaves Mammy
Judy and Daddy Joe contrast sharply with the High Conjurers who
have organized in the Dismal Swamp to carry on the tradition of
Nat Turner (112–14). Henry's followers Andy and Charles, who
combine buffoonery, plans for a violent rebellion, and a Baptist
faith, are set off by impressive figures like the mulatto poet Placido
and the intelligent and powerful chef Gofer Gondolier. Among
the women whites, mulattoes, and blacks appear in an astounding
variety of character. Reticent Mrs. Franks, courageous Mrs. Van
Winter, and sentimental Cornelia Woodward represent a spectrum of white women; gossipy Louisiana slave girls as well as high
society Cuban mulatto ladies are portraits in various shades of
black. "Unlike many other polemicists of his time, Delany discovered good and evil in both races and in both sections. The
northern opportunist and the Negro drunkard appear in the same
gallery with the slave trader and the arrogant aristocrat."[20]

In all this variety, however, Delany does not lose sight of his
main points: that black people of all shades and classes have to be
unified to achieve their freedom, and that the intelligence,
achievement, and character of individual black Americans are not
dependent on the amount of white blood in their veins. If the
mulattoes, quadroons, and octoroons of writers like Stowe and
William Wells Brown would mostly "claim the morals, images,
and symbols of whites as their own," Delany "set about to redefine
the definitions,"[21] to show that a pure African could be superior to

any mulatto, and that the images of Western Christianity and Western morality could not simply be used against, or transferred to, enslaved black Africans.

Blake is not only an efficient organizer, charismatic leader, and dedicated family man. In describing his influence on others Delany sounds an apocalyptic note: Blake is a "messenger of light and destruction" (101), the "Arm of the Lord" (224), a "dread" (207), a "destroying angel" (83), a "King" (104). His personality commands obedience, his mere look seems to influence nature. A Portuguese mate on the ship *Vulture* tells Blake: "By your looks a grin from you would fascinate a mermaid; the flash of your eye obscure the most vivid streak of lightning, and the sound of your voice silence the loudest clap of thunder. Have you ever stayed a tempest and quieted the raging seas?" (200). Blake is as ungraspable as a "flying cloud" (108); a poisonous snake does not harm him (115). His dialogues are authority-commanding catechizations:

> "How do they treat their slaves?"
> "Da boys all mighty haud maustas, de gals all mighty good; sahvants all like 'em."
> "You seem to understand these people very well, aunty. Now please tell me what kind of masters there are generally in the Red River country."
> "Haud 'nough, chile, haud 'nough, God on'y knows!"
> "Do the colored masters treat theirs generally worse than the whites?"
> "No, hunny, 'bout da same."
> "That's just what I want to know. What are the usual allowances for slaves?"   (72)

Blake's style of speaking is not only highly polished and often stilted to distinguish him from ordinary slaves, but in the Cuban "seclusions" or at the secret rebel gatherings his presence gives a ritualistic style to the discussions (256–60, 292).[22] Biblical imagery heightens the character of Blake. An old man named Nathan thanks the Lord for being able to behold Henry, as the biblical Simeon beheld the Christ child: "My eyes has seen, and meh yeahs heahn, an' now Laud! I's willin' to stan' still an' see dy salvation!" (73).[23] The recurring image of standing still and seeing

the Lord's salvation is totally reversed from its traditional inter-
pretation by the actions and the character of Henry. When Daddy
Joe admonishes him to stand still and see the Lord's salvation,
Henry retorts:

> "That's no talk for me, Daddy Joe; I've been 'standing still' long
> enough. . . ."
> " 'Now is the accepted time, today is the day of salvation.' So
> you see, Daddy Joe, this is very different to standing still."
> "Ah boy, I's feahd yeh's losen yeh 'ligion!"
> "I tell you once for all, Daddy Joe, that I'm not only 'losing' but I
> have altogether lost my faith in the religion of my op-
> pressors." (21)

Although the activist Henry rejects the idea of "standing still,"
Andy, a former Baptist preacher and a loyal follower of Henry,
uses the phrase of standing still and seeing the salvation to persuade the rebel Charles to trust and obey Henry (40).

Henry Holland, alias Henricus Blacus, is thus a black revolutionary hero evoking apocalyptic images of salvation as well as
destruction. "Like the biblical Daniel and historical Nat Turner,
[he] wrote off the present age as irredeemably evil, saw the new age
as abruptly replacing, not redeeming, this age and claimed to have
a revealed scheme of things."[24] When Blake is seen as a destroying
angel "more terrible" than the angel commanding the slaughter of
the first-born in Egypt (83), he is the symbol of a black Christian
faith which refused to see obedience to white masters and patient
suffering of slavery as the essence of Christianity. The slaves'
religion, unlike their masters', was a "free" or "whole" gospel.[25]
At times God was regarded as the exclusive agent of imminent
redemption, while at other times the militant agency of the blacks
themselves was deemed essential. The apocalypse was not seen as
an end of all time so much as a sudden destruction of all oppression
and a liberation of the enslaved.

> While white Americans expounded doctrines of progress and con-
> cerned themselves with what Herman Melville (in *Pierre*) called
> horological time, black Americans looked to an absolute, linear
> (chronometrical) time moving from the creation to the judgment

day, which, they felt, would be the day of their liberation. White Americans, as R.W.B. Lewis, Perry Miller, and Leo Marx have demonstrated, considered themselves new Adams in a new Garden of Eden; they believed that thrift and industry, a powerful technology, the dictates of social Darwinism, and a laissez-faire economy would assure the endurance and growth of their paradise. The black American's theological perspective, on the other hand, stressed his own "Egyptian captivity," not his ease in a new Eden. One result of these divergent views has been an opposition between the white and the black American's conceptions of the apocalypse.[26]

Two qualities differentiate Blake from a black Jewish-Christian prophet and leader like Harriet Beecher Stowe's Dred. One is his rationalism, the other—to put it anachronistically—is his quasi-Marxism. Some of his statements express an eighteenth-century rationalistic understanding of nature and the Deity combined with a revolutionary romanticism: "Equality of rights in Nature's plan, / To follow nature is the march of man" (293). The general insurrection which Henry Holland envisions will be as natural as "the whistling of the wind, rustling of the leaves, flashing of lightning, roaring of thunder, and running of streams" (39). Historical change is as inevitable as the flux of nature: "That time to strike was fast verging upon them, from which, like the approach of the evening shadow of the hilltops, there was no escape" (292). Henry's rationalism is also obvious when he becomes a High Conjurer in the Dismal Swamp. He is eager to "enlighten" his friends on his position that conjuring is a foolish superstition which simply puts money in the conjurer's pocket and makes the slaves passive and dependent (136–37). He becomes a conjurer only as a means of being all things to all people, because "I'll do anything not morally wrong, to gain our freedom; and to effect this, we must take the slaves, not as we wish them to be, but as we really find them to be" (126). What Blake considers "morally wrong," however, is not dependent on traditional morality. "I'm incapable of stealing from any one, but I have, from time to time, taken by littles, some of the earnings due me for more than eighteen years service to this man Franks, which at the low rate of two hundred dollars a year, would amount to sixteen hundred dollars more than I secured, exclusive of the interest, which would have more than supplied my clothing, to say nothing of the injury done me by degrading me as a slave" (31).[27] He exhorts the slaves to keep the overriding issue of economics in mind. "God told the Egyptian slaves to 'borrow from their neighbors'—meaning their oppressors—'all their jewels'—meaning to take their money and wealth wherever they could lay hands upon it, and depart from Egypt. So you must teach them to take all the money they can get from their masters to enable them to make the strike without a failure" (43). On the flight north, any white ferryman can be bribed with money (130). "Delany departs radically from the Abolitionist formula of broken families and violated octoroons by treating slavery primarily as an exploitative labor system. It is a remarkable novel, closer in spirit to Karl Marx than to the New England Abolitionists."[28]

The character of the black hero Blake is a unique fusion of revolutionary fervor, mystical religion, rationalism, and economic consciousness, yet he is not the typically tough, "all-masculine" leader. He can shed tears freely, and he conducts himself with great modesty (44, 69, 85, 125, 242). The women in Blake, likewise, are not purely feminine types. Several of them exhibit "male" toughness as well as some of Henry's revolutionary fervor.

The Cuban section offers some outstanding women of mixed blood and a Soudan woman named Abyssa who feels drawn to Blake as a charismatic leader. On the slave ship *Vulture* she is confined under terrible conditions (229), all the more degrading since she is an educated woman who used to be a textile merchant. (Certainly no earlier abolitionist novel had introduced an all-black, African, female merchant!) She is described as "handsome and pleasant, with a meek and humble look" (224). She had been a Mohammedan, then converted to Christianity, and was later taken in warfare and sold to Dahomi (224). She speaks good English and startles Blake by whispering into his ears in passing, "Arm of the Lord, awake!" When she later utters a spontaneous prayer at the soiree in Madam Cordora's house, a wealthy quadroon planter suspects her of being crazy, but one of the guests explains that "her head is as clear as a sunbeam" (249). She is "moaning with joy in African accents" when Blake is chosen as leader of the emancipation army (251). Later she marries the black Gofer Gondolier, who in boyhood attended a Spanish grandee to Genoa and is now "caterer of the police cuisine." Delany uses the occasion of their wedding to point out the innocent faith of Abyssa and—with heavy-handed satire—the seemingly empty rituals of the Roman Catholic church. He considers the priest a "simpleton" and the whole church wedding a superfluous formality, but Abyssa is not criticized for believing in the ceremony (279–81). She prays for her enemies, in contrast to her rather tough, radical, pragmatic husband, Gofer (291), but she believes in the revolution with religious fervor, and that gives her a power different from his. While her traditional Christianity, then, differs from Blake's deism, she has many of his traits: beauty, stateliness, an urge to witness the apocalypse of liberation, and the ability to express emotions freely. As a merchant she must certainly also have his consciousness of economics.

A very different type of woman is Blake's wife, Maggie. In many respects she is a "traditional" figure, the beautiful, victimized mulatto of many abolitionist novels. "She was a dark mulatto of a rich, yellow, autumnlike complexion, with a matchless cushionlike head of hair, neither straight nor curly, but handsomer than either" (6). She is separated from her little son when she is sold without him to Mrs. Ballard, the cold-hearted wife of a Northern judge who is a stereotype of the cruel slave holder. She in turn sells Maggie to a very cruel Cuban "for the worst of designs" (190). When he is unable to subdue her virtue, even through torture, he sends her to his equally cruel sister, Madame Garcia. At the Garcia hacienda Henry finally finds his wife. At first he does not know her because the daily terror she has lived with has aged and disfigured her face. He recognizes her at the moment "when was heard the frightful yelping of approaching dogs, having in chase a large guana, which rushing pass [sic], brushed the skirt of her dress, when screaming Maggie stood supported in the arms of her husband" (180). The guana is a fitting image for the victimized Maggie, but she is a tough, surviving victim, different from those tragic octoroons who die of broken hearts or who take poison to escape disgrace. She has a toughness of resistance in common with Delany's male heroes.

When Henry provides the money to buy his wife's freedom and, according to Cuban laws, her owners have to let her go, the abused

Maggie's spirit gradually revives. She and Henry share a religious faith that has been severely tested but prevails in their final reunion. Maggie now becomes the devoted wife who has to be educated to understand her husband's great tasks and to bear patiently his absences from home in the service of a greater cause. "Henry detailed to her his plans and schemes; and the next day imparted his grand design upon Cuba. At this information she was much alarmed, and could not comprehend that an ordinary man and American slave such as he, should project such an undertaking" (191). She would like to keep him at home, but he explains to her that only she is legally free, while he can yet be recaptured as a fugitive slave, and he has to help others who share his fate. When she tries to dissuade him from his revolutionary plans, he becomes patronizing.

> "My dear wife, you have much yet to learn in solving the problem of this great question of the destiny of our race. I'll give you one to work out at your leisure; it is this: Whatever liberty is worth to the whites, it is worth to the blacks; therefore, whatever it cost the whites to obtain it, the blacks would be willing and ready to pay, if they desire it. Work out this question in political arithmetic at your leisure, wife, and by the time you get through and fully understand the rule, then you will be ready to discuss the subject further with me." Maggie smiled and sighed, but said no more on the subject. (192)

Later, when Blake is elected "General-in-Chief of the army of emancipation of the oppressed men and women of Cuba" (241), Maggie is desperate: " 'I suppose then I may give up all hope of ever having you with me at all!,' she replied with renewed sobs" (242). This time it is Henry's cousin, the rebel poet Placido, who feels called upon to teach her a lesson: "The position of a man carries his wife with him; so when he is degraded, she is also, because she cannot rise above his level; but when he is elevated, so is she also; hence, the wife of Henry the slave was Maggie the slave; but the wife of Mr. Henry Blake will be Mrs. Maggie Blake; and the wife of General Blake will be Mrs. General Blake" (242). Maggie now understands everything and gives the poet a "smile of gratification."

From a twentieth-century perspective, these scenes seem out of place in a revolutionary novel, but they take on a different meaning in light of the rest of the story and Delany's early life experiences. In the later part of the novel Maggie Blake is not the contented housewife who carries on cheerfully without her politically active, mostly absent husband; she takes an active part with other women in the rebel "seclusions," "the misses being admitted by courtesy, they having the confidence of the seclusion" (255). Delany's childhood experiences and the position of black women in his time also helped to form his views on the matter of woman's role and aspirations.

> He established, as a barometer of a people's social health, the occupations of its women and, therefore, of its men. In doing so he aroused the ire of the black women, whose status as domestics and children's nurses was considerably higher than that of their fathers and husbands as unskilled laborers. Delany argued that the reverse should be sought, that the women of his race should aim to become ladies themselves, rather than ladies' maids, and that the economic and professional elevation of the male was the true standard of a people's success. Delany's preoccupation with this theme is obvious. He was the son of a free, enterprising, and ambitious woman. His father had been a slave and was now a laborer.[29]

Thus, if Delany's male heroes are on occasion boringly didactic in their conversations with women, the emphasis on their intelligence and courage is accounted for by the lesser opportunity they had, compared to their wives, to rise above the level of common slaves. At one of the "seclusions" when Madame Cordora rises to ask a question about whether the religious observances of the revolutionaries disagree with those of the Roman Catholic faith in which many of the participants were raised, Blake addresses a long speech to her:

> "I, first a Catholic, and my wife bred as such, are both Baptists; Abyssa Soudan, once a pagan, was in her own native land converted to the Methodist or Wesleyan belief; Madame Sabastina and family are Episcopalians; Camina, from long residence out of the colony, a Presbyterian, and Placido is a believer in the Swedenborgian doctrines. We have all agreed to know no sects, no denomination, and but one religion for the sake of our redemption

from bondage and degradation. . . . The whites accept of nothing but that which promotes their interests and happiness, socially, politically, and religiously. They would discard a religion, tear down a church, overthrow a government, or desert a country, which did not enhance their freedom. In God's great and righteous name, are we not willing to do the same?" (258)

Even though the men act as teachers and women as learners, women, such as Madame Cordora, are shown to possess intelligence (257), and in general the fictional women in *Blake* are as much equal participants at the council-meetings as the real women present at Delany's Emigration Convention.

Several other black and mulatto women besides Abyssa, Maggie, and Madame Cordora show strengths in their characters. Mammy Judy, in spite of being a simple slave and a traditional Christian in a way which Henry cannot accept, is ingenious in covering up the disappearance of Maggie's and Henry's little boy, who has been secretly taken away by his father to go North with other escaped slaves. Mammy Judy fakes a sudden religious inspiration when she is interrogated (45), and her shrewd concealment is true to the spirit of the slave narratives. Ailcey is a simple slave girl who gradually gains in stature. "Ailcey was a handsome black girl, graceful and intelligent, but having been raised on the place, had not the opportunity of a house maid for refinement" (52). She is as clever and unselfish as Mammy Judy in covering up Little Joe's disappearance (48). Phebe Seth, with her husband, Nathan, welcomes Henry during his secret travels in the South (101–7). She sings one of the several spirituals in the story, which contribute a strong folk element to the novel (104).[30] She is as determined as any male to get rid of the slave Tib who betrayed the secret meeting of the revolutionaries. "I wish I was man, I'd break 'is neck, so I would!," she declares (106). On the whole, the black and mulatto women are mostly of equal stature with the black men, except that they often have to be taught before they can fully participate in the liberation struggle. In his work as a reformer Delany pleaded for adequate schools for black women, and his encouraging of career goals beyond the domestic sphere predated the women's rights movement.[31] His fictional black women are to a large extent in accord with his theoretical views.

Delany's treatment of mulattoes is distinctive in that, unlike other abolitionist fiction, *Blake* shows many unamiable mulattoes. When Henry in his travels through Louisiana visits a plantation owned by a mulatto family, he finds out that they treat their slaves very badly (71–72). When he is looking for a job in South Carolina, a "respectable-looking mulatto gentleman" tells him to take off his hat, calls him "boy," and tries to have him arrested (111). Not all mulatto images are negative, however (81, 118). Placido, a historical figure and in real life as well as in fiction a man of mixed blood, is in the novel a highly respected spokesman for the black revolutionaries. He makes it plain to Madame Cordora that the liberation of all people of color, whatever their shade, can only start with pure-blooded Africans, because in acknowledging the equality of the African with themselves, white people would necessarily have to acknowledge the equality of mulattoes (260–61). At one point she declares, "Although I thought I had no prejudices, I never before felt as proud of my black as I did of my white blood" (262). In describing the "Brown Society" of Charleston, Delany shows that mulattoes who believe in the superiority of their own color over that of pure blacks are the unwitting tools of white people (111). Even though he answers the stereotypes of the no-good black and the beautiful mulatto with the counter-stereotype of the pure black hero, he is capable of transcending all types. That Delany considers blacks and mulattoes as well as whites "to be capable of virtue or vice, heroism or villainy, is borne out in the extensive range of characters he utilizes in the novel."[32]

The white women in *Blake* in comparison with male and female blacks are equally varied. If women and blacks in William Wells Brown's work asserted themselves by aspiring to middle-class status and gentility, in Delany's they aspire to self-determination and freedom. In two of the white women in the novel, this drive for independence is perverted. The Northern judge's wife, Mrs. Ballard, wants to wield tyrannical power over the maid Maggie (6, 8), and Madame Garcia, later the mistress of Maggie in Cuba, is the stereotype of a devilish woman who hates nothing more than the rights of black people (168, 185). Two other white women make honest but not very strong attempts to assert themselves. Mrs. Franks, Maggie's original mistress, is to some extent the weak

Southern lady typical of abolitionist novels. She is kind to her maid and treats her almost like a sister, but she is unable to keep her husband from selling Maggie. Although she tries to defend Maggie's and Henry's rights, her husband does not give in. She turns to Mrs. Winter and Major Armsted to have Maggie and Henry bought back and enfranchised (22, 65), but her honest attempts to stand up for what is right prove futile. Cornelia Woodward is more successful in her self-assertion as a woman. Her story, however, is too melodramatic to make her an impressive figure. She is an innocent American Eve victimized by a male intrigue (165). After she sees through the deceptions of the man who wanted to marry her, she vigorously determines "by the purity of unsullied womanhood" (164) that she will no longer let him sport with her misfortune. When he finds a poem by Cornelia expressing her lovesickness for him, however, he repents, she forgives, and they marry the next day (166).

Two other white women are as freedom-loving as any black slave in *Blake*. In fact, they are advocates of the slaves and support them in word and deed. Mrs. Van Winter is known among the plantation owners as the black sheep in the community. She actively helps the slaves to escape (22, 46), and yet she does not isolate herself. She is a friend of Mrs. Franks and gives an affectionate hug to Sheriff Hughes (she is related to his wife) when he searches for information about the fugitive Henry at her house (57). The other lover of freedom and equality is the Frenchwoman Celia Bonselle, who is visiting at the Garcias. "Madame Bonselle was an excellent lady, and loved by all the slaves on the hacienda. Being French, she was an inherent votary of the late revolution and reform, and a believer in the principles espoused by the government of Lamartine, Ludro Rollin and Louis Blanc, and even wore a gold brooch on which the motto was inscribed 'Liberte, Eqalite [sic], Fraternite!' " (168).

Besides blacks and mulattoes, other ethnic minorities appear in the novel. There are first of all the Indians whom Henry visits on his travels through Arkansas. A discussion with the chief shows him that the Indians, in spite of being slave holders, have more respect for their slaves than white people. "Indian work side by side with black man, eat with him, drink with him, rest with him, and both lay down in shade together; white man even won't let you talk. In our Nation Indian and black all marry together. Indian like black man very much, ony he don't fight 'nough."[33] Henry is quick to answer the chief: "You make, Sir, a slight mistake about my people. They would fight if in their own country they were united as the Indians here, and not scattered thousands of miles apart as they are. You should also remember that the Africans have never permitted a subjugation of their country by foreigners as the Indians have theirs . . ." (86). The chief agrees, and when Henry asks where the Indians would stand in case the blacks would rise up, he is told that in Florida, where blacks and Indians have fought side by side in the Seminole Wars, the two groups lived peacefully together. "The squaws of the great men among the Indians in Florida were black women, and the squaws of the black men were Indian women. You see the vine that winds around and holds us together." The chief encourages Henry's revolutionary fervor: "If you want white man to love you, you must fight im!" (87).

While Delany has a favorable image of the Indian, he does not portray other ethnic minorities in a positive way. A Dutchman (119), two Irish gendarmes (274), and especially a German tavern keeper named Slusher are ignorant, primitive characters. When Slusher's attempt to get good business from a party of fugitive slaves is foiled, he pities himself: " 'Convound dish bishnesh! . . . Id alwaysh cosht more dan de ding ish wordt. Mine Got! afder dish I'll mindt mine own bishnesh. Iv tem Soudt Amerigans vill gheep niggersh de musht gedch dem demzelve' " (152).

Foreign immigrants, in *Blake* and in the black novel generally, take the place of funny black slaves in the plantation novel. Providing comic relief, just like the native poor whites, they emphasize the intelligence of black slaves.[34] All nonwhite characters of importance, however, are assertive, crave their freedom, and are willing to pay the highest price for it. It is the same with most of the women, especially the black women. While blacks as well as women are often seen as needing instruction because their knowledge is still limited, their basic intelligence and right to independent judgment are never questioned. Mrs. Garcia is instructed by her brother in the realities of Cuban law and English politics (184–86). Henry instructs his wife, Maggie, and the Cuban ladies at the "seclusions" (242, 258), and he constantly

teaches the slaves about the North Star, the foolishness of superstitions, and the need to get money. But the lack of education or
refinement never implies fewer innate abilities. The simple field
hand Ailcey shows as much shrewdness as Madame Cordora.
Andy, Henry's follower, is just as important for the revolution as
the sophisticated Placido.

Delany widens the perspective on women as well as blacks by
adding exotic scenes and characters. Often there is something
static or closed in the universe of black fiction; the ghetto or the
irony of color caste limits the view.[35] Although the world of blacks
in *Blake* is limited, Delany opens up windows into the world at
large by adding settings and characters that evoke Africa, the
American Indian, the French Revolution, and Cuban culture and
society. This use of exotic elements, inside America and outside,
differs from the use of the exotic in white fiction. Melville finds
the exotic in women and in South Sea islanders, and for him an
exotic setting is an isolated group of tropical islands or the drab
rooms of New York bohemians. An exotic setting in *Blake* is the
high society in the city of Havana. In *The Scarlet Letter*, the exotic
forest wilderness is threatening and tempting; in Delany, as in the
slave narrative, the swamp wilderness is a superb hiding place for a
group of Voodoo believers, exotic conjurers, and mystic revolutionaries (110–15).[36] Thoreau traces the path of the American
Indians to recover their simple life style; Delany wants to learn
from the Indians how slaves can be treated in a "civilized" way.
The most exotic woman in Delany is not a Pacific nymph or a
mentally primitive girl of American-French ancestry, as in
Melville, but a merchant woman from Soudan who supports a
revolutionary council. Among black writers the exotic scenes and
characters exist within the community and civilization, not away
from them.

The slave narratives provided a darker view of the presumably
ideal world of Southern rural life; their authors knew that the
landscaped gardens and opulent villas in the country were made
possible by an inhuman social system. In contrast, a Northern city
seemed like an Eden to them, and therefore some of the slave
narratives reverse the pattern of *Walden, Moby-Dick,* and *Huckleberry Finn,* although often the praises of the city also end in
disillusionment.[37] *Blake,* like the slave narratives, moves from

rural slave cabins and plantations to cities—Windsor, Canada, New York City, and Havana, Cuba; it moves not away from civilization but toward it. Hawthorne's Zenobia eagerly leaves the city for a rural Utopia; Maggie Blake longs to leave a rural hell for a civilized city. The French connection in Melville's *Pierre* points to immorality and exotic temptations; the Frenchwoman Celia Bon-selle in *Blake* stands for civilized *liberté, égalité, fraternité.*

The exotic settings and characters, then, have a special func-tion in the black novel. Just as in *Clotel* the flight to an alien setting (England or France) implies that outside the United States the black person is treated as an equal, so in *Blake* the Cuban setting proves that there are countries where a slave can at least buy his or her freedom and where black people hold positions far above those of house servant, nursemaid, or groom. Through exotic settings within the United States, like the Dismal Swamp or an Indian nation, the author can make use of folk elements (superstitions, songs) and ethnic traditions. The retreats into nature which the characters seek, however, are not individualis-tic, as in *Walden;* they are, rather, a search for community. "The black culture hero's desperate assertion of self does not alienate him from his people, as so often occurs with the protagonists of Melville and Hawthorne; it makes him an example to them of their corporate capacity for liberation. Thus *Blake* links romantic individualism and revolutionary politics in a manner much more akin to the thinking of Shelley and Byron than to the writing of American romantics."[38]

Delany's thinking in *Blake* may also be akin to another roman-tic, William Blake, whose fusion of rationalism, mysticism, and revolutionary fervor foreshadows the black revolt, from Delany to Malcolm X, against a white Christianity that practiced oppression but asked virtue of the slave. "One Law for the Lion & Ox is Oppression," as William Blake laconically phrased it.[39] The ancient Hebrew fervor and prophetic stature of Henry Blake brings to mind Rintrah or other angry prophets in William Blake. They preach the same inversion of ethical values. Henry Blake admits that he simply turns the principles of the slave holders' Christianity upside down: " 'You must make your religion sub-serve your interests, as your oppressors do theirs!' advised Henry. 'They use the Scriptures to make you submit, by preaching to you the texts of "obedience to your masters" and "standing still to see the salvation," and we must now begin to understand the Bible so as to make it of interest to us' " (41). If whites have justified violence to obtain their liberty as a people, blacks should do no less, Delany argues. And so we see Gofer Gondolier, chef-caterer of the Palace police, standing ready with his kitchen carving knife to fight for freedom (253–54) and calling the whites "devils" (312–13), "reptiles" (309), and "alabasters" (253); and Phebe Seth, the slave woman, wishing she were a man so as to break the neck of a traitor to the black people (106).

We do not know, however, how the novel ends. We know only how Delany's life went on, and his life story is not without ambiguities in the later years. He longed for the pure primitiveness of Africa as it had been known many centuries earlier, yet he wanted to civilize, Christianize, and industrialize Africa when he planned the settlement in the Niger Valley. "As he urged blacks to develop an African basis for their identity and freedom, he also realized his deep attachment to America."[40] The dedication of his book *The Condition, Elevation . . .* "to the American people, north and south, by their most devout, and patriotic fellow-citizen, the author" speaks of this attachment. Delany in the person of Henry Blake calls for violence, primitive and simple, to end the evil of slavery (82), but Blake also knows that he could never kill his kind mistress, Mrs. Franks, and that his followers and friends, Andy and Charles, could never "muster up courage enough to injure a 'good master' or mistress." "I cannot find it in my heart to injure an individual except in personal conflict" (128). Delany, like Blake, had a mulatto wife, and his thoughts of violence against whites were naturally tempered by this fact. Delany in his imagination may have raged against whites because he felt compelled to relieve his inner tension and to commit himself unambiguously to "Afra-ka," as the young black sailor Gascar calls it in *Blake* (210).[41] Whether this is true or not, Delany's image of blacks in *Blake* was bound to be ambiguous. The black masses are to be instructed and guided so they will leave their primitive subservience behind. At the same time, they should be even more primitive, sloughing off their inhibitions toward violence in order to affirm their aboriginal strength and unmask the more sophisticated and more far-reaching violence of their masters. The Soudan woman Abyssa admonishes her husband, "You should 'pray for them that de-spitefully use you' " (291), but she supports the plans for a rebel-lion with the repeated shouts, "Arm of the Lord, awake!" (224, 257). This paradox does not imply weakness; it is reminiscent of ancient Hebraic as well as Islamic traditions to which blacks, disenchanted with a perverted Christianity, have tended to return.[42]

No clear-cut solution was possible for the black writers of the mid-nineteenth century. They tried to break the silence which has characterized the black experience even in Nat Turner's story (ironically known only in the words of the white Mr. Gray) and in Melville's "Benito Cereno." "Under American slavery, a black man's speech did not legally exist. His testimony inadmissible at court, his literacy forbidden, quite literally he was made mute."[43] When black writers finally spoke, their voices were still unbal-anced—sentimental as in Brown, violent as in Delany—from the agony of not being heard. Symbolically, perhaps, *Blake*, as we know it, does not have an ending.

6

The Epic of Dekanawida:
Aboriginal Strength in
Native American Narrative

*A primitive people is not a backward or retarded people; indeed it may possess
a genius for invention or action that leaves the achievements of civilized
peoples far behind.* [1]

Claude Lévi-Strauss

*One should begin by assuming that an Indian oral narrative may be a
first-rate work of art. . . .
. . . It is our scholarship, not Indian literature, which is primitive or
undeveloped.* [2]

Karl Kroeber

It may seem odd to interpret an orally transmitted American
Indian narrative alongside novels by Hawthorne and Melville,
among others. What follows is meant to be an explorative essay
that should raise questions about the possibilities of multi-ethnic
perspectives in nineteenth-century studies. In the 1980s Native
American literature has come to be acknowledged as part of
American literature and its criticism. It is no longer possible to see
it as a development of the late nineteenth century when some
intelligent American Indians became "civilized" enough to imitate white literature and enrich it with their tribal touches.
Native American literature is a product of a distinct and rich
cultural heritage that reaches back into the distant past.

The acculturation of American Indians is as much a fact of
American life as the acculturation of black Americans. There can
be no American literature that is ethnically pure, but multi-eth-
nicity is what sustains, enriches, and gives identity to American

literature. If the various ethnic, religious, and cultural roots of "all-American" literature are ignored, it is reduced to a bland universality. The first, truly native Americans had developed, in some of their tribes, a highly sophisticated literature long before Columbus's time. Until Sequoyah invented a syllabary for the Cherokees in 1821, however, no Indian tribe had a written language. As we know from the *Iliad* and the *Odyssey*, oral literature need not be inferior to the written word, but its critical interpretation is more difficult because its original impact was auditory, visual, and emotional, and it served a social, ritual, or educational function. Furthermore, American Indian literature has been recited and recorded in hundreds of different languages many of which have neither grammars nor dictionaries nor native speakers to be consulted. All American Indian tribes today emphasize the great differences between them. Just as in Europe the Swedes, the Portuguese, and the Albanians are thoroughly different from each other, so the more than 300 tribes which are surviving today have very distinct cultures. There were more than 2,000 independent tribes in Columbus's time, and they spoke 500 different languages belonging to fifty distinct language groups, some as different as Chinese and English.[3]

The step from interpreting white fiction to understanding American Indian literature, in oral or written form, is difficult also because tribal art is not the art of individuals. "The purpose of Native American literature is never one of pure self-expression. . . . The tribes seek, through song, ceremony, legend, sacred stories (myths), and tales to embody, articulate, and share reality, to bring the isolated private self into harmony and balance with this reality. . . ."[4] The corporate nature of this art does not imply a lack of artistry, however, as all great epics of the world as well as the Hebrew and Christian Scriptures testify.[5]

What the epic of Dekanawida contributes to an understanding of women and Indians in the minds of mid-nineteenth-century Americans is its unusually high regard for the nature and role of women and the deep faith in the sacredness, intelligence, and power of human beings which they were used to calling "savages." Recognizing these facts does not mean glorifying the American Indians, past or present. The presumption that the Iroquois or any other tribes were perfect ecologists, nonaggressors, nonsexists,

natural democrats, noncompetitive people, and wise because pre-
scientific only reflects the longing of whites to find somebody to be
what they are not.[6] The Iroquois epic is, like the narratives of all
other native tribes, a primeval part of American literature.[7]

The story of Hiawatha was, of course, known to white scholars
in the 1850s. But the main source of information, Henry Rowe
Schoolcraft's *Algic Researches* (1839), was to a large extent a
fictionalized report. Longfellow took over Schoolcraft's inaccur-
acies in writing his famous poem, and so a historical Iroquois
lawgiver of the fifteenth century was confused with an Ojibway
demigod. Every version of the story is, of course, intertwined with
legends, because it constitutes a primeval kind of "fiction." But
accuracy in terms of what the Iroquoian tribes themselves recorded and approved is important. There are two reliable texts of
the narrative, easily available today, which were published
together by William N. Fenton under the title *Parker on the
Iroquois*.[8] Arthur C. Parker, of partly Seneca ancestry, was a
renowned anthropologist of the 1920s and the grandnephew of Ely
S. Parker, an American Indian engineer and general in the Union
army. The elder Parker collaborated with Lewis Henry Morgan,
the "father of American anthropology," in the writing of the first
great book on the Iroquois League in 1851. The younger Parker's
important monographs on Iroquois life, edited by Fenton, include
"The Constitution of the Five Nations," dealing with the Dekana-
wida-Hiawatha story and the Great Law which formed the base of
the League. Parker gives us two principal texts which he discovered in the Six Nations Reservation in Ontario, Canada, in
1910. The first was written down by the Mohawk Seth Newhouse
(1842–1921) in Indian English and reviewed by Albert Cusick, a
New York Onondaga-Tuscarora. The second version is an official
compilation by the chiefs of the Six Nations Council, approved by
them in 1900, which originated in the chiefs' dislike for Newhouse's text. The latter remained the more popular form. In a
shorter version it had been known since about 1880, when the
story was put into writing by Newhouse for the first time.[9]

Dekanawida and Hiawatha, or Hayonwatha (the spelling of
both names varies widely with the dialect of the informants and
the transliteration of the recording scholars) were probably two
distinct beings in the original narrative, but in some legends they

have become fused over the centuries into a single folk hero with the attributes of a demigod. The written texts published by Parker and Fenton agree that Dekanawida was a prophet and mystic born of a poor virgin mother among the Hurons, that he had miraculous powers and through a vision felt compelled to end the continuous fighting between neighboring tribes. They also agree that Hayon-watha, a Mohawk who had experienced serious bereavement, became the disciple of Dekanawida and the practical organizer of the League which comprised the Mohawk, Oneida, Onondaga, Cayuga, and Seneca tribes. (The Tuscarora came under the protection of the League in 1723, and from then on the British called it the League of Six Nations.) The third most important character in the narrative is an evil man, Adodarho, or Tha-do-dah-ho, an Onondaga tyrant and cannibal, crippled and snake-haired on the outside, malicious and perverse inside, who eventually is healed and converted and becomes the "Fire-Keeper" (a kind of speaker or president) of the League's Council.

An integral part of the story is the "Great Law," which outlines all the rules of League politics and rituals, and attached to it is a description of the Condolence Ritual which provided for the funeral ceremony of a deceased sachem and the installation of a successor. Since narrative, laws, and ritual are designed to overcome personal grief as well as hostility among the tribes, the whole body of literature can be understood as the record of a revitalization movement among several tribes.[10] The origin of the League is dated by the Iroquois chiefs around 1390, by white scholars about 1570. White people probably did not know about it until 1640. The League has influenced people as diverse as Benjamin Franklin and Karl Marx, and it may have been one of the models on which the Constitution of the United States was based. Some of its principles resemble those of the United Nations.[11]

The main characters of the myth are images of spiritual, psychological, and intellectual power, not physical prowess. Dekanawida's power is supernatural from birth. As a child he survives his grandmother's attempts to drown him. She does not understand his virgin birth until a messenger tells her in a vision that this is a special child who will bring peace to the nations (14). As a young man he survives a fall from a high tree he ordered to be cut down after climbing to its top. The unbelieving onlookers are sure he has drowned in the chasm below, but they find him nearby, cooking his breakfast. This miracle establishes Dekanawida as a man of power who will be able to bring the peace he prophesies (16, 73). He is also a man of authority who is able to change the character and vocation of his followers. As he declares to one of his disciples: "You shall therefore be called 'Oh-dah-tshe-deh' (meaning, the quiver bearer), as your duty as a guardian of the cornfields is now changed because the Good News of Peace and Power has now come. Your duty hereafter shall now be to see that your children (instead of fields) shall live in peace" (82).

Dekanawida shows political and psychological acumen in choosing special people for special tasks at the right time (84, 88). There is an eschatological note in the chiefs' version of the narrative when the prophetic leader, reminiscent of Henry Blake, moves from settlement to settlement to win over the chiefs and repeatedly hears a voice calling "A-son-kek-ne-eh," "it is not yet," or "it has not yet occurred" (79, 87), while the water of the lake which he and his followers want to cross becomes "very rough and troubled." The voice is that of Tha-do-dah-ho, and the mood of expectation is heightened by an earlier sign that the evil man is beginning to change: he perceived the wrongness of his own nature when he saw Dekanawida's face reflected in a waterkettle (69–70). As long as the tyrant in his derangement is troubling the water, Dekanawida can quiet the waves (89). Finally all the chiefs have crossed the lake and are assembled before Tha-do-dah-ho. Dekanawida asks each one of them to repeat after him ritual words of thanksgiving. But the tyrant is unable to speak, and the chiefs see that his hairs resemble snakes and his hands are contorted (89). When they address him one by one, Tha-do-dah-ho is finally moved to tears, and when they offer to submit to his authority, they have won him over. Thus the converted man becomes the honored Fire-Keeper of the Confederate Council (91), a strong person in his own right. Even his body is straightened and strengthened, as Dekanawida tells the chiefs: " 'We have now accomplished our work and completed everything that was required with the exception of shaping and transforming him (by rubbing him down), removing the snake-like hair from him and circumcising him.' The lords therefore all took part in doing this and Ohdahtshedeh was the first to rub down Thadodahho and

the others followed his example so that the appearance of Thaddo-
dahho [sic] might be like that of other men" (91).

In the Newhouse version, the evil man is healed in a different
way. The chiefs march up to the cannibal's lodge and sing a peace
hymn, but they make mistakes in their ritual singing and only
Dekanawida's song, combined with his healing touch, is powerful
enough to effect a cure in mind and body (28). Earlier, Dekanawida heals Hayonwatha with a similar cure. According to Newhouse's version of the story, Hayonwatha has lost seven daughters
through the wiles of Ohsinoh, a famous shaman. Like Job, he is
utterly grief-stricken. He leaves his tribe to go on a journey.
Meditating on a way to find comfort in his grief and to console
others in his condition, he imagines lifting up a strand of beads and
shell strings and turning each bead or shell into a consoling word.
Obviously, the story is at this point an explanation of the Condolence Ritual and the use of memory devices like beads, shells, or
quills. When Hayonwatha finally meets Dekanawida and the
whole Council, the healing is brought about by such ritual devices. One is reminded of Job's consoling friends or of Roman
Catholics praying a certain number of rosaries: "So then Dekanawida said: 'My younger brother, it has now become very plain to
my eyes that your sorrow must be removed. Your griefs and your
rage have been great. I shall now undertake to remove your
sorrow. . . . I shall string eight more strands [of shells] because
there must be eight parts to my address to you. . . .' When the
eight ceremonial addresses had been made by Dekanawida the
mind of Hayonhwatha [sic] was made clear. He was then satisfied
and once more saw things rightly" (23–24).

The many references in the narrative to dreams, visions, double-
facedness, perversion, and grief make it clear that "the Iroquois
had achieved a great degree of psychological sophistication. They
recognized conscious and unconscious parts of the mind. They
knew the great force of unconscious desires, were aware that the
frustration of these desires could cause mental and physical
(psychosomatic) illness. . . . It would be fair to say that Iroquois
and other Indian cultures in the seventeenth and eighteenth
centuries possessed a deeper understanding of psychodynamics
than most enlightened Europeans of the time."[12] One of the main
points of the Dekanawida myth is the subtle interrelatedness of

psychological and social conditions which is also evident in Hawthorne, Melville, and Stowe. Hayonwatha and Tha-do-dah-ho become powerful leaders because they are able to overcome grief and evil through Dekanawida's vision and charisma, and because they share their power so that from generation to generation the ritual enacted by the whole tribe can contribute to social and individual wholeness.

How does the power of the men in the story compare with that of the women? The only important women figures in the narrative proper are the mother and grandmother of Dekanawida. The virgin birth indicates that life in the fullest and most sacred dimension is life engendered by spirit. Mother and grandmother, both virtuous women, readily accept the message of their visions that a special spirit child and peace-bringer will be born. The official version of the narrative gives us deeper insight into the character of the mother by identifying her with Ji-kon-sah-seh (70–71), the celebrated Huron Peace Queen and "mother of nations."[13] Dekanawida visits her and advises her to stop feeding "bloodthirsty and destructive" travelers who regularly pass by her house. "He then told her that the reason she was to stop this custom was that the Karihwiyoh or Good Tidings of Peace and Power had come. He then said: 'I shall, therefore, now change your disposition and practice.' Then also, 'I now charge you that you shall be the custodian of the Good Tidings of Peace and Power, so that the human race may live in peace in the future' " (71). When four nations have assembled for Council, Dekanawida eagerly awaits his mother's arrival (88). Only when she is present is everything completed so that the ritual which is to heal Tha-do-dah-ho can proceed. Women Faith Keepers (priests) among the Iroquois were in charge of psychiatric cures. Women "were present at all public rituals and joined in the dances."[14] The psychiatric and religious power of the women also entailed political power. When Tha-do-dah-ho has been healed, he cannot officially be commissioned without Ji-kon-sah-seh. As Dekanawida says, " 'You, the chief warrior, and you, our mother, you have the control of the power (the authority), and we will now put upon him a sign, by placing upon his head the horns of a buck deer' " (91). Thus the electoral power of Iroquois women had been established: " 'It shall now, in the future among us, the United

Nations, thus be a custom that whenever a lord is to be created we shall all unite in a ceremony (such as this)' " (92). As the Newhouse version phrases it, " 'The titles [of the chiefs] shall be vested in certain women and the names shall be held in their maternal families forever' " (27). Not only were the women to elect the chiefs; they also were to depose them if, after repeated warnings, they did not perform their duties. The Great Law provides the rules and rituals for this procedure:

> The War Chiefs shall then divest the erring Lord of his title by order of the women in whom the titleship is vested. . . .
> When a Lord is to be disposed, his War Chief shall address him as follows:
> "So you, _____, disregard and set at naught the warnings of your women relatives. So you fling the warnings over your shoulder to cast them behind you.
> "Behold the brightness of the Sun and in the brightness of the Sun's light I depose you of your title and remove the sacred emblem of your Lordship title. . . . I now depose you and return the antlers to the women whose heritage they are. . . .
>
> . . . You shall now go your way alone . . . for we know not the kind of mind that possesses you. As the Creator has nothing to do with wrong so he will not come to rescue you from the precipice of destruction in which you have cast yourself." (34–35)

The ritual indicates that political, religious, and kinship responsibilities are one and the same, and they are shared by men and women. Women did not take care of government affairs, but they could choose, admonish, and depose the men who did. Women did not go to war, but no war could take place without their consent. They also decided the fate of a prisoner of war.[15] All property belonged to the women. As the Great Law phrases it: "The lineal descent of the people of the Five Nations shall run in the female line. Women shall be considered the progenitors of the Nation. They shall own the land and the soil. Men and women shall follow the status of the mother" (42).

The complex Iroquois system of blood relationship and female descent cannot really be summed up by the term "matriarchy." It was an intricate division as well as sharing of rights and responsibilities between the sexes. Horatio Hale, an expert on Iroquoian

rites, observed in 1883: "The complete equality of the sexes in
social estimation and influence is apparent in all the narratives of
the early missionaries. . . . The Iroquois does not give up his seat
to a woman, or yield her precedence on leaving a room; but he
secures her in the possession of her property, he recognizes her
right to the children she has borne, and he submits to her decision
the choice of his future rulers."[16] More recent scholars realize that
there was no "complete equality." Women hardly left home and
fireside and were in the end dependent on the men's willingness to
act on their advice.[17] Nevertheless, Iroquois culture as expressed
in the Dekanawida myth, the Great Law, and the ancient rites
achieved the same balance of power between the sexes which
anthropologists have confirmed for most hunting and gathering
societies.[18] The achievement was not a feat of intellect only; it
had grown organically out of ancient religious and psychological
wisdom.

The images connected with all the sachems in the Dekanawida
myth are those of power, peace, and thanksgiving. The pine tree
which Dekanawida plants, the eagle in its top, the bundle of
arrows (101), and the Council fire are images of strength and
unity. When the sachems uproot the tree they had planted, throw
all weapons into the chasm below, and then replant the tree, they
symbolically enact their desire for peace. Iroquois festivals and
rites are primarily rites of thanksgiving. Just as grandmothers hold
family prayers of thanksgiving in the home,[19] so the chiefs begin
their government affairs with an expression of thankfulness.
When Dekanawida assembles the representatives of four nations
and is getting ready to win over the fifth, he proclaims: "We shall
now first give thanks to the Great Ruler. We will do this because
our power is now completed" (90).

The spiritual strength of Indian characters is also discernible in
other American Indian literature of the 1850s. An example is
Chief Seattle's famous speech of 1853:

> And when the last Red Man shall have perished, and the memory
> of my tribe shall have become a myth among the White Men, these
> shores will swarm with the invisible dead of my tribe, and when
> your children's children think themselves alone in the field, the
> store, the shop, upon the highway, or in the silence of the pathless

woods, they will not be alone. In all the earth there is no place dedicated to solitude. At night when the streets of your cities and villages are silent and you think them deserted, they will throng with the returning hosts that once filled them and still love this beautiful land. The White Man will never be alone.

Let him be just and deal kindly with my people, for the dead are not powerless. Dead, did I say? There is no death, only a change of worlds.[21]

Very little American Indian "fiction" in the modern sense existed in the middle of the nineteenth century. Elias Boudinot's *Poor Sarah*, the story of a converted Indian woman, published in the Cherokee language in 1833, is actually the translation of a New England missionary tract.[22] John Rollin Ridge's *The Life and Adventures of Joaquín Murieta*, the largely fictional account of a California bandit, published in 1854, could be considered the first American Indian novel.[23] The genuine Native American narrative genius, however, is much more alive in the epic of Dekanawida and in countless other Indian myths, legends, and oratory. The Great Law of Dekanawida, the Condolence Ceremony, and the installation rite are still Iroquois rituals in the 1980s, not memorized verbatim but re-enacted by each celebrant, newly composed out of the ancient prescribed rules and ritual phrases.[24]

The American Indians of the mid-nineteenth century, like their ancestors in the time of the League's founding and their descendants living today, wanted to salvage the strength and nobility of their ancient culture and religion in the midst of their nations' ruthless destruction. Their emphasis on nonrational, "feminine," spiritual values was the same that made Hawthorne and Melville turn against the current of their optimistic technological culture. Their active concern for justice and democracy was the same as that of the first black novelists. In regard to equality between the sexes, the epic of the Great League was far ahead of the white as well as the black fiction of the time, because the tribes were not encumbered by either the European hierarchical structures or the uprootedness of slaves. The Great League embodied many American ideals before whites as well as blacks found ways to enact them. No literature is more genuinely American than that of the American Indian.

When this continent erupted onto the literary scene, the whole range of humankind's means of communication were represented simultaneously, from tribal myths to modern novels. In tribal telling and listening "a great deal of the story is believed to be inside the listener."[25] Teller and audience are almost inseparable, and the stories confirm community. The beginnings of black fiction show a groping for group identity and solidarity. White fiction writers in America emerged as individual artists, and their protagonists were often separated or elevated from society. A few white authors realized that the loss of community means lack of wholeness and that the dominance of one group or one sex damages the subtle social fabric of a new society as it damages the individual. Thus they tried to regain the mysterious wholeness of a dim human past, and their romantic yearnings united them with black and American Indian narrators. None of them simply tells stories that move "from point A to point B to point C," but like American Indian myths they spin "something like a spider's web—with many little threads radiating from a center, criss-crossing each other" until finally "the structure will emerge . . . and . . . meaning will be made."[26]

Definite historical processes underlie the development of literature from its aboriginal spider-web nature to an expression of individualistic progress. In the epic of Dekanawida, the powerful images of women and of Iroquois people in general can be explained by the social and historical circumstances common to all hunting and gathering tribes in preindustrial and precolonial times. Authority was widely dispersed among male as well as female members of the larger kinship group. Women were regarded highly not only through the matrilineal descent of titles and property but also through their role in rituals and the arts of healing, their contribution of essential foods like roots, herbs, vegetables, berries, or fish, and their handcrafting of baskets, leather-goods, fabrics, and shelters. With more advanced techniques of weaving and smelting ores and of keeping herds instead of relying exclusively on the hunt, the tribes acquired goods beyond their immediate needs. Private ownership of goods led to trade, mostly by males as a substitute for the hunt, the employment of prisoners of war as slaves to tend and increase these goods, and the downgrading of the women's contribution to the family's livelihood as more incidental and decorative. With the dissolution of wider kinship ties, the individual male household head acquired greater responsibility for his family. With herds and slaves under his command, the patriarch acquired the exchange value of these possessions in the form of money. Thus the difference between classes of masters and slaves, owners and laborers developed simultaneously with the widening gap between male and female authority. Colonizers and missionaries did not create this development, but they intensified it since they brought with them the European notions of feudalism and ecclesiastical as well as racial and familial hierarchy.[27]

What happens to a people's literature during the transformation from aboriginal to modern society? An epic, tale, or myth spontaneously created and continually recreated by a group for a group, expressing common faith, common history, and common goals, becomes the consciously designed artistic work of an individual for like-minded individuals. This is an inevitable process, in itself neither good nor bad. It goes wrong only when these individuals belong mostly to one social class, one race, or one sex and fail to discern the subtle ways in which they reinforce a pattern of social domination and cultural alienation.

Hawthorne realized that American Puritanism had contributed heavily to such a debilitating pattern of development. Melville in the South Seas experienced a society in which male and female values pervaded the common life in equal measure and where private acquisitiveness and competition were unknown. Stowe, Brown, and Delany were conscious of the human power hidden in groups long excluded from the decision-making processes of their society. The fiction of all these authors reflects a very aboriginal human notion, that good literature expresses the sacredness of all of life. Even where it simply entertains, it retains its vitality only as long as it keeps its human integrity, accountable to all facets and conditions of life. As long as American literature retains the spider web-nature of its primeval background, that is, its ethnic and cultural diversity, it will retain its strength and identity.[28]

Conclusion

The problem posed by the interpretation of oral Native American literature raises the broader issue of the strengths and weaknesses in mid-nineteenth-century American fiction as a whole. The examples given of "white," "black," and "red" narrative art are, of course, only part of the all-American literary scene in the 1850s. European immigrant fiction, and in particular Jewish fiction, was also appearing. Yiddish narrative, which emerged in the middle of the nineteenth century, is an interesting counterpoint to Native American and black narrative for it combined both legend and history. It retained a strong legendary element even into the twentieth century. Yiddish writers "have produced many stories, narratives, legends, but until our day, very little fiction."[1] The element of ethnic narrative is what gives the fiction of an Isaac Bashevis Singer a universal strength. Anglo-Saxons had distinguished fiction from history and legend three hundred years before the American Renaissance, in the time of Sidney and Spenser.[2] It was the great chance of the newly emerging, distinctly American fiction, however, to incorporate into a novel some "prefictional" elements offered by Colonial Puritans or aboriginal tribes, as in Hawthorne; by Afro-American slaves, as in Stowe, Brown, and Delany; and by Oriental cultures, as in Melville. The "raw romance" elements in Hawthorne, the allegory and mysticism in Melville, and the autobiographical, historical, or folk elements in Stowe, Brown, and Delany kept these writers from elevating a male Anglo-Saxon hero above the women and "primitive" races around him. Some aspects of prefictional mythical strength found in the Iroquois epic are alive in the fiction of the five writers mentioned.[3] They share a concern for psychological and social wholeness in an age of individualistic upward mobility, ruthless imperialism, and technological fragmentation. Instead of imitating the whole "faustian fustian," they would like to put the Humpty Dumpty of a progress-loving, atomistic society together again.[4] They find strength at the bottom of the social ladder, not the top; in myth, not in logic; in liberation, not in domination.

Their voices were not heeded. Instead, the nation drifted into the Civil War. White supremacy was practically as taken for granted in the North as it was in the South since even Northern abolitionists frequently believed in the intellectual inferiority of blacks. The appeal for the slaves' human rights was accepted by a broad spectrum of Northerners only when they feared the slave holders' competition for capital, land, labor, and political power.[5] In order to strengthen white supremacy and to comply at least in part with America's democratic principles, Southern slave holders extended the franchise to lower-class whites, and some Northerners fought for the political rights of immigrants. But the color line remained as insurmountable as the sexual line: the black vote and the women's vote were equally excluded.

The abolitionist and feminist writers of the mid-nineteenth century did not invent the connection between the woman question and the race question. Charles Brockden Brown's *Alcuin,* for example, draws the comparison as early as 1798.[6] In a negative way, the historians of the mid-nineteenth century fused the two issues of sex and race or social group. Bancroft, Parkman, Motley, and Prescott ascribed feminine wiles to Catholics and Jews. They contended that ultimately the blacks and Native Americans as well as the French, Spaniards, and Portuguese, would be overcome by honest, energetic, masculine Anglo-Saxons.[7]

The popular imagery which connected women and ethnic or exotic characters found expression in the sentimental novels. Their authors reacted to the technological and political problems of the day by extolling the virtues of domesticity. The more perceptive writers realized that the sentimentalists' ideal of domesticity was an illusion because it did not correspond to just social relations outside the home. Domestic life for a Hester Prynne was a lonely, stigmatized existence. The dark Indian element in her nature was suppressed by an authority that also suppressed the Indians themselves, and Hawthorne arouses our sympathy for her exotic vitality. In *The House of the Seven Gables* the reader may at first suspect a glorification of domesticity in Phoebe, a woman very different from Hester Prynne. Domestic peace and happiness, however, can occur only after private greed and social pretensions have died with Jeffrey Pyncheon, and even an imbecile like Clifford Pyncheon is accepted as a free human being. A precarious new domestic Eden may be established at the end of this novel, but Melville's *Pierre* presents the complete breakdown of home and family life. Pierre has been shaped by an excess of domesticity. His identity is his family's identity. The world of Saddle Meadows is a self-serving world of daydreams. As family property the idyllic place is made possible by Pierre's grandfather's slaughter of Indians. Domesticity with Isabel and Lucy in New York is even more of a travesty, because Pierre cannot single-handedly redeem his father's failings and society's injustice toward Isabel.

In *Uncle Tom's Cabin*, domestic peace is impossible for torn-apart slave families and always endangered for white slave-holding families. In *Clotel* and *Blake*, family happiness is at best a fleeting possibility. The Dekanawida myth pleads for an end to warfare and hostility so that families and clans can live in peace, but in the 1850s, the surviving tribes were uprooted, forced into reservations, or in other ways deprived of their traditional home life.

Given this dim view of domesticity, none of the works discussed here shows an American Eve as the angel in the house who keeps her Adam from becoming totally absorbed by the immoral world outside which harbors the dangerous Eves and other primitive forces. Private life and social life are tied up in an "intricate knot," to use Melville's term. No Taji can be happy with his Yillah if he wins her by murdering a few natives. No Hollingsworth can harbor true sympathy for the prisoners he wants to reform if he uses two women solely for his own purposes. Hawthorne and Melville, therefore, take the old images of women and nonwhite races and hold them up for what they are worth, asking: Is Miriam a dangerous dark woman who spells doom for a man? Is Donatello a primitive child of nature who commits murder by instinct? Are

South Sea natives never to be trusted? Is Lucy a model of selfless-ness? And the answer to such questions can only be: Yes, but . . . , because Miriam is also a victimized woman and a radiant, creative, loving person; Donatello is also a very subtle, conscien-tious human being; South Sea natives can be trusted as little as Westerners, but they are also as capable of true humanity; Lucy is selfless but psychologically blind. In Hawthorne and Melville the standard images are not only corrected but sometimes totally reversed. Scowling, weak, old Hepzibah is the one person to stand up to greedy Judge Pyncheon, to fight for her brother Clifford's life and happiness. Gorgeous, majestic Mrs. Glendinning dies a mad-woman filled with hate.

Such reversals of value are even more pronounced in Stowe, Brown, and Delany. They, too, start out with traditional images: an obedient black slave, a beautiful mulatto woman, a devilish slave holder's wife. But then the slave resists white inhumanity to the point of his own death or fights for his freedom at any cost; the victimized mulatto woman forcefully takes her fate into her own hands; and the devilish slave holder's wife is overshadowed by another white woman who emancipates her slaves. The old Eve becomes the new, and Sambo becomes first Uncle Tom and George Harris, then Babo, Jerome, and Henry Blake. Those who have been ignored are shown as powerful, and those formerly in power turn into ghosts or maniacs, like the superstitious Legree. There is a psychological price to be paid for social wrong. Thus, in the Iroquois epic, Tha-do-dah-ho, evil, ugly, and despised, can be an effective leader only when he becomes accepted and accepting within his society.

How far the works discussed transcended the stereotypes of their day may be shown by comparing them with another kind of American art in the mid-nineteenth century. William Wetmore Story (1819–1895) was a popular and internationally known sculptor. His most famous sculptures illuminate the prevalent images of women and exotic characters in the 1850s and 1860s. Hawthorne, James Russell Lowell, Henry James, and the Brown-ings were frequent guests at Story's studio in Rome in the 1850s, and the sculptor's *Cleopatra* became the statue that Hawthorne ascribed to Kenyon in *The Marble Faun*. The original statue, however, does not reveal the fierce passion, "full of poisonous and rapturous enchantment" (127), which Hawthorne describes in Kenyon's masterpiece. Story's woman figure is impressive but represents merely a romantic heroine in meditative repose. In fact, art critics have found that the statue owes its fame more to Hawthorne's *The Marble Faun* than to its intrinsic artistic quality.[8] Story conceived the idea for his other famous sculpture, the "Libyan Sibyl," after Harriet Beecher Stowe visited the Storys in 1856 and told them of her meeting with Sojourner Truth, imitating her wild prophetic utterances. In 1860 when Stowe returned to Rome, Story asked her to tell him once more about Sojourner Truth. She told him the story as dramatically as before, and shortly afterwards he brought her his model of the "Libyan Sibyl." Again, the statue does not at all evoke the powerful image of the black woman orator, as Harriet Beecher Stowe described her in the *Atlantic Monthly*.[9] She could be any intelligent poetess of antiquity, perhaps even a "Libyan Sibyl," but not the black American Sojourner Truth recently escaped from slavery, or even Stowe's Cassy in *Uncle Tom's Cabin.* Story and other American sculptors of his time preferred exotic and antique classical images to anything that was native American or contemporary. Hiram Powers's various Eve figures and his idealized *Greek Slave,* Harriet Hosmer's *Zenobia* and her fauns, Thomas Crawford's *Chief Contemplating the Progress of Civilization,* and his *Dying Mexican Princess* all express the stereotypes of the time. Above all, Horatio Greenough, who frankly admitted his prejudices against blacks and American Indians, created in his *Rescue Group* (1837–1850) an image of white male supremacy at its worst. Certainly American writers were ahead of the sculptors in their portraits of women and other cultures and races.[10]

Blacks and women have been characterized by silence in several of the works we have looked at, for example *Pierre* and "Benito Cereno." Hester standing silent at the scaffold and the native of Typee staring speechless at the narrator who may have just killed him are symbols of the voicelessness of women, slaves, American Indians, and Orientals in nineteenth-century fiction. Nonwhite women experienced a double handicap. "Two-thirds of the illiterate in the world today are women. Frederick Douglass was able to leave for us the legacy of his life and thoughts as he chose to write it; Harriet Tubman and Sojourner Truth . . . come to us filtered through the words of others: words they were not able to read to correct or change."[11]

Since melodrama can be described as an "echo of the historically voiceless," it is not surprising that the first important novels by a woman like Stowe or black writers like Brown and Delany still contain much melodrama. For an inarticulate audience and an inexperienced writer, a melodrama had the function of a morality play. Psychological and social surface detail was firmly subordinated to a moral world order in which reward depended on the righteousness of one's conduct. Last minute rescues, surprising reunions, and the foiling of a villain's plot pointed to an impartial divine justice, a universe ruled after all by moral law.[12] Stowe and Brown were among the first to articulate the voice of the voiceless, and they were not able to leave melodrama behind. Delany freed himself to a much larger extent from this tradition. The first American Indian "novels" were also characterized by sensationalism or sentimentality, but Native Americans had an advantage over black slaves in that their tribal culture was still directly available to them, though only in tragic remnants, and their myths and narratives provided a very unsentimental survival power. For white society, American Indians were another silent minority. In fact, an Indian appearing in white fiction was, more often than not, "inaudible."[13]

Recently, women critics have commented on the scarcity of articulate female voices in the American literature of the nineteenth century and the special quality of the few great voices that were heard. Tillie Olsen contemplates all the silences which have kept writers, male and female, from expressing their thoughts and visions. She considers silences as long as Hawthorne's and Melville's "uncreative" decades and other silences imposed by audiences, publishers, governments, families, or poverty. Olsen decides: "The power and the need to create, over and beyond reproduction, is native in both women and men. Where the gifted among women (*and men*) have remained mute, or have never attained full capacity, it is because of circumstances, inner and outer, which oppose the needs of creation."[14]

The first fictional works which manage to overcome strongly adverse circumstances will usually retain some marks of the struggle. The image of the "madwoman in the attic" (derived from

Bertha Mason, the insane wife of Rochester in *Jane Eyre*) has been used to show that women in nineteenth-century fiction were adept at camouflage and double talk. The madwoman, serving as a double, acted out the author's camouflaged guilt or rage. The writers we have considered used many images of confinement and masking. Cassy of *Uncle Tom's Cabin*, for example, becomes a true "madwoman in the attic." She "exploits impersonation of madness and confinement to escape maddening confinement." She is a black woman wearing white, a ghost of herself, because Legree has killed much of her through his abuse, but she haunts him victoriously.[15]

Thus the silences in Melville become tentative, unbalanced, or camouflaged voices in the works of women and early black novelists. Like Cassy, these authors turn their handicap into imaginative action. Louis D. Rubin, Jr., has described the "experience of difference" as the most creative force in American literature. Writers who feel alienated in their society often become superior artists.[16] Stowe, Brown, and Delany were aliens in the established world of letters, and they were therefore able to portray other aliens in their fiction. Hawthorne and Melville felt rejected in different ways, but they, too, could portray characters who were different because they themselves went against the tide of their time. It is noteworthy that both of them were considered to have feminine traits. James Russell Lowell writes of Hawthorne:

> When nature was shaping him, clay was not granted
> For making so full-sized a man as she wanted,
> So, to fill out her model, a little she spared
> From some finer-grained stuff for a woman prepared,
> And she could not have hit a more excellent plan
> For making him fully and perfectly man.[17]

And Newton Arvin writes of Melville, "There was a deep strain of the tropical, the indolent, the sensual and the feminine in Melville."[18] Both Hawthorne and Melville thus represented what Lewis Mumford has seen as a counterweight to the mechanical, the automatic, and the compulsive in American culture.

> It is associated with a worship of the vitalities of nature, particularly as expressed in primitive people, primitive customs and usages,

185

primitive occupations like hunting and fishing, and a rough, simple, hearty life, lived in utmost freedom from human restrictions, in direct communion with the wilderness. To be willing to live under such conditions was, indeed, a primary condition for survival in the New World during the period of pioneering. . . . The life of the frontier in the New World called, not for a docile mechanical discipline, but for animal energy and audacity: the romantic impulse thus offered an alternative to those hardy spirits who refused to be imprisoned in the new mechanical routine of the counting house and the factory.[19]

The authors discussed here wanted to bring the primitive vitalities of culture into the American consciousness to have them acknowledged as equal in value to man's rational potential. Primitive powers had been relegated to women and ethnic groups who were thereby stereotyped into sub-human or superhuman beings, very savage or very noble. This process deprived individual man of human wholeness, because, as Melville shows in Captain Ahab, his rational will came to stifle his feeling. Ahab's wife and a motley crew of all races are of little consequence to him. He is the Faustian hunter. In D.H. Lawrence's terms, what he hunts in the whale is "the deepest blood-being of the white race." Moby-Dick "is hunted, hunted by the maniacal fanaticism of our white mental consciousness. We want to hunt him down. To subject him to our will. And in this maniacal conscious hunt of ourselves we get dark races and pale to help us, red, yellow, and black, east and west, Quaker and fire-worshipper, we get them all to help us in this ghastly maniacal hunt which is our doom and our suicide."[20] Hawthorne and Melville show the effect of this hunt on the hunter, whereas Stowe, Brown, and Delany are mostly concerned with the hunted.

In all of these writers the individual, the interpersonal (male and female), and the wider social level are interwoven. None of them wants the "blood-principle" to take over all power: Hawthorne's primitive Donatello has to gain rationality; Melville's Ishmael figures return from Pacific islands to their Western home; Stowe wants blacks and women to be equal with men, not superior; Brown tries to assimilate primitive blackness into white culture; and Delany tries to assimilate white intellectual and commercial achievement into black culture. Even Delany in his thoughts on black violence is intensely rational in his approach. Black writers felt that the ghetto, in spite of its oppressiveness, had preserved the black person's "link with the world of healthy instinct", whereas the white world of "Philistines and Babbits" is dehumanized by "the scramble for gain and the repression of natural desires."[21] The traditional Native American culture, in particular, sought to balance the "blood-principle" with rational order, as the epic of Dekanawida shows. The mythic, corporate nature of this art preceded all fragmentation into feminine and masculine, psychological and social, spiritual and political concerns. To many whites, American Indian faces could often not be distinguished as either male or female. For the Native Americans themselves, such opposites as matter and spirit simply did not exist. J.N.B. Hewitt, one of the foremost scholars on Iroquois mythology, has explained that for the Iroquois "all things . . . were thought to have life and to exercise will, whose behests were accomplished through orenda—that is, through magic power, reputed to be inherent in all things."[22] It is this view of the universe which aligns American Indians and American romantic writers.

Thoreau, the American writer most strongly drawn to the American Indian (apart from the anthropologist Lewis Henry Morgan), valued the Indians for their closeness to nature and to original human nature, though he did not point out any relationship between Indians and women. "Significantly, the single consequential reference to a woman in all [of] Thoreau's works of art is to one who kills, in cowardice and savagery, human representatives of the natural realm."[23] Hannah Dustan, first prisoner and then scalper of Indians, in Thoreau's portrayal appears fiercer than any woman in Delany's *Blake*. At the end of the seventeenth century, Cotton Mather reported Hannah Dustan's story and pointed out how lavishly the authorities recompensed the woman for taking Indian scalps.[24] Hawthorne, too, was intrigued by the image of this savage white woman from American history, but she appears in a very different light in his account: "Would that the bloody old hag had been drowned . . . or that she had sunk over head and ears in a swamp, and been there buried, till summoned forth to confront her victims at the day of Judgment."[25] Hawthorne admires Mr. Dustan, who with seven of his children quietly accepts death from wild Indians when resistance no longer seems possible.

Certainly Thoreau felt as little sympathy with Hannah Dustan's savagery as Hawthorne does, but he felt intensely drawn to the Indians. What Hawthorne found in women like Hester, Zenobia, or Miriam was similar to what Thoreau found in the Indians of the Maine Woods: they were representative of the original human nature, much more so than Emerson's "Representative Men," Plato, Shakespeare, Napoleon, or Goethe.[26] They were not naturally noble but represented human beings closer to reality than civilized men. Hawthorne's women and Thoreau's Indians, just like many of Melville's South Sea natives, illuminated the basic and enduring nature of human beings. Hannah Dustan thought she could imitate the Indian's unreflective, aboriginal savageness. Such imitations are perversions, however, because they lack the integrity and "innocence" of the primitive world. For example, scalping may have been unknown until white people offered bounties for Indian scalps.[27] Hannah Dustan's story in Thoreau's version is the story of a Paradise Lost. After the bloody deed, Hannah and her two companions feel fear and estrangement from nature which to them is now dangerous and must be tamed. Thoreau can refrain from any moral judgment—seen in its context, the story speaks for itself.[28]

Black American novelists, from William Wells Brown and Martin Delany to Ralph Ellison and Ernest Gaines, are caught in the dilemma of choosing between a primitive instinct for justice and a civilized mind of compassion. They can neither responsibly make Hannah Dustan's choice of blind revenge nor adjust to the illusions and injustices of the dominant civilization. The same dilemma has often made black women, in fiction as well as in reality, into Eves or Madonnas, temptresses or saviors; they had to encourage their sons and husbands to fight for their rights while also restraining their zeal in order to preserve their lives and their humanity in a hostile society.[29]

In white writers the problem of instinct and intellect takes a somewhat different form. Especially in Melville, the primitive is, at once, "a regenerative force and a mysterious source of evil."[30] White and black writers struggle with similar issues under very different circumstances. Both know that savagery or primitivism represents "the qualities of life and nature which give human beings "the ability to act" and that "it is the duty of the intellect to keep such energy in check."[31] Lewis Mumford has described the necessity of balancing the rational and the instinctive, as it pertains to relationships between different races and nationalities on the American continent:

> With this special susceptibility to the natural and the primitive in every form, the American has not merely returned to a source of vitality: he has symbolically, by his receptivity if not by his humility, performed an act that may prove important in the development of a common culture: he has recognized and transmitted values derived from peoples who were once despised because they had existed outside the circle of European tradition. As with the development of the machine, the opening of Western culture to more primitive impulses was not without grave dangers; for if it was accompanied by a great surge of vitality, by a vast increase in the food supply and the population, it likewise multiplied the powers and claims of the id. To make the primitive elements dominate the more cultivated elements is a sort of reversed imperialism. . . . But to accept the primitive as an active component in life, even in its highest manifestations, was a gain, not merely for human wisdom, but for the more universal culture that mankind has still to create.[32]

The powers of the id are not only present in other races and cultures of America but in women. The great Romantic writers acknowledged this fact. The American Eve was not simply another version of the American Adam, just as the black or red Adam could not simply be subsumed under a "generic" white Adam.[33] Only an individualistic tradition that disregarded primitive roots and relationships could ignore the different life-forces that have to balance each other. No single American Eve, and certainly no double Eve in the sense of a temptress–virgin mother, has evolved from the American melting pot. Innumerable, different Eves have emerged whose integrity should be as carefully acknowledged and preserved as that of ethnic groups.

The writers discussed here "tried with a noble generosity to imagine a world in which other persons really counted,"[34] even invisible blacks, inaudible Indians, and inconspicuous women. American literature gained strength whenever it drew on the power of the powerless. It can still learn a lesson from Dekanawida.

Notes

Notes for Introduction

[1]Nathaniel Hawthorne, *The Scarlet Letter*, ed. Fredson Bowers (Columbus: Ohio State Univ. Press, 1962), 199. All Hawthorne quotations are from the Centenary Edition, unless otherwise indicated.

[2]Herman Melville, *Moby-Dick or, The Whale*, ed. Harrison Hayford and Hershel Parker (New York: Norton, 1976), 28–29. See the interpretation of this passage in Mark Hennelly, "Ishmael's Nightmare and the American Eve," *American Imago*, 30 (Feb. 1973), 274–93.

[3]Arthur O. Lovejoy, *The Great Chain of Being: A Study of the History of an Idea* (1936; rpt. Cambridge, Mass.: Harvard Univ. Press, 1964), 326. It is noteworthy that William Gilmore Simms still used the "degree" theory of the Great Chain of Being concept when he defended slavery, in his criticism as well as in his fiction. See his critique of Harriet Martineau's *Society in America* (1837) and the ordering of social relationships in his novel *Woodcraft* (1852). Jean Fagan Yellin makes this point in *The Intricate Knot: Black Figures in American Literature, 1776–1863* (New York: New York Univ. Press, 1972), 74.

[4]H. Bruce Franklin, *The Wake of the Gods: Melville's Mythology* (Stanford, Calif.: Stanford Univ. Press, 1963), 2. Franklin also points out that in the later 18th century the primitive mind was located in the collective popular mind as well, whereas in the 19th and 20th centuries it was located below the conscious part of each mind and in the collective unconscious of all minds. Ibid., 2–3.

[5]Susan P. Conrad, *Perish the Thought: Intellectual Women in Romantic America, 1830–1860* (New York: Oxford Univ. press, 1976), 38.

[6]William Wasserstrom, *Heiress of All the Ages: Sex and Sentiment in the Genteel Tradition* (Minneapolis: Univ. of Minnesota Press, 1959), 24.

[7]Leslie Fiedler, *No! In Thunder: Essays on Myth and Literature* (London: Eyre and Spottiswood, 1963), 266.

[8]See Hoxie Neale Fairchild, *The Noble Savage: A Study in Romantic Naturalism* (New York: Russell & Russell, 1961), 124, 131. Fairchild gives a good summary of the whole history of the Noble Savage concept. It arose from a fusion of the following ideas: observations of explorers, various classical and medieval con-

ventions like the Golden Age concept, and deductions of philosophers and men of letters. Ibid., 2.

On Rousseau, see Arthur O. Lovejoy, "The Supposed Primitivism of Rousseau's *Discourse on Inequality*," in his *Essays in the History of Ideas* (Baltimore: Johns Hopkins Univ. Press, 1948), 14–37; J.H. Broome, *Rousseau: A Study of His Thought* (London: Edward Arnold, 1963), 48–49; and Leo Marx, *The Machine in the Garden: Technology and the Pastoral Ideal in America* (New York: Oxford Univ. Press, 1964), 101–2.

[9]Richard Slotkin, *Regeneration Through Violence: The Mythology of the American Frontier, 1600–1860* (Middletown, Conn.: Wesleyan Univ. Press, 1973), 384.

[10]Arthur O. Lovejoy and George Boas, *Primitivism and Related Ideas in Antiquity* (Baltimore: Johns Hopkins Univ. Press, 1935), 1, 7.

[11]Ibid., 7, 24–26, 289.

[12]My discussion of Romantic primitivism is based on Michael Bell, *Primitivism* (London; Methuen, 1972), 57–59.

[13]See Edith A. Runge, *Primitivism and Related Ideas in Sturm und Drang Literature* (Baltimore: Johns Hopkins Univ. Press, 1946), 1.

[14]See James R. Baird, *Ishmael: A Study of the Symbolic Mode in Primitivism* (Baltimore: Johns Hopkins Univ. Press, 1956), 13, 101. The Melville quotation is from ch. lvii of *Moby-Dick.*

[15]R.W.B. Lewis, *The American Adam: Innocence, Tragedy, and Tradition in the Nineteenth Century* (Chicago: Univ. of Chicago Press, 1955), 5.

[16]Daniel G. Hoffman, *Form and Fable in American Fiction* (New York: Oxford Univ. Press, 1961), 7, 78.

[17]Many women authors and abolitionists like Lydia Maria Child or the Grimké sisters fought for the slaves' rights, and black leaders like Frederick Douglass and William Wells Brown championed women's rights. For another example, see Eleanor Ransome, ed., *The Terrific Kemble: A Victorian Self-Portrait from the Writings of Fanny Kemble* (London: Hamish Hamilton, 1978), 81, 107–13, 145, 172, 232.

[18]See George Santayana, *The German Mind: A Philosophical Diagnosis* (New York: Crowell, 1968), xiv: "Egotism—subjectivity in thought and wilfullness in morals . . . is the soul of German philosophy."

[19]See Donald D. Stone, "Victorian Feminism and the Nineteenth-Century Novel," *Women's Studies* 1, no. 1 (1972), 65–91.

[20]Fred Lewis Pattee, *The Feminine Fifties* (New York: D. Appleton-Century, 1940).

[21]Ann Douglas, *The Feminization of American Culture* (New York: Knopf, 1977). See also Barbara Welter, "The Feminization of American Religion 1800–1860" in her *Dimity Convictions: The American Woman in the Nineteenth Century* (Athens: Ohio Univ. Press, 1976), 83–102.

[22]Helen Papashvily, *All the Happy Endings* (New York: Harper, 1956). See also Ernest Earnest, *The American Eve in Fact and Fiction, 1755–1914* (Urbana: Univ. of Illinois Press, 1974), 141; and Douglas, *Feminization*, 45, who says Sarah Hale of *Godey's Lady's Book* and her followers "pursued partially feminist goals by largely anti-feminist means."

[23]Nina Baym, *Woman's Fiction: A Guide to Novels by and About Women in America, 1820–1870* (Ithaca, N.Y.: Cornell Univ. Press, 1978), 18, 25–26.

[24]Quoted in Conrad, *Perish the Thought*, 1, as one of the epigrams of this book. For the discussion of True Womanhood, see Barbara Welter, "The Cult of True Womanhood: 1820–1860," *American Quarterly*, 18 (Summer 1966), 151–74; rpt. in her book *Dimity Convictions*, 21–41. She based her findings mostly on the more important women's magazines, on gift books, religious tracts, sermons, cookbooks, diaries, and autobiographies. The novels dealing with true womanhood had been discussed earlier in Herbert Ross Brown, *The Sentimental Novel in America 1789–1860* (New York: Pageant Books, 1959). Welter's article on True Womanhood should be read together with her later articles in *Dimity Convictions* in which she describes the complexity of the feminization process and the positive strength women gained from the limitations imposed upon them.

[25]Harriet Beecher Stowe, *The Minister's Wooing*, quoted in Brown, *Sentimental Novel*, 281.

[26]Margaret Fuller, *Woman in the Nineteenth Century* (New York: Norton, 1971), 6–7. Italics mine.

[27]For all the imagery mentioned, see Brown, *Sentimental Novel*, 294, 338, 293.

[28]Ibid., 142.

[29]Baym, *Woman's Fiction*, 181, 183.

[30]Ann S. Stephens, *Malaeska: The Indian Wife of the White Hunter* (New York: John Day, 1929), 157, 107.

[31]Earnest, *American Eve*, 79.

[32]Franklin, *Wake of the Gods*, 114.

[33]See Edward Wagenknecht, *Cavalcade of the American Novel: From the Birth of the Nation to the Middle of the Twentieth Century* (New York: Henry Holt, 1952), 94.

[34]Harriet Beecher Stowe, *Uncle Tom's Cabin or, Life Among the Lowly*, ed. Kenneth S. Lynn (Cambridge, Mass.: Harvard Univ. Press, 1962), 152, 185, 236, 210, 149, 33, 100, 213.

[35]Addison Gayle, Jr., *The Way of the New World: The Black Novel in America* (Garden City, N.Y.: Anchor-Doubleday, 1976), 8.

[36]Ibid., 11.

[37]Ibid., 21.

[38]Herbert Marshall McLuhan, *War and Peace in the Global Village* (New York: McGraw-Hill, 1968), 115–16, 120.

[39]See Anne Firor Scott, *The Southern Lady: From Pedestal to Politics, 1830–1930* (Chicago: Univ. of Chicago Press, 1970), 100.

[40]Quentin Anderson says this about Hawthorne in *The Imperial Self: An Essay in American Literary and Cultural History* (New York: Knopf, 1971), 87.

Notes for Chapter 1

[1]Nathaniel Hawthorne, Mosses from an Old Manse (Columbus: Ohio State Univ. Press, 1974), 120. Hereafter, page numbers in parentheses within the text refer to the work under discussion (Centenary Edition).

[2]James Mellow, Nathaniel Hawthorne in His Times (Boston: Houghton Mifflin, 1980), 237.

[3]Judith Fetterley, The Resisting Reader: A Feminist Approach to American Fiction (Bloomington: Indiana Univ. Press, 1978), 24.

[4]Nina Baym, The Shape of Hawthorne's Career (Ithaca, N.Y.: Cornell Univ. Press, 1976), 109.

[5]See Mellow, Nathaniel Hawthorne, 102–26. If "Rappaccini's Daughter" is a reflection of Hawthorne's ambiguous relationship to Mary Crowninshield Silsbee, his judgment is all the more surprising.

[6]Hawthorne, Scarlet Letter, 49.

[7]Richard Harter Fogle, Hawthorne's Fiction: The Light and the Dark, rev. ed. (Norman: Univ. of Oklahoma Press, 1964), 136.

[8]See Robert E. Todd, "The Magna Mater Archetype in The Scarlet Letter," New England Quarterly, 45 (Sept. 1972), 423. "In the first third of the book (chs. i–viii) Hester is referred to at least a half dozen times as pedestalled."

[9]See Claudia D. Johnson, The Productive Tension of Hawthorne's Art (Tuscaloosa: Univ. of Alabama Press, 1981), 49, 58, 63, 65. Claudia Johnson rightly sees that this is the same demonic power that Hawthorne felt within himself as a writer of fiction. He could identify with Hester as the narrator of "The Custom House" trying on the burning red letter A in a lifeless world of "customs" which did not understand him. His "pearl" is always some "devil in manuscript," as he titled one of his sketches. But, just like Hester, he turns demonic into creative forces.

[10]See William Bysshe Stein, Hawthorne's Faust: A Study of the Devil Archetype (Gainesville: Univ. of Florida Press, 1953), 112.

[11]In Nina Baym's estimation, Hester is meant as an "admirable character, . . . while of course in Christian terms she is from first to last an unredeemed sinner." However, an unredeemed sinner can be, in human terms, an admirable character. Hester has sinned, is admirable, and is redeemed, as far as redemption is humanly possible. The "virtual absence of God from the text" does not imply at all that Hester's and Dimmesdale's relationship is nothing but "a social crime" unrelated to divine law. Interestingly, the biblical book of Esther also does not mention God even once, and that certainly does not imply that it is not concerned with divine law. We cannot impose on Hawthorne a secularized 20th-century world view, however ambiguous his religious ideas may have been. Especially the last pages of the novel point in another direction. See Baym, Shape of Hawthorne's Career, 9, 125–26, and The Westminster Dictionary of the Bible (Philadelphia: Westminster Press, 1944), s.v. "Esther."

[12]See Michael T. Gilmore, The Middle Way: Puritanism and Ideology in American Romantic Fiction (New Brunswick, N.J.: Rutgers Univ. Press, 1977), 93–112; and Johnson, Productive Tension, 130.

[13]Kenneth Dauber, *Rediscovering Hawthorne* (Princeton, N.J.: Princeton Univ. Press, 1977), 38.

[14]Richard Brodhead, *Hawthorne, Melville, and the Novel* (Chicago: Univ. of Chicago Press, 1976), 22, 60.

[15]See Henry Nash Smith, *Virgin Land: The American West as Symbol and Myth* (New York: Vintage Books–Random House, 1950), 127. Charles W. Webber was one of the first to introduce the custom of making a heroine of questionable repute a European instead of an American. The violation of propriety was less shocking when the girl was not an American.

[16]On the causes and implications of stigmatizing, see Marjorie Pryse, *The Mark and the Knowledge: Social Stigma in Classic American Fiction* (Columbus: Ohio State Univ. Press, 1979).

[17]Joel Porte, *The Romance in America: Studies in Cooper, Poe, Hawthorne, Melville, and James* (Middletown, Conn.: Wesleyan Univ. Press, 1969), 104.

[18]Slotkin, *Regeneration*, 205, 356, 358, 363–65, 519–23.

[19]See Louise K. Barnett, *The Ignoble Savage: American Literary Racism, 1790–1890* (Westport, Conn.: Greenwood Press, 1975), 150.

[20]Cf. Judith Fryer, *The Faces of Eve: Women in the Nineteenth-Century American Novel* (New York: Oxford Univ. Press, 1976), 84, who maintains that Hester is "wonderfully individualistic" and that "her own brand of lawlessness . . . threatens with destruction" the society of her day.

[21]Clark Griffith, "Substance and Shadow: Language and Meaning in *The House of the Seven Gables*," in *The House of the Seven Gables*, by Nathaniel Hawthorne, ed. Seymour L. Gross (New York: Norton, 1967), 394. See also *House of the Seven Gables*, 27, 169, 295, where the relationship of house and heart is implied.

[22]Hoffman, *Form and Fable*, 195–97.

[23]Gilmore, *Middle Way*, 127.

[24]Dorothy Y. Deegan, *The Stereotype of the Single Woman in Novels: A Social Study with Implications for the Education of Women* (New York: King's Crown Press–Columbia Univ. Press, 1951), 40. My sketch of the single woman is based on ibid., 83–114.

[25]Brodhead, *Hawthorne, Melville*, 72.

[26]Ibid., 71. Brodhead compares Hester's and Hepzibah's emergence from isolation. Harry Levin, Introd., *House of the Seven Gables* (Columbus, Ohio: Merrill, 1969), xi, mentions the "mock-heroic reverberations" of Hawthorne's style.

[27]Jane Lundblad, *Nathaniel Hawthorne and European Literary Tradition* (New York: Russell & Russell, 1965), 164. Lundblad simplifies the differences of the characters' origins to a certain extent, since Dimmesdale is not quite an American, just the official representative of the American Puritan establishment, and Zenobia is American in spite of being a "cosmopolitan."

[28]Hoffman, *Form and Fable*, 195–97. Hoffman also notes that Hawthorne had read Sir Walter Scott's *Letters on Demonology and Witchcraft* in 1837.

[29]Griffith, "Substance and Shadow," 387.

[30]See Randall Stewart, ed. and introd. *The American Notebooks*, by Nathaniel

Hawthorne (New Haven, Conn.: Yale Univ. Press, 1932), lvif.; and *Love Letters of Nathaniel Hawthorne* (Washington, D.C.: Microcard Editions, 1972), 113–219.

[31]Griffith, "Substance and Shadow," 387. In comparison with Phoebe, Sophia Peabody was much more intellectual and strong-willed. "Sophia became proficient in Greek, Latin, and Hebrew. In Salem, she was taught French . . . , she studied Italian as well." See Mellow, *Nathaniel Hawthorne*, 134. On Sophia's strong-willed nature, see ibid., 205.

[32]H.N. Smith, *Democracy and the Novel: Popular Resistance to Classic American Writers* (New York: Oxford Univ. Press, 1978), 32–33. See also Edwin M. Eigner, *The Metaphysical Novel in England and America: Dickens, Bulwer, Melville, and Hawthorne* (Berkeley: Univ. of California Press, 1978). Eigner's work emphasizes the fusion of realism and symbolism in the authors he discusses. He sees the "household Virgin, the hearthside Madonna, the domestic angel" in many of the American romances as a conscious and purposeful use of an old stereotype (the redeeming woman). Authors like Hawthorne and Melville, he argues, wanted to counter the flat rationalism of their time (120, 122).

[33]Rudolph von Abele, "Holgrave's Curious Conversion," in *House of the Seven Gables*, by Hawthorne, ed. Gross, 401.

[34]Richard Harter Fogle, *Hawthorne's Imagery: The "Proper Light and Shadow" in the Major Romances* (Norman: Univ. of Oklahoma Press, 1969), 49.

[35]Eigner, *Metaphysical Novel*, 102.

[36]See Gilmore, *Middle Way*, 127.

[37]Edgar A. Dryden, *Nathaniel Hawthorne: The Poetics of Enchantment* (Ithaca, N.Y.: Cornell Univ. Press, 1977), 171.

[38]See Brook Thomas, "*The House of the Seven Gables*: Reading the Romance of America," *PMLA*, 97 (Mar. 1982), 208.

[39]Roy Harvey Pearce, Introd., Centenary Edition of *Blithedale Romance*, xxv.

[40]See Edith Roelker Curtis, *A Season in Utopia: The Story of Brook Farm* (New York: Thomas Nelson, 1961), 91–92, 105.

[41]See, e.g., Irving Howe, "Hawthorne: Pastoral and Politics," in *The Blithedale Romance*, by Nathaniel Hawthorne, eds. Seymour Gross and Rosalie Murphy (New York: Norton, 1978), 290.

[42]On the equivocal role of Coverdale as narrator, see, e.g., Robert C. Elliott, "*The Blithedale Romance*," in *Hawthorne Centenary Essays*, ed. Roy Harvey Pearce (Columbus: Ohio State Univ. Press, 1964), 111; Brodhead, *Hawthorne, Melville*, 100; Frederick C. Crews, *The Sins of the Fathers: Hawthorne's Psychological Themes* (New York: Oxford Univ. Press, 1966), 196–212; also James H. Justus, "Hawthorne's Coverdale: Character and Art in *The Blithedale Romance*," and Kent Bales, "The Allegory and the Radical Romantic Ethic of *The Blithedale Romance*," in *The Blithedale Romance*, eds. Gross and Murphy. Fogle, *Hawthorne's Fiction*, 185, and Dauber, *Rediscovering Hawthorne*, 155, consider Coverdale reliable.

[43]Marius Bewley, *The Eccentric Design: Form in the Classic American Novel* (New York: Columbia Univ. Press, 1959), 156; D.H. Lawrence, *Studies in Classic American Literature* (New York: Viking, 1923), 107; Baym, *Shape of*

Hawthorne's Career, 191; Stewart, ed., *American Notebooks*, by Hawthorne, xxix; and Peter B. Murray, "Mythopoesis in *The Blithedale Romance*," in *Critics on Hawthorne*, ed. Thomas J. Rountree (Coral Gables, Fla.: Univ. of Miami Press, 1972), 109.

[44]See Murray, "Mythopoesis," 113; Daniel Hoffman, "Myth, Romance, and the Childhood of Man," in *Hawthorne Centenary Essays*, ed. Pearce, 217; and Fogle, *Hawthorne's Fiction*, 170. "The movement is definite, heavy, and ritualistic, like a ceremonial dance which celebrates a myth." Ibid.

[45]Cf. Hawthorne, *The American Notebooks*, Centenary Edition, VIII, 197. In the journal entry of Sept. 26, 1841, Hawthorne describes the same phenomenon of a clinging and choking vine. The notebook entry of Oct. 9, 1841, describes the wild "little sempstress from Boston" who was the prototype of Priscilla: "[S]he romps with the boys. . . ." On the following day, Oct. 10, Hawthorne records: "I visited my grape vine. . . . This vine climbs around a young maple tree." Ibid., 209–13. The same image can be found in the *Italian Notebooks*. In June 1858 Hawthorne describes an old grapevine "imprisoning . . . the friend that supported its tender infancy." See *The French and Italian Notebooks*, Centenary Edition, XIV, 274. These references support the identification of Priscilla with the climbing vine as well as the ambiguity of the image in Hawthorne's mind: something natural and beautiful becomes unintentionally choking.

[46]Murray, "Mythopoesis," 112.

[47]Edith Hamilton, *Mythology* (New York: New American Library, 1969), 70.

[48]Bales, "Allegory and Radical Romantic Ethic," 407–13.

[49]Ibid., 411. For Priscilla as symbol of a misunderstood "Spirit," see Russell M. Goldfarb and Clare R. Goldfarb, *Spiritualism and Nineteenth-Century Letters* (Rutherford, N.J.,: Fairleigh Dickinson Univ. Press; London: Associated Univ. Presses, 1978), 166–67. Priscilla is one of the typical female mediums of the 19th century who were controlled by an assertive male figure. Hawthorne rejected the "old humbug" (Coverdale's expression) of Spiritualism and especially the exploitation of mediumistic heroines by villainous necromancers.

[50]See Fogle, *Hawthorne's Imagery*, 119. Priscilla is "a touchstone of truth and a test of faith and imagination."

[51]William Van O'Connor, "Conscious Naiveté in *The Blithedale Romance*," *Revue des Langues Vivantes*, 20 (Feb. 1954), 40. For the argument that Priscilla may have been a prostitute, see Allan Lefcovitz and Barbara Lefcovitz, "Some Rents in the Veil: New Light on Priscilla and Zenobia in *The Blithedale Romance*," *Nineteenth-Century Fiction*, 21 (Dec. 1966), 263–75; and Fryer, *Faces of Eve*, 90–91.

[52]Hawthorne, *True Stories from History and Biography*, 43–44.

[53]Helena Kane Finn, "Design of Despair: The Tragic Heroine and the Imagery of Artifice in Novels by Hawthorne, James, and Wharton." Diss. St. John's Univ. 1976, 45–46. See also Hawthorne's comment in his preface to *The Marble Faun* on "Miss Hosmer's noble statue of Zenobia" (4).

[54]Hawthorne, *The French and Italian Notebooks*, Centenary Edition, XIV, 174. In the entry of April 22, 1848, Hawthorne contemplated the creation of a *female* fictional faun (179).

[55]Fogle, *Hawthorne's Fiction*, 192.

[56]See Jonathan Auerbach, "Executing the Model: Painting, Sculpture and Romance Writing in Hawthorne's The Marble Faun," E.L.H., 47 (Spring 1980), 117. Some of my comments about Kenyon derive from this article.

[57]Bernard J. Paris, "Optimism and Pessimism in The Marble Faun," in The Merrill Studies in The Marble Faun, comp. David B. Kesterson (Columbus, Ohio: Merrill, 1971), 64.

[58]Sacvan Bercovitch, "Of Wise and Foolish Virgins: Hilda versus Miriam in Hawthorne's Marble Faun," in Merrill Studies in The Marble Faun, comp. Kesterson, 79–83.

[59]Baym, Shape of Hawthorne's Career, 248.

[60]See Fogle, Hawthorne's Fiction, 210.

[61]Cf. Paradise Lost, Book IX, 1.1099.

[62]Eigner, Metaphysical Novel, 188.

[63]Mellow, Nathaniel Hawthorne, 495. Cf. Bell Gale Chevigny, The Woman and the Myth: Margaret Fuller's Life and Writings (New York: Feminist Press, 1976), 417–18. Chevigny suggests that Julian Hawthorne, who published his father's remarks on Fuller, may have incorrectly transcribed a part of the notes.

[64]Ursula Brumm, Geschichte und Wildnis in der amerikanischen Literatur (Berlin: Erich Schmidt, 1980), 160–62.

[65]Edwin Fussell, "Neutral Territory: Hawthorne on the Figurative Frontier," in Hawthorne Centenary Essays ed. Pearce, 304–6.

[66]Virginia Ogden Birdsall, "Hawthorne's Fair-haired Maidens: The Fading Light," PMLA, 75 (1960), 250–56.

[67]Randall Stewart, Nathaniel Hawthorne: A Biography (New Haven, Conn.: Yale Univ. Press, 1948), 54.

[68]Ibid., 55–56.

[69]William J. Scheick, The Half-Blood: A Cultural Symbol in 19th-Century American Fiction (Lexington: Univ. Press of Kentucky, 1979), 58–59.

Notes for Chapter 2

[1]Q.D. Leavis, "Melville: The 1853–6 Phase," in New Perspectives on Melville, ed. Faith Pullin (Kent, Ohio: Kent State Univ. Press, 1978), 205.

[2]Carolyn L. Karcher, Shadow over the Promised Land: Slavery, Race, and Violence in Melville's America (Baton Rouge: Louisiana State Univ. Press, 1980), 8; Richard Chase, Herman Melville: A Critical Study (New York: Hafner, 1971), 295. Statements similar to the latter quote, by Chase, can be found in William H. Gilman, Melville's Early Life and Redburn (New York: New York Univ. Press; London: Oxford Univ. Press, 1951), 164; and Alan Lebowitz, Progress into Silence: A Study of Melville's Heroes (Bloomington: Indiana Univ. Press, 1970), 212.

[3]See Walter D. Kring and Jonathan S. Carey, "Two Discoveries Concerning Herman Melville," Proceedings of the Massachusetts Historical Society, 87 (1975), 137–41. Cf. Charles J. Haberstroh, Jr., Melville and Male Identity (Rutherford, N.J.: Fairleigh Dickinson Univ. Press; London: Associated Univ. Presses,

1980), 70, 71. Haberstroh conjectures that Melville's marriage was unfulfilling from the beginning, and he tries to prove this, for example, by identifying Melville with the fictional Taji in *Mardi*. Taji, however, is seen very critically by Melville.

[4]Chase, *Herman Melville*, 19.

[5]Ibid., 295. See also Leslie Fiedler, *Love and Death in the American Novel*, rev. ed. (New York: Stein and Day, 1975), 341–42, 348, 362–63; Edwin Haviland Miller, *Melville* (New York: Braziller, 1975), 44–51.

[6]Robert Scott Kellner, "Toads and Scorpions: Women and Sex in the Writings of Herman Melville," Diss. Univ. of Mass. 1977, passim.

[7]See Jay Leyda, *The Melville Log: A Documentary Life of Herman Melville, 1819–1891* (New York: Harcourt, Brace, 1951), II, 694.

[8]Herman Melville, *The Works of Herman Melville*, XI, *Israel Potter* (London: Constable, 1923), 82.

[9]Herman Melville, *Typee: A Peep at Polynesian Life* (Evanston, Ill.: Northwestern Univ. Press and Newberry Library, 1968), 125. All following quotations from *Typee, Omoo, Mardi*, and *Pierre* are from this edition, with page numbers given in parentheses within the text.

[10]Richard Harter Fogle, *Melville's Shorter Tales* (Norman: Univ. of Oklahoma Press, 1960), 145. Fogle uses this phrase in reference to the slaves in "Benito Cereno."

[11]See Charles Roberts Anderson, *Melville in the South Seas* (New York: Columbia Univ. Press, 1939), 121, 178; and James Baird, *Ishmael: A Study of the Symbolic Mode in Primitivism* (Baltimore: Johns Hopkins Univ. Press, 1956), 100–15. Cf. Milton Stern, *The Fine Hammered Steel of Herman Melville* (Urbana: Univ. of Illinois Press, 1968), 20.

[12]Eleanor Melville Metcalf, *Herman Melville: Cycle and Epicycle* (Cambridge, Mass.: Harvard Univ. Press, 1953), 91.

[13]Faith Pullin, "Melville's *Typee*: The Failure of Eden," in *New Perspectives on Melville*, ed. Pullin, 2.

[14]Miller, *Melville*, 130; and Baird, *Ishmael*, 252.

[15]Baird, ibid.

[16]Robert Stanton, "*Typee* and Milton: Paradise Well Lost," *Modern Language Notes*, 74 (May 1959), 411.

[17]Miller, *Melville*, 47–49. The worship of Apollo played a significant part in 19th-century life and art: "Benjamin West and the painters of his school depicted the human body according to the Apollonian idealization. George Catlin found Apollo in the wilds of America among the Indians, as did James Fenimore Cooper before him . . . Everywhere in the 19th century there were plaster replicas of Apollo Belvedere and inexpensive engravings of the famous sculpture."

[18]Stern, *Fine Hammered Steel*, 46.

[19]Ibid., 40.

[20]Edgar A. Dryden, *Melville's Thematics of Form: The Great Art of Telling the Truth* (Baltimore: Johns Hopkins Univ. Press, 1968), 45. See also Edward S. Grejda, *The Common Continent of Men: Racial Equality in the Writings of Herman Melville* (Port Washington, N.Y.: Kennikat, 1974), 14: "Melville [in *Typee*]

constantly blends the voice of the subjective narrator with that of the travel-book writer and propagandist"; and William B. Dillingham, *An Artist in the Rigging: The Early Work of Herman Melville* (Athens: Univ. of Georgia Press, 1972), 12, 17.

[21] Baird, *Ishmael*, 370.

[22] Fogle, *Melville's Shorter Tales*, 138.

[23] Edwin M. Eigner, "The Romantic Unity of Melville's *Omoo,*" *Philological Quarterly*, 46 (Jan. 1967), 99.

[24] Lebowitz, *Progress into Silence*, 44, shows that Bembo foreshadows Ahab. "As in the later works . . . the moral implications are ambiguous. Bembo's savagery is matched immediately by the crew's howling for his life." Grejda, *Common Continent*, 37, states that Melville does not condone Bembo's savagery but justifies it. Baird, *Ishmael*, 281, suggests that Bembo foreshadows "the dark, primitive attributes of Fedallah."

[25] The following discussion is based on Eigner, "Romantic Unity," 107–8.

[26] Ironically, according to later gossip, at the time Melville was fascinated by a single glimpse of Mrs. Dell on horseback she had already taken to drink and was even then riding toward an early grave. See Leon Howard, *Herman Melville: A Biography* (Berkeley: Univ. of California Press, 1951), 63.

[27] See Kellner, "Toads and Scorpions," 23–29.

[28] F.O. Matthiessen, *American Renaissance: Art and Expression in the Age of Emerson and Whitman* (London: Oxford Univ. Press, 1941), 466. (In the last quote, Matthiessen is using T.S. Eliot's words.)

[29] For Melville on *Mardi*, see Metcalf, *Herman Melville*, 62. For the critics, see Merrell R. Davis, "The Flower Symbolism in Mardi," *Modern Language Quarterly*, 2 (Dec. 1941), 625–38; idem, *Melville's Mardi: A Chartless Voyage* (New Haven, Conn.: Yale Univ. Press, 1952); Franklin, *Wake of the Gods*; Mildred K. Travis, "*Mardi*: Melville's Allegory of Love," *Emerson Society Quarterly*, 43 (Second Quarter 1966), 88–94; Maxine Moore, *That Lonely Game: Melville, Mardi, and the Almanac* (Columbia: Univ. of Missouri Press, 1975); Karcher, *Shadow over the Promised Land*; and Joyce Sparer Adler, *War in Melville's Imagination* (New York: New York Univ. Press, 1981).

[30] Milton R. Stern, "Melville's Tragic Imagination: The Hero Without a Home," in *Patterns of Commitment in American Literature*, ed. Marston LaFrance (Toronto: Univ. of Toronto Press, 1967), 46. "Heaven hath no roof" is a quotation from *Mardi*, 636. See also Richard Harter Fogle, *The Permanent Pleasure: Essays on Classics of Romanticism* (Athens: Univ. of Georgia Press, 1974), 152, 154, for Melville's "distrust of affirmations" and his idea of "Cosmic jest or Anarch blunder" in his poem "After the Pleasure Party."

[31] See Stern, *Fine Hammered Steel*, 76.

[32] Blaise Pascal, *Pensées and The Provincial Letters* (New York: Random, 1941), 55.

[33] See Moore, *Lonely Game*, 126. The reference to Belshazzar is ambiguous because only to the narrator does Jarl seem to be a frightened Belshazzar; he is actually a Daniel who can accurately discern the handwriting on the wall.

[34] Ibid., 49.

[35]Melville, "Benito Cereno," in *The Complete Stories of Herman Melville*, ed. Jay Leyda (New York: Random, 1949), 307.

[36]Stern, *Fine Hammered Steel*, 104.

[37]Ibid., 106.

[38]See Dillingham, *Artist in the Rigging*, 116.

[39]Davis, "Flower Symbolism in *Mardi*," 632.

[40]See Dillingham, *Artist in the Rigging* 112. Taji "lost the comfortable advantage of death when his humanity died within him." See also ibid., 124. The idea of endless circularity as a kind of damnation is the opposite of Emerson's joyful discovery that "Line in nature is not found." "*Mardi* is Emerson's *Nature* turned inside out." Cf. Hennig Cohen, introd. to Moore, *Lonely Game*, xxiv. Cohen, like Dillingham, speculates that Taji does not die, but lives on to tell the story of his suicidal quest.

[41]See, e.g., Matthiessen, *American Renaissance*, 384; and Frederic I. Carpenter, "Puritans Preferred Blondes: The Heroines of Melville and Hawthorne," *New England Quarterly*, 9 (June 1936), 258–60.

[42]See John Seelye, *Melville: The Ironic Diagram* (Evanston, Ill.: Northwestern Univ. Press, 1970).

[43]Adler, *War in Melville's Imagination*, 21.

[44]See, e.g., Travis, "*Mardi*: Melville's Allegory of Love," 89–91; Miller, *Melville*, 149; and Haberstroh, *Melville and Male Identity*, 53–66. Kellner, "Toads and Scorpions," 38–41, sees positive marriage imagery only in the relationship of Taji and Yillah (144, 287 of *Mardi*).

[45]Fogle, *Melville's Shorter Tales*, 132.

[46]See David W. Pancost, "Donald Grant Mitchell's *Reveries of a Bachelor* and Herman Melville's 'I and my Chimney,' " *American Transcendental Quarterly*, 42 (Spring 1979), 129–36.

[47]Matthiessen, *American Renaissance*, 466.

[48]Many aspects of the grotesque value reversals in Melville foreshadow similar processes in the fictional world of Faulkner. See Stern, *Fine Hammered Steel*, 171.

[49]In her article on "Melville's Quarrel with Fiction, *PMLA*, 94 (Oct. 1979), 909–23, Nina Baym states that there "seems to be no evidence that Melville had read any of the sentimental or domestic romances then coming into vogue, and in all likelihood *Pierre* is modeled not on ladies' fiction, but on the bildungsroman." The question is, what quality of bildungsroman did he have in mind? He also may have picked up sentimental clichés from serialized fiction in periodicals, or perhaps from the books his sisters and his wife circulated among them.

[50]See Max Frank, *Die Farb- und Lichtsymbolik im Prosawerk Herman Melvilles* (Heidelberg: Carl Winter, 1967), 144, 149. See also ch. xlii of *Moby-Dick*, "The Whiteness of the Whale." On whiteness in *Pierre*, see Charles Moorman, "Melville's Pierre in the City," in *The Merrill Studies in* Pierre, comp. Ralph Willett (Columbus, Ohio: Merrill, 1971), 41.

[51]The serpent imagery is all-pervasive in *Pierre*. Even a thought of Lucy can be "serpent-like" (104). See Charles Moorman, "Melville's Pierre and the Fortunate Fall," *The Merrill Studies in* Pierre, comp. Willett, 36.

[52]Henry A. Murray, Introd., *Pierre or, The Ambiguities*, by Herman Melville (New York: Hendricks, 1949), li. See also Goldfarb and Goldfarb, *Spiritualism*, 156–57, on Isabel as described by spiritualistic and mesmeristic imagery.

[53]Murray, Introd., Pierre, by Melville, lxxxiii.

[54]See Fryer, Faces of Eve, 54. See also Baym, "Melville's Quarrel with Fiction," 920: In Pierre, Melville himself came to the point where he no longer thought it possible to utter truth in long fiction.

[55]Chase, Herman Melville, 127–29.

[56]Cf. Rev. 22:20, 21:3; Matt. 12:49, 16:18. It is not surprising to find a woman with "Christlike" traits in Melville. The Chola Widow in "The Encantadas" is a similar figure, and even in Clarel, as Richard Harter Fogle has shown, Melville's Christ is "relatively feminine and passive," because "God the Father is too purely male, the stern sky-god," and "there is no room in [Melville's] system for the virgin mother of God." See Fogle, "Melville's Clarel: Doubt and Belief," in The Permanent Pleasure, 181.

[57]Murray, for example, sees Isabel's face as Pierre's "anima" in the Jungian sense. See Introd., Pierre, by Melville, xliv.

[58]Howard, Herman Melville, 187; Lebowitz, Progress into Silence, 169.

[59]In terms of the famous Plinlimmon pamphlet in Book xiv of Pierre, one could say that Pierre, like other Melville protagonists, finally has to recognize the impossibility of harmonizing "chronometrical" and "horological" truth. For a good discussion of these concepts in Pierre, see Sacvan Bercovitch, The American Jeremiad (Madison: Univ. of Wisconsin Press, 1978), 28–30.

[60]Only in Billy Budd was Melville able to express in a single primitive figure destructive instinct as well as saving grace. See Ray B. West, Jr., "Primitivism in Melville," Prairie Schooner, 30 (Winter 1956): 383.

[61]Matthiessen, American Renaissance, 508.

[62]Yellin, Intricate Knot, 224.

[63]Kermit Vanderbilt, " 'Benito Cereno': Melville's Fable of Black Complicity," Southern Review, NS 12 (Spring 1976), 311–22.

[64]Karcher, Shadow over the Promised Land, 128.

[65]Page numbers in the text refer to Melville, "Benito Cereno," in The Complete Stories, ed. Leyda.

[66]See H. Bruce Franklin, "Apparent Symbol of Despotic Command: Melville's Benito Cereno," New England Quarterly, 34 (Dec. 1961), 462–77.

[67]See Adler, War in Melville's Imagination, 104.

[68]Marvin Fisher, Going Under: Melville's Short Fiction and the American 1850's (Baton Rouge: Louisiana State Univ. Press, 1977), 112.

[69]The reference is most likely to tuberculosis, which ravaged urban and rural America throughout the 19th century. About the historical circumstances and working conditions of female factory workers, see Thomas Dublin, "Women, Work, and the Family: Female Operatives in the Lowell Mills, 1830–1860," Feminist Studies, 3 (Fall 1975), 30–35; and Benita Eisler, ed., The Lowell Offering: Writings by New England Mill Women (1840–1845) (Philadelphia: Lippincott, 1977), 13–41.

[70]Douglas, Feminization, 239. Douglas refers to Irving's Sketchbook, Willis's Pencillings by the Way, Mitchell's Reveries of a Bachelor, and Curtis's Prue and I.

[71]H. Bruce Franklin, The Victim as Criminal and Artist: Literature from the American Prison (New York: Oxford Univ. Press, 1978), 34.

[77]Maurita Willett, "The Silences of Herman Melville," in Studies in the Minor and Later Works of Melville, ed. Raymona Hull (Hartford, Conn.: Transcenden-

tal Books, 1970), 90. Melville's portrayal of Hunilla is historically "true" and prophetic as a symbol of Chola women's exploitation, courage, and enduring humanity, in past enturies as well as in ours. See Ruby Rohrlich-Leavitt, ed., *Women Cross-Culturally: Change and Challenge* (The Hague: Mouton, 1975), 165, 264, 623, 630, 636.

Notes for Chapter 3

[1]William R. Taylor, *Cavalier and Yankee: The Old South and American National Character* (New York: Harper, 1961), 172–74.

[2]Ibid. Taylor is quoting Beverly Tucker's *George Balcombe* (1836).

[3]Jean Willoughby Ashton, *Harriet Beecher Stowe: A Reference Guide* (Boston: Hall, 1977), xi.

[4]See Kenneth S. Lynn, Introd., *Uncle Tom's Cabin or, Life among the Lowly*, by Harriet Beecher Stowe (Cambridge, Mass.: Harvard Univ. Press, 1962), xiv, xxvi, xxviii. All page numbers in parentheses within the text refer to this edition. See also John A. Woods, Introd., *Uncle Tom's Cabin* (London: Oxford Univ. Press, 1965), vii–xx. "It has been estimated that in the first century of *[Uncle Tom's Cabin's]* existence more than six and a half million copies had been printed throughout the world." Woods attributes the novel's success in the United States to the state of domestic politics, in foreign countries to the fact that an attack on slavery was read as an attack on oppression everywhere.

[5]Elizabeth Ammons, "Heroines in *Uncle Tom's Cabin*," in *Critical Essays on Harriet Beecher Stowe*, ed. Elizabeth Ammons (Boston: Hall, 1980), 163.

[6]Douglas, *Feminization*, 253.

[7]Lynn, Introd., *Uncle Tom's Cabin*, by Stowe, xi. See also Richard Beale Davis, "Mrs. Stowe's Characters-in-Situations and a Southern Literary Tradition," in *Essays on American Literature in Honor of Jay B. Hubbell*, ed. Clarence Gohdes (Durham, N.C.: Duke Univ. Press, 1967), 109, and Edward Charles Wagenknecht, *Harriet Beecher Stowe: The Known and the Unknown* (New York: Oxford Univ. Press, 1965), 5.

[8]Ellen Moers, *Harriet Beecher Stowe and American Literature* (Hartford, Conn.: Stowe-Day foundation, 1978). 15.

[9]Edmund Wilson, *Patriotic Gore: Studies in the Literature of the American Civil War* (New York: Oxford Univ. Press, 1962), 5.

[10]Alice C. Crozier, *The Novels of Harriet Beecher Stowe* (New York: Oxford Univ. Press, 1969), 73. Cf. Woods, Introd., *Uncle Tom's Cabin*, by Stowe, ix. "It would be unwise to assume that any book could become as popular as *Uncle Tom's Cabin*—and preserve that popularity for more than a century—without having marked literary and artistic qualities."

[11]Moers, *Harriet Beecher Stowe*, 1, 4.

[12]See William Gilmore Simms, *Woodcraft* (New York: Norton, 1961), 500. Joseph V. Ridgely, "*Woodcraft*: Simms's First Answer to *Uncle Tom's Cabin*," *American Literature*, 31 (Jan. 1960): 421–33, has convincingly argued that

Simms wrote this novel in order to answer Harriet Beecher Stowe's abolitionism with a picture of happy plantation life and contented slaves who are never ill-treated, torn from their family, or desiring their freedom. Cf. also Yellin, *Intricate Knot*, 77–81, on Simms and Stowe.

[13]J.C. Furnas, *Goodbye to Uncle Tom* (New York: Sloane, 1956), 53–54. Furnas's book is valuable for some historical information, but the author has a confused, if not allergic, attitude toward Harriet Beecher Stowe, and his material on slavery is only very vaguely related to his diatribes against her.

[14]Yellin, *Intricate Knot*, 137.

[15]Moody E. Prior, "Mrs. Stowe's Uncle Tom," *Critical Inquiry*, 5 (Summer 1979): 650.

[16]Yellin, *Intricate Knot*, 136, 145. About *Archy Moore* (first version 1836), see ibid., 87–120. Yellin rates the novel considerably higher than *Uncle Tom's Cabin* and thinks Stowe used it as a source. Cf. also Charles Nichols, "The Origins of *Uncle Tom's Cabin*," *Phylon*, 19 (Fall 1958): 328–34. E. Bruce Kirkham, *The Building of* Uncle Tom's Cabin (Knoxville: Univ. of Tennessee Press, 1977), 96–97, points out that Nichols's "proofs" that *Uncle Tom's Cabin* is a poor imitation of *Archy Moore* are self-contradictory.

[17]Moers, *Harriet Beecher Stowe*, 15. See Yellin, *Intricate Knot*, 126–30, about the differences between the slave narratives of Josiah Henson and Lewis and Milton Clarke on the one hand and *Uncle Tom's Cabin* on the other. Besides the slave narratives, a main source for *Uncle Tom's Cabin* was Theodore Weld, *American Slavery as It Is* (1839), a powerful collection of facts relating to slavery and possibly the only source Stowe consulted intensively before writing the novel. The other sources may have been used only for writing the *Key to* Uncle Tom's Cabin (1853), an attempt to defend the facts behind the novel. See Kirkham, *Building of* Uncle Tom's Cabin, 102; and Yellin, *Intricate Knot*, 142.

[18]Judith R. Berzon, *Neither White nor Black: The Mulatto Character in American Fiction* (New York: New York Univ. Press, 1978), 35.

[19]Lynn, Introd., *Uncle Tom's Cabin*, by Stowe, xii.

[20]Ellen Moers, *Literary Women* (Garden City, N.Y.: Anchor-Doubleday, 1977), 57. Cf. Catherine Juanita Starke, *Black Portraiture in American Fiction: Stock Characters, Archetypes, and Individuals* (New York: Basic Books, 1971), 65, who sees Topsy as a stock character, a black buffoon.

[21]Moers, *Literary Women*, 57.

[22]See Georg Lukács's statement, in his *Studies in European Fiction*, that those novelists are great who can set aside their own most cherished prejudices in order to describe what they really see. "This ruthlessness toward their own subjective world-picture is the hallmark of all great realists. . . . No . . . truly good writer . . . can direct the evolution of his own characters at will." Quoted in Georg Lukács, "Historical Truth in Fiction," in *The Modern Tradition: Backgrounds of Modern Literature*, ed. Richard Ellman and Charles Feidelson, Jr. (New York: Oxford Univ. Press, 1965), 354.

[23]John William Ward, *Red, White, and Blue: Men, Books, and Ideas in American Culture* (New York: Oxford Univ. Press, 1969), 88.

[24]See Caroline Rush in *The North and South* (1852). "As a general thing, the greatest slave on a plantation is the mistress. She is like the mother of an

immense family, of some fifty up to five or six hundred children." See also Mrs. M. Eastman in her *Aunt Phillis's Cabin* (1852): "This is the era of mental and bodily emancipation. Take advantage of it, wives and negroes! But, alas for the former! There is no society formed for their benefit . . . they must wear their chains." Quoted in Brown, *Sentimental Novel*, 227, 263. Mary Boykin Chestnut, in her famous diary, also speaks of the "martyrdom" of planters' wives who are "forced to have a negro village walk through their houses whenever they see fit, dirty, slatternly, idle, ill-smelling by nature. . . . These women . . . have less chance to live their own lives in peace than if they were African missionaries." C. Vann Woodward, ed., *Mary Chestnut's Civil War* (New Haven, Conn.: Yale Univ. Press, 1981), 245.

[25]Stowe herself has been accused of caring only about blacks' souls. See, e.g., Yellin, *Intricate Knot*, 135.

[26]See Johanna Johnston, *Runaway to Heaven: The Story of Harriet Beecher Stowe* (Garden City, N.Y.: Doubleday, 1963), 6–7. See *Chestnut's Civil War*, ed. Woodward, 168. " 'I hate slavery. . . . What do you say to this? A magnate who runs a hideous black harem and its consequences under the same roof with his lovely white wife and his beautiful and accomplished daughters? He holds his head as high and poses as the model of all human virtues to these poor women whom God and the laws have given him. . . . 'You see, Mrs. Stowe did not hit the sorest spot. She makes Legree a bachelor. . . .' " (Quotation marks are used erratically in Chestnut's diary.)

[27]See Papashvily, *All the Happy Endings*, 194–95. Papashvily sees the death of a child (and sometimes of several children in one family) as so horrible for mothers in the 19th century because children were the only expressions of a woman's creativity. Douglas, *Feminization*, 205, regards the death of children in popular novels only as a sentimental device. Baym, *Woman's Fiction*, 15–16, considers the glorification of childhood innocence a reaction against the Puritan idea of natural depravity.

[28]Johnston, *Runaway to Heaven*, 72.

[29]Douglas, *Feminization*, 74.

[30]Harriet Beecher Stowe, *Oldtown Folks*, ed. Henry F. May (Cambridge, Mass.: Harvard Univ. Press, 1966), 456.

[31]Ibid., 458.

[32]Wagenknecht, *Cavalcade of the American Novel*, 101.

[33]George M. Fredrickson, *The Black Image in the White Mind: The Debate on Afro-American Character and Destiny, 1817–1914* (New York: Harper & Rowe, 1971), 103. Fredrickson mentions that James Russell Lowell in his *Anti-Slavery Papers* also held the view that Caucasians could only gain from being influenced by the "gentler and less selfish" character qualities of the Negroes. Ibid., 107–8.

[34]Fredrickson, *Black Image in the White Mind*, 113.

[35]See Jean Lebedun, "Harriet Beecher Stowe's Interest in Sojourner Truth, Black Feminist," *American Literature*, 46 (Nov. 1974): 359–63.

[36]See Charles Edward Stowe, comp. *Life of Harriet Beecher Stowe, Compiled from Her Letters and Journals* (Boston: Houghton Mifflin, 1891), 198.

[37]Ammons, "Heroines in *Uncle Tom's Cabin,*" in *Critical Essays*, ed. Ammons, 152.

[38]See John C. Ruoff, "Frivolity to Consumption: Or, Southern Womanhood in Antebellum Literature," *Civil War History*, 18 (Sept. 1972): 222, 228.
[39]Ammons, "Heroines in *Uncle Tom's Cabin*," in *Critical Essays*, ed. Ammons, 154.
[40]Ward, *Red, White, and Blue*, 79. Italics mine.
[41]Letter xxxiv, Jan. 1843; quoted in Gail Parker, *The Oven Birds: American Women on Womanhood 1820–1920* (Garden City, N.Y.: Anchor Books, 1972), 90. Stowe and Childs were not the only writers in the mid-19th century to discover the feminine potential in man and the masculine potential in woman. Catherine Beecher, for example, thought that for women to cultivate their true femininity they had to add the traditional masculine virtues like calm judgment, steady efficiency, habitual self-control, to their natural feminine traits of imagination and warm sympathy. See Conrad, *Perish the Thought*, 32.
[42]Gayle Kimball, "Harriet Beecher Stowe's Revision of New England Theology," *Journal of Presbyterian History*, 58 (Spring 1980): 64. See also Johnston, *Runaway to Heaven*, 5; and John R. Adams, *Harriet Beecher Stowe* (New York: Twayne, 1963), 20.
[43]Douglas, *Feminization*, 245.
[44]Welter, "The Feminization," 102. In another article Welter states that women's novels "often served as a vehicle of protest." See "Defenders of the Faith: Women Novelists of Religious Controversy in the Nineteenth Century," in her *Dimity Convictions*, 103.
[45]Jane P. Tompkins, "Sentimental Power: *Uncle Tom's Cabin* and the Politics of Literary History," in *Glyph* 8, Johns Hopkins Textual Studies (Baltimore: Johns Hopkins Univ. Press, 1981), 81.
[46]See Dorothy Berkson, "Millennial Politics and the Feminine Fiction of Harriet Beecher Stowe," in *Critical Essays*, ed. Ammons, 245–47.

Notes for Chapter 4

[1]H. Bruce Franklin, "Animal Farm Unbound Or, What the *Narrative of the Life of Frederick Douglass, An American Slave*, Reveals about American Literature," *New Letters: A Magazine of Fine Writing*, 43 (Apr. 1977): 25.
[2]Among the hopeful recent attempts is the excellent essay by William L. Andrews, "The 1850s: The First Afro-American Literary Renaissance," in *Literary Romanticism in America*, ed. William L. Andrews (Baton Rouge: Louisiana State Univ. Press, 1981), 38–60.
[3]The presence of Africans in North America begins even earlier with the Spanish and Portuguese explorers and settlers in the second half of the 16th century. See Lerone Bennett, Jr., *Before the Mayflower: A History of the Negro in America 1619–1964* (Baltimore: Penguin Books, 1966), 35. See also Blyden Jackson, Introd., *Black Poetry in America: Two Essays in Historical Interpretation*, ed. Blyden Jackson and Louis D. Rubin, Jr. (Baton Rouge: Louisiana State Univ. Press, 1974), xiii. "Before there was a United States, there were black poets."

[4]Edward Margolies, *Native Sons: A Critical Study of Twentieth-Century Black American Authors* (Philadelphia: Lippincott, 1968), 14–15.

[5]*Clotel* is the first novel written by a black American, Frank Webb's *The Garies and Their Friends* is the second, and *Blake* is the third. Webb's work was published only in England in 1857 whereas *Blake* was, at least partially, published in the United States in 1859. The second version of *Clotel* under the title of *Miralda: or, the Beautiful Quadroon* appeared in the United States in 1860–61. Since *Clotel* was first written and published in England in 1853, it precedes the other two works, but *Blake* is, in fragmentary form, "the first novelistic offering of a black writer to be published in the United States." See Floyd J. Miller, Introd., *Blake or The Huts of America,* by Martin R. Delany (Boston: Beacon Press, 1970), xii.

[6]Kenny J. Williams, *They Also Spoke: An Essay on Negro Literature in America, 1787–1930* (Nashville: Townsend, 1970), 85. For other evaluations of the slave narratives, see Edward Margolies, "Ante-Bellum Slave Narratives: Their Place in American Literary History," *Studies in Black Literature,* 4 (Autumn 1973): 1–8; M. Thomas Inge, Maurice Duke, and Jackson R. Bryer, *Black American Writers: Bibliographical Essays* (New York: St. Martin's, 1978), 30–33; and Frances Smith Foster, *Witnessing Slavery* (Westport, Conn.: Greenwood, 1979).

[7]See Dorothy Sterling, *Black Foremothers: Three Lives* (Old Westbury, N.Y.: Feminist Press; New York: McGraw-Hill, 1979), 24. Sterling notes that at this time "Harriet Tubman was still in Maryland, her escape some months away, and Sojourner Truth's powerful voice was just beginning to be heard in western Massachusetts."

[8]Robin W. Winks, Introd., *Four Fugitive Slave Narratives* (Reading, Mass.: Addison-Wesley, 1969), vi.

[9]J. Noel Heermance, *William Wells Brown and Clotelle: A Portrait of the Artist in the First Negro Novel* (Hamden, Conn.: Shoestring Press, 1969), 79–81.

[10]Frederick Douglass, *Narrative of the Life of Frederick Douglass, an American Slave, Written by Himself,* introd. William Lloyd Garrison (Boston 1845; rpt. Garden City, N.Y.: Doubleday, 1963), 1.

[11]Williams, *They Also Spoke,* 81–83. See also Andrews, "The 1850s," 39–44.

[12]See Gilbert Osofsky, ed., *Puttin' On Ole Massa: The Slave Narratives of Henry Bibb, William Wells Brown, and Solomon Northrup* (New York: Harper & Row, 1969), 16–17.

[13]Winks, Introd., *Four Fugitive Slave Narratives,* vi.

[14]Ronald T. Takaki has speculated that Brown's preoccupation with female tragic mulattoes arises from his psychologial need to be in fiction what he could not be in reality, a man who is able to protect black women. See his *Violence in the Black Imagination: Essays and Documents* (New York: Putnam's 1972), 223.

[15]Robert A. Bone, *The Negro Novel in America,* rev. ed. (New Haven, Conn.: Yale Univ. Press, 1965), 21.

[16]Blyden Jackson, "A Golden Mean for the Negro Novel," *College Language Association Journal,* 3 (Dec. 1959): 81–87, and Yellin, *Intricate Knot,* 174, think that the sentimental romance was a very inappropriate form for the message of a protest novel. About some underlying reasons for using melodrama, see David

Grimsted, "Melodrama as Echo of the Historically Voiceless," in *Anonymous Americans*, ed. Tamara K. Hareven (Englewood Cliffs, N.J.: Prentice-Hall, 1971), 80–98.

[17]Jules Zanger, "The 'Tragic Octoroon' in Pre–Civil War Fiction," *American Quarterly*, 18 (Spring 1966): 65–67. See also Penelope Bullock, "The Mulatto in American Fiction," *Phylon*, 6 (First Quarter 1945): 78–82; and Theodore R. Hudson, "In the Eye of the Beholder: The First Black Novelist," *Negro Digest*, 19 (Dec. 1969): 43–48. Hudson is uncertain whether Brown's preoccupation with beautiful mulattoes instead of all-black characters is a "power-group imitation," a phenomenon common in all minority cultures, or whether Brown simply wished to give his audience what it wanted.

[18]William Wells Brown, "A Lecture Delivered Before the Female Anti-Slavery Society of Salem," in *Four Fugitive Slave Narratives*, introd. Robin W. Winks, 84. In certain passages in *Clotel* marriage is described as the foundation of all civilization and culture.

[19]See R.G. Walters, "The Erotic South: Civilization and Sexuality in American Abolitionism," *American Quarterly*, 25 (May 1973): 182–85.

[20]Sterling A. Brown, "Negro Character as Seen by White Authors," *Journal of Negro Education*, 2 (Apr. 1933): 180.

[21]William Gardner Smith, "The Negro Writer—Pitfalls and Compensations," in *The Black Novelist*, ed. Robert Hemenway (Columbus, Ohio: Merrill, 1970), 198.

[22]See Robert B. Stepto, *From Behind the Veil: A Study of Afro-American Narrative* (Urbana: Univ. of Illinois Press, 1979), 26–30.

[23]Williams, *They Also Spoke*, 98.

[24]See Arthur Davis, Introd., *Clotel, or The President's Daughter*, by William Wells Brown (New York: Macmillan, 1970), vii. All page numbers in parentheses within the text refer to this edition. See also William Edward Farrison, *William Wells Brown: Author and Reformer* (Chicago: Univ. of Chicago Press, 1969), x; Maxwell Whiteman, Introd., *The Anti-Slavery Harp: A Collection of Songs*, by William Wells Brown, Afro-American History Series, Rhistoric Publication No. 206, ed. Maxwell Whiteman (Boston: Bela Marsh, 1848; rpt. Philadelphia: n.d.); and Heermance, *William Wells Brown and* Clotelle, passim.

[25]William Wells Brown, *The Black Man: His Antecedents, His Genius, and His Achievements* (Boston: James Redpath, 1863; rpt. New York: Kraus Reprint, 1969), 11. Farrison, *William Wells Brown*, 4, doubts that Brown was a descendant of Boone. Cf. J. Saunders Redding, *To Make a Poet Black* (Chapel Hill: Univ. of North Carolina Press, 1939), 25, for a discussion of the reasons for different versions of Brown's childhood memories and ancestry.

[26]Farrison, *W.W. Brown*, 5. See also William Wells Brown, "The Narrative of William Wells Brown, A Fugitive Slave," introd. Larry Gara, in *Four Fugitive Slave Narratives*, introd. Winks, 2, 28–29, 31–32, 35.

[27]William Wells Brown, *Black Man*, 18–19.

[28]William Wells Brown, "Narrative," 43.

[29]Bernard W. Bell, "Literary Sources of the Early Afro-American Novel,"

College Language Association Journal, 18 (Sept. 1974): 42. See also Arlene Elder, *The "Hindered Hand": Cultural Implications of Early African-American Fiction* (Westport, Conn.: Greenwood, 1978), xii.

[30]See Quincy's introductory letter for the 1847 edition of the *Narrative* in William Wells Brown, "Narrative," xxiii.

[31]See Farrison, *W. W. Brown*, 176.

[32]Ibid., 217–18. For a thorough investigation into the historical circumstances on which the story is based, see William Edward Farrison, "Clotel, Thomas Jefferson and Sally Hemings," *College Language Association Journal*, 17 (Dec. 1973): 147–74. Fawn M. Brodie, in her biography, *Thomas Jefferson: An Intimate History* (Toronto: Bantam, 1974), regards Jefferson's paternity of Sally Hemings's children and his deep love for her as historical fact. For her detailed documentation, see, for example, 293–302. For a more recent contrasting opinion, see John Chester Miller, *The Wolf by the Ears: Thomas Jefferson and Slavery* (New York: Free Press; London: Collier Macmillan, 1977), 154–76. Miller renews the old argument that Sally Hemings's children were fathered by Jefferson's nephews, Peter and Samuel Carr. He states that Jefferson inherited many miscegenation problems from his wife's family and seems to have been unable to keep close relatives from fathering children of mixed blood who looked so much like the President that rumors made him the father.

[33]Farrison, *W. W. Brown*, 218–19.

[34]The story first appeared in *The Liberty Bell* of 1842 but was later included in Lydia Maria Child's *Fact and Fiction: A Collection of Stories* (New York: C.S. Francis; Boston: J.H. Francis, 1846), 61–76.

[35]Thomas Wentworth Higginson, quoted in Fredrickson, *Black Image*, 119. Italics mine.

[36]Brown leaves out only one (unimportant) word in Child's sentence. For all quotations from "The Quadroons," see Child, "The Quadroons," in *Fact and Fiction*, 61–63.

[37]Cf. Tony Trent, "Stratification Among Blacks by Black Authors," *Negro History Bulletin*, 34 (Dec. 1971): 179–81.

[38]Pryse, *Mark and Knowledge*, 164, 169.

[39]See Farrison, *W. W. Brown*, 98.

[40]Davis, Introd., *Clotel*, by Brown, xvi.

[41]Brown later changed his mind on the colonization issue. Up to 1860 he argued against it, but in 1861 he promoted a mass immigration of Negroes to Haiti. See Farrison, *W. W. Brown*, 336.

[42]Yellin, *Intricate Knot*, 174.

[43]See Starke, *Black Portraiture*, 88.

[44]Sterling Brown, *The Negro in American Fiction* (Washington, D.C.: Associates in Negro Folk Education, 1937), 28. An example of the "intractable" Negro is the powerful slave Randall in Brown's "Narrative" who refuses to be whipped and cannot be subdued until he is fired at, rushed upon with clubs and chained with a ball attached to his leg. See William Wells Brown, "Narrative," 3–4. Cf. also the slave Harry in Brown, *Clotel*, 107.

[45]Blyden Jackson, "The Negro's Image of the Universe as Reflected in His Fiction," in *Black Voices: An Anthology of Afro-American Literature*, ed. Abraham

Chapman (New York: New American Library; London: New English Library, 1968), 627.

[46]See Robert E. Fleming, "Humor in the Early Black Novel," *College Language Association Journal*, 17 (Dec. 1973): 250.

[47]Brown used this story again for another catechism scene in his play, *The Escape; or, A Leap for Freedom, A Drama in Five Acts*, Afro-American History Series, Rhistoric Publication No. 207, ed. Maxwell Whiteman, (Boston: R.F. Wallcut, 1858; rpt. Philadelphia: n.d.)

[48]Bernard Bell has noted the influence of the Bible on Brown's work. See Bell, "Literary Sources," 30, 33, 36.

[49]Roger Whitlow, *The Darker Vision: A Socio-Critical History of Nineteenth-Century Fiction Written by Black Americans* (New York: Gordon, 1977), 88.

[50]Addison Gayle, Jr., *The Way of the New World: The Black Novel in America* (Garden City, N.Y.: Anchor-Doubleday, 1976), 11.

[51]William Wells Brown, *Clotelle; or, The Colored Heroine: A Tale of the Southern States* (Miami, Fla.: Mnemosyne, 1969), 114. The various versions of Brown's novel have been differently evaluated. Farrison, *W.W. Brown*, 328, suggests that Brown "did not improve upon *Clotel* by writing *Miralda*, neither in art nor in argument." Yellin, *Intricate Knot*, 174, calls *Miralda* a "marked improvement," partly because of the figure of Jerome. Heermance, *W.W. Brown and Clotelle*, 133, states that the last version "gives us our understanding of the artist who is finally pleased enough with his work so that he does not revise it again." Heermance practically ignores *Miralda*, and his contention that the last version must have pleased the author most is beside the point in appraising artistic quality.

[52]Whitlow, *Darker Vision*, 89. Actually, Jerome's values are not necessarily Horatio Alger values. Even celibacy in loyalty to a distant spouse was not unusual among slaves. See Stephen E. Brown, "Sexuality and the Slave Community," *Phylon*, 42 (Mar. 1981): 4.

[53]Redding, *To Make a Poet Black*, 28.

[54]See especially William Wells Brown, *Black Man*; and *The Rising Son; or, The Antecedents and Advancement of the Colored Race* (Boston: Brown, 1874). Also of interest is his pamphlet, *St. Domingo: Its Revolutions and Its Patriots, A Lecture, Delivered Before the Metropolitan Athenaeum*, 1854. In *Clotel*, Brown used passages from the Rev. John Beard's *Life of Toussaint L'Ouverture*, a biography he used more extensively in his *St. Domingo*. See Farrison, *W.W. Brown*, 255-56.

[55]See Rosalyn Terborg-Penn, "Black Male Perspectives on the Nineteenth-Century Woman," in *The Afro-American Woman: Struggles and Images*, ed. Sharon Harley and Rosalyn Terborg-Penn (Port Washington, N.Y.: Kennikat, 1978), 39.

Notes for Chapter 5

[1]Theodore L. Gross, "The Idealism of Negro Literature," in *The Heroic Ideal in*

American Literature (New York: Free Press; London: Collier Macmillan, 1971), 125–26.

[2]Gayle, *Way of New World*, 24, speaks of the picaresque aspect of the novel. The term is not quite appropriate, but it describes the work's episodic and often satiric character, the sense of heroic adventure, and the realistic description of detail. It does not fit the serious, almost apocalyptic note of *Blake*. For the designation of the novel as an epic, see Allan D. Austin, "The Significance of Martin Robison Delany's *Blake or The Huts of America*," (Diss. Univ. of Massachusetts 1975), 73. The rhetorical aspect is analyzed in Roger W. Hite, " 'Stand Still and See the Salvation': The Rhetorical Design of Martin Delany's *Blake*," *Journal of Black Studies*, 5 (Dec. 1974): 192–202.

[3]Dorothy Sterling, *The Making of an Afro-American: Martin Robison Delany, 1812–1885* (Garden City, N.Y.: Doubleday, 1971), 28.

[4]Matthiessen, *American Renaissance*, 16, 551, 553.

[5]See Victor Ullman, *Martin R. Delany: The Beginnings of Black Nationalism* (Boston: Beacon, 1971), 193, 197; and Floyd J. Miller, Introd., *Blake or The Huts of America*, by Martin R. Delany, ed. Floyd J. Miller (Boston: Beacon, 1970), xx, xxviii. All page numbers given in parentheses within the text refer to this edition. For a critical view of Miller's edition, see Austin, "Significance of *Blake*," 95–96, 296–302.

[6]Lorenzo Dow Turner, *Anti-Slavery Sentiment in American Literature Prior to 1865* (1929; rpt. Port Washington, N.Y.: Kennikat, 1966), 78.

[7]Quoted in Gayle, *Way of New World*, 20.

[8]Ullman, *Martin R. Delany*, 3. Sterling, *Making of an Afro-American*, 2, mentions that the Mandingos ruled the richest empire in West Africa 150 years before the discovery of America. Although in the following centuries invading armies destroyed their power, they still were noted throughout the African world as craftsmen and traders.

[9]Miller, Introd., *Blake*, by Delany, xiii. See also Penelope L. Bullock, *The Afro-American Periodical Press, 1838–1909* (Baton Rouge: Louisiana State Univ. Press, 1981), 15, 19, 20–21, 54, 60, about Delany's contributions to journalism.

[10]See Ullman, *Martin R. Delany*, 50. Four of the children died in infancy. The legal denial of Catherine Richard's substantial inheritance was one of the heavy blows Delany suffered on account of his race. See Austin, "Significance of *Blake*," 2.

[11]The Patent Office had become a controversial exponent of the rising faith in technology and progress. Melville commented on it satirically a few years later in *The Confidence Man*. Delany's application was received during the time that Thomas Ewbanks served as Patent Commissioner, 1849–52. Ewbanks talked about the "melting away of the red race" because of their idleness, and he disregarded the dire consequences of mechanization for the poor working class. See Karcher, *Shadow over Promised Land*, 248–49. On Delany's invention, see Sterling, *Making of an Afro-American*, 139; and Frank A. Rollin [Frances E. Rollin Whipper], *Life and Public Services of Martin R. Delany* (Boston: Lee and Shepard, 1883), 77.

[12]Ullman, *Martin R. Delany*, 199–200. Cf. Yellin, *Intricate Knot*, 196.

[13]Floyd Miller, Introd., *Blake*, xi, suggests that either Delany lost confidence in the *Anglo-African Magazine* when he halted the serialization in 1859 or he did

not want to see his work published while he was in Africa. Yellin, *Intricate Knot,* 20, doubts the latter possibility since in an 1859 installment headnote his leaving was announced, and the last segment appeared two months after he sailed to Africa.

[14]Ullman, *Martin R. Delany,* 208.

[15]Sterling, *Making of an Afro-American,* 243.

[16]Miller, Introd., *Blake,* by Delany, xvii.

[17]Ibid., xx. About the dating of the beginnings of *Blake,* see also Austin, "Significance of *Blake,*" 4.

[18]Gayle, *Way of New World,* 29.

[19]See Miller, Introd., *Blake,* by Delany, ix. Miller himself discovered chs. 24–28 and 32–74.

[20]Hugh M. Gloster, *Negro Voices in American Fiction* (New York: Russell & Russell, 1965), 29.

[21]Gayle, *Way of New World,* 11, 21.

[22]See Yellin, *Intricate Knot,* 206. Yellin thinks this language may be reminiscent of the Chatham proceedings with John Brown. Robert E. Fleming calls the language of the Delany hero "the overly-correct, priggish language associated with the heroes of melodrama." See "Black, White, and Mulatto in Martin R. Delaney's [sic] *Blake,*" *Negro History Bulletin,* 36 (Feb. 1975): 38.

[23]Delany's use of dialect is inconsistent and of varying quality. Some transcriptions seem awkward. Julianne Malveaux, however, suggests that Delaney accurately captured the dialect of the slaves. See "Revolutionary Themes in Martin Delaney's [sic] *Blake,*" *The Black Scholar,* 4 (July–Aug. 1973): 56. Cf. Austin, "Significance of *Blake,*" 96, 229–34. Austin finds the rendering of the dialect on the whole consistent and attributes some inconsistencies to flaws in Miller's edition.

[24]Bell, "Literary Sources," 35.

[25]Houston A. Baker, Jr., *Long Black Song: Essays in Black American Literature and Culture* (Charlottesville: Univ. Press of Virginia, 1972), 46. See also Andrews, "The 1850s," 49, on apocalypticism in Delany, Poe, Hawthorne, Melville, and Mark Twain.

[26]Baker, *Long Black Song,* 46.

[27]Cf. Franklin, "Animal Farm Unbound," 36–38, on the moral inversions in the slave narratives: to survive the slave often had to steal; to attain his humanity he had to use deceit and trickery.

[28]Bone, *Negro Novel,* 30.

[29]Ullman, *Martin R. Delany,* 53. Ullmann is commenting on Delany's views expressed in his newspaper, *The Mystery.*

[30]See Sterling Stuckey, "Through the Prism of Folklore: The Black Ethos in Slavery," *Massachusetts Review,* 9 (Summer 1968): 417–34. Stuckey explains that slave singing was a kind of group therapy. Slaves usually did not sing because they were happy and easy-going, as the plantation romancers assumed, but because they needed a release for their heartache. "Slaves were able to fashion a life style and set of values—an ethos—which prevented them from being imprisoned altogether by the definitions which the larger society sought to impose. This ethos was an amalgam of Africanisms and New World elements" (418). See also Austin, "Significance of *Blake,*" ch. iv, on songs and poems in the novel.

[31]Terborg-Penn, "Black Male Perspectives," 31.

[32]Fleming, "Black, White, and Mulatto," 39.

[33]Interestingly, in "The Narrative of the Life and Adventures of Henry Bibb, An American Slave," the experiences with the Indians are described in a similar way. Bibb, sold for a while to a very wealthy half-Indian (Cherokee), found that slaves are treated with more respect by Indians than by whites. Osofsky, *Puttin' on Ole Massa*, 140–44.

[34]See Fleming, "Humor in the Early Black Novel," 253–54.

[35]Jackson, "Negro's Image of the Universe," 628–31.

[36]Cf. Stephen Butterfield, *Black Autobiography in America* (Amherst: Univ. of Massachusetts Press, 1974), 55. The wilderness with heathens, black men, devil, and serpents was a terror to Cotton Mather. For Nat Turner it was an inspiration.

[37]Edward Halsey Foster, *The Civilized Wilderness: Backgrounds to American Romantic Literature, 1817–1860* (New York: Free Press; London: Collier Macmillan, 1975), 149. See also Blyden Jackson, "The Ghetto of the Negro Novel," in *The Waiting Years: Essays on American Negro Literature* (Baton Rouge: Louisiana State Univ. Press, 1976), 180. "The Negro novel is a city novel. It almost always has been." On exotic elements, see Mukhtar Ali Isani, "The Exotic and Protest in Earlier Black Literature: The Use of Alien Setting and Character," *Studies in Black Literature*, 5 (Summer 1974): 9–14.

[38]Andrews, "The 1850s," 48. Delany quotes Byron in *Blake*, 227.

[39]William Blake, *The Marriage of Heaven and Hell*, quoted in *English Romantic Writers*, David Perkins, ed. (New York: Harcourt, Brace, 1967), 75. The title of Delany's newspaper, *The Mystery*, could also be understood in the Blakean sense. See "The Book of Ahania," ibid., 89.

[40]Takaki, *Violence in Black Imagination*, 81. Cf. Austin, "Significance of *Blake*," 290–94, who criticizes Takaki's interpretation of ambivalence in Delany.

[41]Takaki, ibid.

[42]R. Baxter Miller defines the ethics of black literature as a black humanism. See R. Baxter Miller, introd., *Black American Literature and Humanism*, ed. Miller (Lexington: Univ. Press of Kentucky, 1981), 1–7. In the same work, Trudier Harris, "Three Black Women Writers and Humanism: A Folk Perspective," 50–74, sees this black humanism represented in black folk traditions. While she discovers in three contemporary black novels a sharp contrast between Christianity and black folk traditions, often only a perverted Christianity is opposed in black literature of the 19th century, not the Christian faith as such.

[43]Yellin, *Intricate Knot*, 207.

Notes for Chapter 6

While this book was in print, I reworked and extended the above chapter under the perspective of "Women, Religion, and Peace in a Native American Ritual" for a paper presented at the American Academy of Religion meeting in New York, Dec. 19–22, 1982, and for an article to be published in 1984. The following titles have been important in my continuing research on the Iroquois epic. For an up-to-date edition of the Condolence Ritual: John Bierhorst, ed., *Four Masterworks of American Indian Literature: Quetzalcoatl/The Ritual of Condolence/Cuceb/The Night Chant* (New York: Farrar, Straus, 1974), 121–83. For an evaluation of the different versions of the epic: William N. Fenton, "The Lore of the Longhouse: Myth, Ritual, and Red Power," *Anthropological Quarterly*, 48 (Fall 1975), 131–47. For an older, but informed retelling of the story and its background, making use of printed as well as manuscript versions: Paul A.W. Wallace, *The White Roots of Peace* (Philadelphia: Univ. of Pennsylvania Press, 1946). For up-to-date, extensive information on Iroquois history and present conditions: Bruce G. Trigger, ed., *Handbook of North American Indians*, vol. 15 (Washington, D.C.: Smithsonian Institution, 1978).

[1]Quoted in the epigram of Alvin M. Josephy, Jr., *The Indian Heritage of America* (New York: Knopf, 1968).

[2]Karl Kroeber, "An Introduction to the Art of Traditional American Indian Narration," in *Traditional Literatures of the American Indian*, ed. Karl Kroeber (Lincoln: Univ. of Nebraska Press, 1981), 2–3, 9.

[3]See Alan R. Velie, *American Indian Literature: An Anthology* (Norman: Univ. of Oklahoma Press, 1979), 3; and Michael Dorris, "Native American Literature in an Ethnohistorical Context," *College English* 41 (Oct. 1979): 147–62. Dorris even doubts the appropriateness of the generic term "American Indian literature."

[4]Paula Gunn Allen, "The Sacred Hoop: A Contemporary Indian Perspective on American Indian Literature," in *Literature of the American Indians: Views and Interpretations*, ed. Abraham Chapman (New York: New American Library, 1975), 112–13.

[5]Although using the term "epic" to describe the Dekanawida myth may not be entirely appropriate, "narrative" and "myth" are too general and do not suggest the function of the story.

[6]See Frederick W. Turner, III, ed., *The Portable North American Indian Reader* (New York: Viking, 1973), 10.

[7]When the story of Dekanawida was passed from one generation to the next over many centuries, some Christian elements were incorporated, and scholars of American literature should be as interested in analyzing its Christian and Native American aspects as they are in analyzing the Christian and non-Christian facets of *Beowulf*. See Thomas E. Sanders and Walter W. Peek, eds., *Literature of the American Indian* (Hollywood, Calif.: Glencoe, 1973), 9.

[8]William N. Fenton, *Parker on the Iroquois* (Syracuse, N.Y.: Syracuse Univ. Press, 1968).

[9]Ibid., Introd., 46; and Book III, 12. The more compact Newhouse version is conveniently available, with a good introduction, in the anthology by Sanders and Peek (n7). The page references in parentheses within the text are to Book III of Fenton-Parker, containing also the "official" version.

[10]See Anthony F.C. Wallace, "The Dekanawideh [sic] Myth Analyzed as the Record of a Revitalization Movement," *Ethnohistory*, 5 (Spring 1958): 118–30.

[11]See Sanders and Peek, *Literature of the American Indian*, 187; and Peter Farb,

Man's Rise to Civilization: The Cultural Ascent of the Indians of North America, rev. 2nd ed. (New York: Dutton, 1978), 90–91.

[12]Wilcomb E. Washburn, *The Indian in America* (New York: Harper & Row, 1975), 24.

[13]See the chiefs' version of the narrative, in *Parker on the Iroquois*, ed. Fenton, 71n.

[14]Ruth M. Underhill, *Red Man's Religion: Beliefs and Practices of the Indians North of Mexico* (Chicago: Univ. of Chicago Press, 1965), 176, 179.

[15]See Thomas R. Henry, *Wilderness Messiah: The Story of Hiawatha and the Iroquois* (New York: William Sloane, 1955), 76.

[16]Horatio Hale, *The Iroquois Book of Rites* (New York: AMS Press, 1969), 65–66.

[17]See Irene Schumacher, *Gesellschaftsstruktur und Rolle der Frau: Das Beispiel der Irokesen* (Berlin: Duncker & Humblot, 1972), 136.

[18]See Rohrlich-Leavitt, ed., *Women Cross-Culturally*, 601–16 and passim.

[19]See Underhill, *Red Man's Religion*, 176.

[20]When Henry Rowe Schoolcraft observed an Iroquois Council in 1846, he was impressed with the way the Council said grace before their meal and thought they would be amazed to see Christians eating without giving thanks. He also observed the Great Law in action, witnessing, for example, the installation of two new sachems and the "impeachment and deposition" of three unfaithful ones. See Appendix B of Fenton, ed., *Parker on the Iroquois*, 127–28.

[21]Quoted in Sanders and Peek, eds., *Literature of the American Indian*, 285.

[22]The story is incorrectly labeled as a fictional work of Boudinot's by the *Dictionary of American Biography* (New York: Scribner's, 1929), s.v. "Boudinot, Elias." Cf. also Bernd C. Peyer, "A Bibliography of Native American Prose Prior to the 20th Century," *The Indian Historian*, 13 (Sept. 1980): 23–25. The story was published in Newburyport by W. & J. Gilman in 1820, probably as a reprint of Tract 128 of the American Tract Society, and appeared also in the *Religious Intelligencer*, 1 and 8 January 1820, pp. 493–95, 510–512, and in the *Boston Recorder*, 11 March 1820, p. 44, as "Religion Exemplified in the Life of Poor Sarah."

[23]See A. LaVonne Brown Ruoff, rev. of *O-GÎ-MÄW-KWĚ MIT-I-GWÄ-KÎ: Queen of the Woods*, by Simon Pokagon, *American Literary Realism*, 13 (Autumn 1980): 317–19; and J.H. Jackson, Introd., *The Life and Adventures of Joaquín Murieta*, by John Rollin Ridge [Yellow Bird] (Norman: Univ. of Oklahoma Press, 1955).

[24]See Michael K. Foster, *From the Earth to Beyond the Sky: An Ethnographic Approach to Four Longhouse Iroquois Speech Events* (Ottawa: National Museums of Canada, 1974), vi–vii, 7.

[25]Leslie Marmon Silko, "Language and Literature from a Pueblo Indian Perspective," in *English Literature: Opening up the Canon*, ed. Leslie A. Fiedler and Houston A. Baker, Jr. Selected Papers from the English Institute, New Series, No. 4 (Baltimore: Johns Hopkins Univ. Press, 1981), 57.

[26]Ibid., 54.

[27]See Eleanor Leacock, "Class, Commodity, and the Status of Women," in *Women Cross-Culturally*, ed. Rohrlich-Leavitt, 607–611; and Frederick Engels, *The Origin of the Family, Private Property and the State, in the Light of the Researches*

of *Lewis H. Morgan*, ed. Eleanor Burke Leacock (New York: International Publishers, 1942, 1972), 33–37, 117f., 220–25, 263.

[28]Michael Dorris has pointed out that the Native Americans before Columbus were much more familiar with cultural and linguistic diversity than the invading Europeans. "Native American Literature," 147f.

Notes for Conclusion

[1]Alfred Kazin, *New York Times Book Review* (Nov. 3, 1973): 1, quoted from John Murray Cuddihi, *The Ordeal of Civility: Freud, Marx, Lévi-Strauss, and the Jewish Struggle with Modernity* (New York: Dell, 1974), 228.

[2]Ibid.

[3]"That work of fiction . . . has most authority which most abundantly opens itself to . . . the mythic." Warner Berthoff, *Fictions and Events: Essays in Criticism and Literary History* (New York: Dutton, 1971), 54.

[4]McLuhan, *War and Peace*, 15, 185.

[5]See George M. Fredrickson, *White Supremacy: A Comparative Study in American and South African History* (New York: Oxford Univ. Press, 1981), 150–51, 156.

[6]Charles Brockden Brown, *Alcuin: A Dialogue*, ed. Lee R. Edwards (New York: Grossman, 1971), 32–33. See also Earnest, *American Eve*, 31–32, on Brown's *Ormond* and *Alcuin*.

[7]See Peter N. Carroll and David W. Noble, *The Free and the Unfree: A New History of the United States* (Harmondsworth, England: Penguin, 1977), 247.

[8]See Wayne Craven, *Sculpture in America* (New York: Crowell, 1968), 277–79; and *200 Years of American Sculpture* (New York: Whitney Museum, 1976), 314.

[9]Harriet Beecher Stowe, "Sojourner Truth, the Libyan Sibyl," *Atlantic Monthly*, 11 Apr. 1863, pp. 473–81. See also Margaret Farrand Thorp, *The Literary Sculptors* (Durham, N.C.: Duke Univ. Press, 1965), 144.

[10]See Sylvia E. Crane, *White Silence: Greenough, Powers, and Crawford: American Sculptors in Nineteenth Century Italy* (Coral Gables, Fla.: Univ. of Miami Press, 1972), 134, 201–2, 218–22, 235, 331, 362; and Cornelia Carr, ed., *Harriet Hosmer: Letters and Memories* (New York: Moffat, Yard, 1912). About the American sculptors' special problems, see Michele Bogart, "The Development of a Popular Market for Sculpture in America, 1850–1880," *Journal of American Culture*, 4 (Spring 1981): 3–27.

[11]Tillie Olsen, *Silences* (New York: Delacorte, 1978), 184.

[12]Grimsted, "Melodrama as Echo," 82–83.

[13]See Geoffrey Rans, "Inaudible Man: The Indian in the Theory and Practice of White Fiction," *Canadian Review of American Studies*, 8 (Fall 1977): 103–15.

[14]Olsen, *Silences*, 16–17.

[15]Sandra M. Gilbert and Susan Gubar, *The Madwoman in the Attic: The Woman Writer and the Nineteenth-Century Literary Imagination* (New Haven, Conn.: Yale Univ. Press, 1979), 534, 621.

[16]Louis D. Rubin, Jr., "The Experience of Difference: Southerners and Jews."

In *The Curious Death of the Novel: Essays in American Literature* (Baton Rouge: Louisiana State Univ. Press, 1967), 281.

[17]James Russell Lowell, "A Fable for Critics," quoted in *The Romantic Movement in American Writing*, ed. Richard Harter Fogle (New York: Odyssey, 1966), 528.

[18]Newton Arvin, *Herman Melville* (New York: William Sloane, 1950), 55.

[19]Lewis Mumford, *The Human Prospect*, ed. Harry T. Moore and Karl W. Deutsch (Carbondale: Southern Illinois Univ. Press, 1955), 194–95.

[20]D.H. Lawrence, *Studies in Classic American Literature* (New York: Viking, 1923), 160.

[21]Jackson, "Ghetto of Negro Novel," 184.

[22]J.N.B. Hewitt, "Iroquoian Cosmology." First Part. *Twenty-first Annual Report of the Bureau of American Ethnology*, (Washington, D.C.: GPO, 1903), 134.

[23]Elizabeth I. Hanson, "The Indian Metaphor in Henry David Thoreau's *A Week on the Concord and Merrimack Rivers*," *Thoreau Journal Quarterly*, 10 (Jan. 1978): 4. Thoreau tells the story of Hannah Dustan in the "Thursday" chapter of *A Week on the Concord and Merimack Rivers* (1849).

[24]The story from Cotton Mather's *Narratives of the Indian Wars* (1675–1699), is reprinted in Nancy B. Black and Bette S. Weidman, eds., *White on Red: Images of the American Indian*, (Port Washington, N.Y.: Kennikat, 1976), 64–66. Leslie Fiedler gives a thorough interpretation of the various Hannah Dustan stories in his *The Return of the Vanishing American* (New York: Stein and Day, 1968), 90–108. Robert F. Sayre, *Thoreau and the American Indians* (Princeton, N.J.: Princeton Univ. Press, 1977), 47–54, provides an excellent evaluation of Thoreau's account.

[25]Black and Weidman, *White on Red*, 190. (Hawthorne's story is reprinted from *The American Magazine of Useful and Entertaining Knowledge*, 9 May 1836, pp. 395–97.

[26]See Philip F. Gura, "Thoreau's Maine Woods Indians: More Representative Men," *American Literature*, 49 (Nov. 1977): 366–84.

[27]Fiedler, *Return of Vanishing American*, 42.

[28]Sayre, *Thoreau and the American Indians*, 52.

[29]See Daryl C. Dance, "Black Eve or Madonna? A Study of the Antithetical Views of the Mother in Black American Literature," in *Sturdy Black Bridges: Visions of Black Women in Literature*, ed. Roseann P. Bell, Bettye J. Parker, and Beverly Guy-Sheftall (Garden City, N.Y.: Anchor Press-Doubleday, 1979), 127–28.

[30]West, "Primitivism in Melville," 378.

[31]Ibid., 377.

[32]Mumford, *Human Prospect*, 196.

[33]On the impossibility of fitting a "black Adam" into a generic Adam, see Richard Gilman, "White Standards and Negro Writing," in *The Black American Writer*, ed. C.W.E. Bigsby, vol. I (Deland, Fla.: Everett/Edwards, 1969), 37. "The Negro has found it almost impossible in America to experience the universal as such." Cf. also Curtis W. Ellison, "Black Adam: The Adamic Assertion and the Afro-American Novelist," (Diss. Univ. of Minnesota 1970).

[34]See note 40 in the Introduction.

Bibliography

Primary Sources

Nathaniel Hawthorne

Fiction

The Centenary Edition of the Works of Nathaniel Hawthorne (Columbus: Ohio State Univ. Press) was used for all the novels and tales discussed.

Other Edition

The Writings of Nathaniel Hawthorne, Vol. XVII: *Miscellanies: Biographical and Other Sketches and Letters.* Boston: Houghton Mifflin, 1900.

Non-Fiction

The American Notebooks. Ed. Claude M. Simpson. Vol. VIII of the Centenary Edition, 1972.
The French and Italian Notebooks. Ed. Thomas Woodson. Vol. XIV of the Centenary Edition, 1980.
Letters of Hawthorne to William D. Ticknor, 1851–1864. Newark, N.J.: Carteret Bookclub, 1910; rpt. Washington, D.C.: NCR/Microcard Editions, 1972.
Love Letters of Nathaniel Hawthorne. Washington, D.C.: Microcard Editions, 1972.

Herman Melville

Fiction

The Northwestern-Newberry Edition (Evanston, Ill.: Northwestern Univ. Press and the Newberry Library) was used for *Typee, Omoo, Mardi,* and *Pierre.*

Other Editions

The Complete Stories of Herman Melville. Ed. Jay Leyda. New York; Random House, 1949.
The Confidence Man: His Masquerade. Ed. Hershel Parker. New York: Norton, 1971.
Moby-Dick or, The Whale. Ed. Harrison Hayford and Hershel Parker. New York: Norton, 1976.

Non-Fiction

Davis, Merrell R., and William H. Gilman. *The Letters of Herman Melville.* New Haven, Conn.: Yale Univ. Press, 1960.

Harriet Beecher Stowe

Dred; A Tale of the Great Dismal Swamp. 2 vols. 1856; rpt. New York: AMS Press, 1970.
Oldtown Folks. Ed. Henry F. May. Cambridge, Mass.: Harvard Univ. Press, 1966.
"Sojourner Truth, the Libyan Sibyl." *Atlantic Monthly,* 11 (Apr. 1863): 473–81.
Uncle Tom's Cabin or, Life Among the Lowly. Ed. Kenneth S. Lynn. Cambridge, Mass.: Harvard Univ. Press, 1962.

William Wells Brown

The Anti-Slavery Harp: A Collection of Songs. Afro-American History Series, Rhistoric Publication No. 206. Ed. by Maxwell Whiteman. Boston: Bela Marsh, 1848; Philadelphia: n.d. rpt.
The Black Man: His Antecedents, His Genius, and His Achievements. Boston: James Redpath, 1863; rpt. New York: Kraus Reprint, 1969.
Clotel, or The President's Daughter: A Narrative of Slave Life in the United States. Ed. with an introd. by Arthur Davis. New York: Macmillan, 1970.

Clotelle; or, The Colored Heroine: A Tale of the Southern States. Boston: Lee & Shepard, 1867; rpt. Miami, Fla.: Mnemosyne Publishing, 1969.

The Escape; or, A Leap for Freedom. A Drama in Five Acts. Afro-American History Series, Rhistoric Publication No. 207. Ed. Maxwell Whiteman. Boston: R.F. Wallcut, 1858; rpt. Philadelphia: n.d.

"A Lecture Delivered before the Female Anti-Slavery Society of Salem." In *Four Fugitive Slave Narratives.* Introd. Robin W. Winks. Reading, Mass.; Addison-Wesley, 1969, pp. 81–98.

"The Narrative of William Wells Brown, A Fugitive Slave." Introd. Larry Gara. In *Four Fugitive Slave Narratives.* Introd. Robin W. Winks. Reading, Mass.: Addison-Wesley, 1969, pp. ix–xvii, 1–81.

Martin R. Delany

Blake or The Huts of America. Ed. with an introd. by Floyd J. Miller. Boston: Beacon Press, 1970.

The Condition, Elevation, Emigration, and Destiny of the Colored People of the United States, Politically Considered. 1852; rpt. New York: Arno Press, 1969.

The Epic of Dekanawida

The two principal versions

Fenton, William N., ed. *Parker on the Iroquois.* Syracuse, N.Y.: Syracuse Univ. Press, 1968.

Other Primary Sources

Hale, Horatio. *The Iroquois Book of Rites.* New York: AMS Press, 1969.

Sanders, Thomas E., and Walter W. Peek, eds. *Literature of the American Indian.* Hollywood, Calif.: Glencoe Press, 1973.

Secondary Sources
(Including Minor Fiction by Other Authors)

Abrams, Robert. "*Typee* and *Omoo*: Melville and the Ungraspable Phantom of Identity." *Arizona Quarterly,* 31 (1975): 33–50.

Adams, John R. *Harriet Beecher Stowe.* New York: Twayne, 1963.

Adler, Joyce Sparer. *War in Melville's Imagination.* New York: New York Univ. Press, 1981.

Allen, Paula Gunn. "The Sacred Hoop: A Contemporary Indian Perspective on American Indian Literature." In *Literature of the American Indians: Views and Interpretations.* Ed. Abraham Chapman. New York: New American Library, 1975, pp. 111–35.

Ammons, Elizabeth. "Heroines in *Uncle Tom's Cabin.*" In *Critical Essays on Harriet Beecher Stowe.* Ed. Elizabeth Ammons. Boston: G.K. Hall, 1980, pp. 152–65.

————, ed. *Critical Essays on Harriet Beecher Stowe.* Boston: G.K. Hall, 1980.

Anderson, Charles Roberts. *Melville in the South Seas.* New York: Columbia Univ. Press, 1939.

Anderson, Quentin. *The Imperial Self: An Essay in American Literary and Cultural History.* New York: Knopf, 1971.

Andrews, William L. "The 1850s: The First Afro-American Literary Renaissance." In *Literary Romanticism in America.* Ed. William L. Andrews. Baton Rouge: Louisiana State Univ. Press, 1981, pp. 38–60.

Angoff, Charles, and Meyer Levin, eds. *The Rise of American Jewish Literature: An Anthology of Selections from the Major Novels.* New York: Simon & Schuster, 1970.

Arvin, Newton. *Herman Melville.* New York: William Sloane, 1950.

Ashton, Jean Willoughby. *Harriet Beecher Stowe: A Reference Guide.* Boston: G.K. Hall, 1977.

Auerbach, Jonathan. "Executing the Model: Painting, Sculpture, and Romance-Writing in Hawthorne's *The Marble Faun.*" *ELH,* 47 (Spring 1980): 103–20.

Austin, Allan D. "The Significance of Martin Robison Delany's *Blake or The Huts of America.*" Diss. Univ. of Massachusetts 1975.

Baird, James R. *Ishmael: A Study of the Symbolic Mode in Primitivism.* Baltimore: Johns Hopkins Univ. Press, 1956.

Baker, Houston A., Jr. *The Journey Back: Issues in Black Literature and Criticism.* Chicago: Univ. of Chicago Press, 1980.

————. *Long Black Song: Essays in Black American Literature and Culture.* Charlottesville: Univ. Press of Virginia, 1972.

Baldwin, James. "Everybody's Protest Novel." In *The Black Novelist.* Ed. Robert Hemenway. Columbus, Ohio: Charles E. Merrill, 1970, 218–26.

Baldwin, Kenneth, and David K. Kirby, eds. *Individual and Community: Variations on a Theme in American Fiction.* Durham, N.C.: Duke Univ. Press, 1975.

Bales, Kent. "The Allegory and the Radical Romantic Ethic of *The Blithedale Romance.*" In *The Blithedale Romance.* Ed. Seymour L. Gross and Rosalie Murphy. New York: Norton, 1978, 407–13.

Barnett, Louise K. *The Ignoble Savage: American Literary Racism, 1790–1890.* Westport, Conn.: Greenwood Press, 1975.

Barthold, Bonnie J. *Black Time: Fiction of Africa, the Caribbean, and the United States.* New Haven, Conn.: Yale Univ. Press, 1981.

Baym, Nina. "Hawthorne's Women: The Tyranny of Social Myths." *Centennial Review,* 15 (Summer 1971): 250–72.

————. "Melville's Quarrel with Fiction." *PMLA,* 94 (Oct.979): 909–23.

————. *The Shape of Hawthorne's Career.* Ithaca, N.Y.: Cornell Univ. Press, 1976.

————. *Woman's Fiction: A Guide to Novels By and About Women in America, 1820–1870.* Ithaca, N.Y.: Cornell Univ. Press, 1978.

Beaver, Harold. "The Drama of Disorientation." Rev. of *Marquesan Encounters,* by T. Walter Herbert. *Times Literary Supplement.* 24 Apr. 1981, pp. 451–52.

Bell, Bernard W. "Literary Sources of the Early Afro-American Novel." *College Language Association Journal,* 18 (Sept. 1974): 29–43.

Bell, Michael. *Primitivism.* London: Methuen, 1972.

Bennett, Lerone, Jr. *Before the Mayflower: A History of the Negro in America, 1619–1964.* Baltimore: Penguin Books, 1966.

Bercovitch, Sacvan. *The American Jeremiad.* Madison: Univ. of Wisconsin Press, 1978.

————. "Of Wise and Foolish Virgins: Hilda Versus Miriam in Hawthorne's *Marble Faun.*" In *The Merrill Studies in* The Marble Faun. Comp. David B. Kesterson. Columbus, Ohio: Charles E. Merrill, 1971, pp. 79–83.

Berg, Barbara G. *The Remembered Gate: Origins of American Feminism: The Woman and the City, 1800–1860.* New York; Oxford Univ. Press, 1978.

Berkson, Dorothy. "Millennial Politics and the Feminine Fiction of Harriet Beecher Stowe." In *Critical Essays on Harriet Beecher Stowe.* Ed. Elizabeth Ammons. Boston: G.K. Hall, 1980, pp. 244–58.

Berthoff, Warner. *Fictions and Events: Essays in Criticism and Literary History.* New York: Dutton, 1971.

Berzon, Judith R. *Neither White nor Black: The Mulatto Character in American Fiction.* New York: New York Univ. Press, 1978.

Bewley, Marius. *The Complex Fate: Hawthorne, Henry James, and Some Other American Writers.* London: Chatto and Windus, 1952.

_____. *The Eccentric Design: Form in the Classic American Novel.* New York: Columbia Univ. Press, 1959.

Birdsall, Virginia Ogden. "Hawthorne's Fair-Haired Maidens: The Fading Light." *PMLA,* 75 (June 1960): 250–56.

Black, Nancy B., and Bette S. Weidman, eds. *White on Red: Images of the American Indian.* Port Washington, N.Y.: Kennikat Press, 1976.

Bogart, Michele. "The Development of a Popular Market for Sculpture in America, 1850–1880." *Journal of American Culture,* 4 (Spring 1981): 3–27.

Bone, Robert A. *The Negro Novel in America.* Rev. ed. New Haven, Conn.: Yale Univ. Press, 1965.

Bontemps, Arna, ed. *Great Slave Narratives.* Boston: Beacon Press, 1969.

"Boudinot, Elias." *Dictionary of American Biography.* New York: Scribner's, 1929.

Branch, Watson G. *Melville: The Critical Heritage.* London: Routledge & Kegan Paul, 1974.

New York: Octagon Books, 1973.

Brock, William R. *Conflict and Transformation: The United States, 1844–1877.* Harmondsworth, England: Penguin Books, 1973.

Brodhead, Richard H. "Creating the Creative." In *New Perspectives on Melville.* Ed. Faith Pullin. Kent, Ohio: Kent State Univ. Press, pp. 29–53.

_____. *Hawthorne, Melville, and the Novel.* Chicago: Univ. of Chicago Press, 1976.

Brodie, Fawn M. *Thomas Jefferson: An Intimate History.* Toronto: Bantam Books, 1974.

Broome, J.H. *Rousseau: A Study of His Thought.* London: Edward Arnold, 1963.

Brown, Herbert Ross. *The Sentimental Novel in America 1789–1860.* New York: Pageant Books, 1959.

Brown, Stephen E. "Sexuality and the Slave Community." *Phylon,* 42 (Mar. 1981): 1–10.

Brown, Sterling. "A Century of Negro Portraiture in American Literature." In *Black Voices: An Anthology of Afro-American Literature.* Ed. Abraham Chapman. New York: New American Library, 1968, pp. 564–89.

_____. *The Negro in American Fiction.* Washington, D.C.: Associates in Negro Folk Education, 1937.

_____. "Negro Character as Seen by White Authors." *Journal of Negro Education,* 2 (Apr. 1933): 179–203.

Brumm, Ursula. *American Thought and Religious Typology*. Trans. John Hooglund. New Brunswick, N.J.: Rutgers Univ. Press, 1970.
————. *Geschichte and Wildnis in der amerikanischen Literatur*. Berlin: Erich Schmidt, 1980.
Bullock, Penelope L. *The Afro-American Periodical Press, 1838–1909*. Baton Rouge: Louisiana State Univ. Press, 1981.
————. "The Mulatto in American Fiction." *Phylon*, 6 (First Quarter 1945): 78–82.
Butcher, Philip, ed. *The Minority Presence in American Literature, 1600–1900: A Reader and Course Guide*. 2 vols. Washington, D.C.: Howard Univ. Press, 1977.
Butterfield, Stephen. *Black Autobiography in America*. Amherst: Univ. of Massachusetts Press, 1974.
Canfield, William W. *The Legends of the Iroquois: Told by "The Cornplanter."* Port Washington, N.Y.: Ira J. Friedman, 1902.
Capps, Walter Holden, ed. *Seeing with a Native Eye: Essays on Native American Religion*. New York: Harper & Row, 1976.
Carpenter, Frederick I. "Puritans Preferred Blondes: The Heroines of Melville and Hawthorne." *New England Quarterly*, 9 (June 1936): 253–72.
Carr, Cornelia, ed. *Harriet Hosmer: Letters and Memories*. New York: Moffat, Yard, 1912.
Carroll, Peter N., and David W. Noble. *The Free and the Unfree: A New History of the United States*. Harmondsworth, England: Penguin books, 1977.
Chapman, Abraham, ed. *Black Voices: An Anthology of Afro-American Literature*. New York: New American Libaray; London: New English Library, 1968.
Chapman, Abraham ed. *Literature of the American Indians: Views and Interpretations*. New York: New American Library, 1975.
Chase, Richard. *Herman Melville: A Critical Study*. New York: Hafner, 1971.
Chevigny, Bell Gale. *The Woman and the Myth: Margaret Fuller's Life and Writings*. New York: Feminist Press, 1976.
Child, Lydia Maria. *Fact and Fiction: A Collection of Stories*. New York: C.S. Francis; Boston: J.H. Francis, 1846.
————. *Hobomok: A Tale of Early Times. By an American*. Boston: Cummings, Hilliard, 1824. In *Wright American Fiction*. Vol. I (1774–1850). Research Publication Microfilm no. 520.
Cicardo, Barbara Ann. "The Mystery of the American Eve: Alienation of the Feminine as a Tragic Theme in American Letters." Diss. Saint Louis Univ. 1971.

Clark, Harry Hayden. "Hawthorne: Tradition *Versus* Innovation." In *Patterns of Commitment in American Literature.* Ed. Marston LaFrance. Toronto: Univ. of Toronto Press, 1967, pp. 19–37.

Cochran, Robert. "The 'Little Lower Layer': Herman Melville's Carefully Disguised Heroes." *Phylon,* 40 (Sept. 1979): 217–23.

Conrad, Susan P. *Perish the Thought: Intellectual Women in Romantic America, 1830–1860.* New York: Oxford Univ. Press, 1976.

Cornillon, Susan Koppelman, ed. *Images of Women in Fiction: Feminist Perspectives.* Bowling Green, Ohio: Bowling Green Univ. Popular Press, 1972.

Cornplanter, Jesse J. *Legends of the Longhouse.* Port Washington, N.Y.: Ira J. Friedman, 1938.

Craft, William, and Ellen Craft. *Running a Thousand Miles for Freedom.* New York: Arno Press and New York Times, 1969.

Crane, Sylvia E. *White Silence: Greenough, Powers, and Crawford: American Sculptors in Nineteenth-Century Italy.* Coral Gables, Fla.: Univ. of Miami Press, 1972.

Craven, Wayne. *Sculpture in America.* New York: Thomas Y. Crowell, 1968.

Crews, Frederick C. *The Sins of the Fathers: Hawthorne's Psychological Themes.* New York: Oxford Univ. Press, 1966.

Crozier, Alice C. *The Novels of Harriet Beecher Stowe.* New York: Oxford Univ. Press, 1969.

Cuddihi, John Murray. *The Ordeal of Civility: Freud, Marx, Lévi-Strauss, and the Jewish Struggle with Modernity.* New York: Dell, 1974.

Cunliffe, Marcus. *The Literature of the United States.* Baltimore, Md.: Penguin Books, 1967.

Curtis, Edith Roelker. *A Season in Utopia: The Story of Brook Farm.* New York: Thomas Nelson, 1961.

Dance, Daryl C. "Black Eve or Madonna? A Study of the Antithetical Views of the Mother in Black American Literature." In *Sturdy Black Bridges: Visions of Black Women in Literature.* Ed. Roseann P. Bell, Bettye Parker, and Beverly Guy-Sheftall. Garden City, N.Y.: Anchor Press-Doubleday, 1979, pp. 123–32.

Dauber, Kenneth. *Rediscovering Hawthorne.* Princeton, N.J.: Princeton Univ. Press, 1977.

Davis, Arthur, Inrod. *Clotel, or The President's Daughter.* By William Wells Brown. New York: Macmillan, 1970.

Davis, Merrell R. "The Flower Symbolism in *Mardi.*" *Modern Language Quarterly,* 2 (Dec. 1941): 625–38.

————. *Melville's Mardi: A Chartless Voyage.* New Haven, Conn.: Yale Univ. Press, 1952.

Davis, Richard Beale. "Mrs. Stowe's Characters-in-Situations and a Southern Literary Tradition." In *Essays on American Literature in*

Honor of Jay B. Hubbell. Ed. Clarence Gohdes. Durham, N.C.: Duke Univ. Press, 1967, pp. 108–25.

Deegan, Dorothy Y. *The Stereotype of the Single Woman in Novels: A Social Study With Implications for the Education of Women.* New York: King's Crown Press–Columbia Univ. Press, 1951.

Dichman, Mary E. "Absolutism in Melville's *Pierre.*" *PMLA,* 67 (Sept. 1952): 702–15.

Dillingham, William B. *An Artist in the Rigging: The Early Work of Herman Melville.* Athens: Univ. of Georgia Press, 1972.

————. *Melville's Short Fiction, 1853–1856.* Athens: Univ. of Georgia Press, 1977.

————. "Structure and Theme in *The House of the Seven Gables.*" In *The House of the Seven Gables.* By Nathaniel Hawthorne. Ed. Seymour L. Gross. New York: Norton, 1967, pp. 449–59.

Dorris, Michael. "Native American Literature in an Ethnohistorical Context." *College English,* 41 (Oct. 1979): 147–62.

Douglas, Ann. *The Feminization of American Culture.* New York: Knopf, 1977.

Douglass, Frederick. *Narrative of the Life of Frederick Douglass, an American Slave, Written by Himself.* Introd. William Lloyd Garrison. Boston, 1845; rpt. Garden City, N.Y.: Doubleday, 1963.

Dryden, Edgar A. *Melville's Thematics of Form: The Great Art of Telling the Truth.* Baltimore: Johns Hopkins Univ. Press, 1968.

————. *Nathaniel Hawthorne: The Poetics of Enchantment.* Ithaca, N.Y.: Cornell Univ. Press, 1977.

Dublin, Thomas. "Women, Work, and the Family: Female Operatives in the Lowell Mills, 1830–1860." *Feminist Studies,* 3 (Fall 1975): 30–35.

Duvall, Severn. "*Uncle Tom's Cabin:* The Sinister Side of the Patriarchy." In *Images of the Negro in American Literature.* Ed. Seymour L. Gross and John Edward Hardy. Chicago: Univ. of Chicago Press, pp. 163–80.

Earnest, Ernest. *The American Eve in Fact and Fiction, 1775–1914.* Urbana: Univ. of Illinois Press, 1974.

Eigner, Edwin M. *The Metaphysical Novel in England and America: Dickens, Bulwer, Melville, and Hawthorne.* Berkeley: Univ. of California Press, 1978.

————. "The Romantic Unity of Melville's *Omoo.*" *Philological Quarterly,* 46 (Jan. 1967): 95–108.

Eisler, Benita, ed. *The Lowell Offering: Writings by New England Mill Women (1840–1845).* Philadelphia: Lippincott, 1977.

Elder, Arlene A. *The "Hindered Hand": Cultural Implications of Early African-American Fiction.* Westport, Conn.: Greenwood Press, 1978.

Elliott, Robert C. "*The Blithedale Romance.*" In *Hawthorne Centenary*

Essays. Ed. Roy Harvey Pearce. Columbus: Ohio State Univ. Press, 1964, pp. 103–17.

Ellison, Curtis W. "Black Adam: The Adamic Assertion and the Afro-American Novelist." Diss. Univ. of Minnesota 1970.

————, and E.W. Metcalf, Jr. *William Wells Brown and Martin R. Delany: A Reference Guide.* Boston: G.K. Hall, 1978.

Ellison, Ralph. "The Art of Fiction: An Interview." In *The Black Novelist.* Ed. Robert Hemenway. Columbus, Ohio: Charles E. Merrill, 1970, pp. 205–17.

Engels, Frederick. *The Origin of the Family, Private Property and the State, in the Light of the Researchers of Lewis H. Morgan.* Introd. and notes by Eleanor Burke Leacock. New York: International Publishers, 1972.

Fairchild, Hoxie Neale. *The Noble Savage: A Study in Romantic Naturalism.* New York: Russell & Russell, 1961.

Farb, Peter. *Man's Rise to Civilization: The Cultural Ascent of the Indians of North America.* Rev. 2nd ed. New York: Dutton, 1978.

Farrison, William Edward. "Clotel, Thomas Jefferson, and Sally Hemings." *College Language Association Journal,* 17 (Dec. 1973): 147–74.

————. *William Wells Brown: Author and Reformer.* Chicago: Univ. of Chicago Press, 1969.

Fenton, William N., ed. *Parker on the Iroquois.* Syracuse, N.Y.: Syracuse Univ. Press, 1968.

————, and John Gulick eds. *Symposium on Cherokee and Iroquois Culture.* Washington, D.C.: GPO, 1961.

Fetterley, Judith. *The Resisting Reader: A Feminist Approach to American Fiction.* Bloomington: Indiana Univ. Press, 1978.

Fiedler, Leslie A. *The Inadvertent Epic: From* Uncle Tom's Cabin *to* Roots. Toronto: Canadian Broadcasting Corp., 1979.

————. *Love and Death in the American Novel.* Rev. ed. New York: Stein and Day, 1966.

————. *No! In Thunder: Essays on Myth and Literature.* London: Eyre and Spottiswoode, 1963.

————. *The Return of the Vanishing American.* New York: Stein and Day, 1968.

————, and Houston A. Baker, Jr., eds. *English Literature: Opening Up the Canon.* Selected Papers from the English Institute, New Series, No. 4. Baltimore: Johns Hopkins Univ. Press, 1981.

Finkelstein, Dorothee Metlitsky. *Melville's Orienda.* New Haven, Conn.: Yale Univ. Press, 1961.

Finn, Helena Kane. "Design of Despair: The Tragic Heroine and the Imagery of Artifice in Novels by Hawthorne, James, and Wharton." Diss. St. Johns Univ. 1976.

Fisher, Marvin. *Going Under: Melville's Short Fiction and the American 1850's*. Baton Rouge: Louisiana State Univ. Press, 1977.

Fleming, Robert E. "Black, White, and Mulatto in Martin R. Delaney's [sic] *Blake*." *Negro History Bulletin*, 36 (Feb. 1973): 37–39.

————. "Humor in the Early Black Novel." *College Language Association Journal*, 17 (Dec. 1973): 250–62.

Fogle, Richard Harter. *Hawthorne's Fiction: The Light and the Dark*. Rev. ed. Norman: Univ. of Oklahoma Press, 1964.

————. *Hawthorne's Imagery: The "Proper Light and Shadow" in the Major Romances*. Norman: Univ. of Oklahoma Press, 1969.

————. *Melville's Shorter Tales*. Norman: Univ. of Oklahoma Press, 1960.

————. *The Permanent Pleasure: Essays on Classics of Romanticism*. Athens: Univ. of Georgia Press, 1974.

————. Ed. *The Romantic Movement in American Writing*. New York: Odyssey Press, 1966.

Foster, Charles Howell. *The Rungless Ladder: Harriet Beecher Stowe and New England Puritanism*. Durham, N.C.: Duke Univ. Press, 1954.

————. "Something in Emblems: A Reinterpretation of *Moby-Dick*." *New England Quarterly* (Mar. 1961):3–35.

Foster, Edward Halsey. *The Civilized Wilderness: Backgrounds to American Romantic Literature, 1817–1860*. New York: Free Press; London: Collier Macmillan, 1975.

Foster, Frances Smith. *Witnessing Slavery*. Westport, Conn.: Greenwood Press, 1979.

Foster, Michael K. *From the Earth to Beyond the Sky: An Ethnographic Approach to Four Longhouse Iroquois Speech Events*. Ottawa: National Museums of Canada, 1974.

Frank, Max. *Die Farb- und Lichtsymbolik im Prosawerk Herman Melvilles*. Heidelberg: Carl Winter, 1967.

Franklin, H. Bruce. "Animal Farm Unbound: Or What the *Narrative of Frederick Douglass, An American Slave* Reveals about American Literature." *New Letters: A Magazine of Fine Writing*, 43 (Apr. 1977): 25–46.

————. "Apparent Symbol of Despotic Command: Melville's *Benito Cereno*." *New England Quarterly*, 34 (Dec. 1961): 462–77.

————. *The Victim as Criminal and Artist: Literature from the American Prison*. New York: Oxford Univ. Press, 1978.

————. *The Wake of the Gods: Melville's Mythology*. Stanford, Calif.: Stanford Univ. Press, 1963.

Fredrickson, George M. *The Black Image in the White Mind: The Debate on Afro-American Character and Destiny, 1817–1914*. New York: Harper & Row, 1971.

_____. *White Supremacy: A Comparative Study in American and South African History*. New York: Oxford Univ. Press, 1981.

Fryer, Judith. *The Faces of Eve: Women in the Nineteenth-Century American Novel*. New York: Oxford Univ. Press, 1976.

Fuller, Margaret. *Woman in the Nineteenth Century*. New York: Norton, 1971.

Furnas, J.C. *Goodbye to Uncle Tom*. New York: William Sloane, 1956.

Fussell, Edwin. "Neutral Territory: Hawthorne on the Figurative Frontier." In *Hawthorne Centenary Essays*. Ed. Roy Harvey Pearce. Columbus: Ohio State Univ. Press, pp. 297–314.

Gabriel, Ralph Henry. *Elias Boudinot, Cherokee, and his America*. Norman: Univ. of Oklahoma Press, 1941.

Gara, Larry, introd. "Narrative of William Wells Brown, A Fugitive Slave." By William Wells Brown. In *Four Fugitive Slave Narratives*. Ed. Robin W. Winks. Reading, Mass.: Addison-Wesley, 1969, pp. ix–xvii.

Gay, Dorothy. "The Tangled Skein of Romanticism and Violence in the Old South: The Southern Response to Abolitionism and Feminism, 1830–1861." Diss. Univ. of North Carolina 1975.

Gayle, Addison, Jr. *The Way of the New World: The Black Novel in America*. Garden City, N.Y.: Anchor-Doubleday, 1976.

_____, ed. *Black Expression: Essays by and about Black Americans in the Creative Arts*. New York: Weybright and Talley, 1969.

Gilbert, Olive, ed. *The Narrative of Sojourner Truth*. Final ed. with materials added by Francis Titus. Battle Creek, Mich.: 1875; rpt. Chicago: Johnson, 1970.

Gilbert, Sandra M., and Susan Gubar. *The Madwoman in the Attic: The Woman Writer and the Nineteenth-Century Literary Imagination*. New Haven, Conn.: Yale Univ. Press, 1979.

Gilbertson, Catherine Peebles. *Harriet Beecher Stowe*. New York: D. Appleton-Century, 1937.

Gilman, Richard. "White Standards and Negro Writing." In *The Black American Writer*. Vol. I. Ed. C.W.E. Bigsby. Deland, Fla.: Everett/Edwards, 1969, pp. 35–49.

Gilman, William H. *Melville's Early Life and Redburn*. New York: New York Univ. Press; London: Oxford Univ. Press, 1951.

Gilmore, Michael T. *The Middle Way: Puritanism and Ideology in American Romantic Fiction*. New Brunswick, N.J.: Rutgers Univ. Press, 1977.

Gloster, Hugh M. *Negro Voices in American Fiction*. New York: Russell & Russell, 1965.

Goldfarb, Russell M., and Clare R. Goldfarb. *Spiritualism and Nineteenth-*

Century Letters. Rutherford, N.J.: Fairleigh Dickinson Univ. Press; London: Associated Univ. Presses, 1978.

Graham, Thomas. "Harriet Beecher Stowe and the Question of Race." *New England Quarterly,* 46 (Dec. 1973): 614–22.

Green, J. Lee. "Black Literature and the American Literary Mainstream." In *Minority Language and Literature: Retrospective and Perspective.* Ed. Dexter Fisher. New York: Modern Language Association of America, 1977, pp. 20–28.

Green, Rayna. "The Pocahontas Perplex: the Image of Indian Women in American Culture." *The Massachusetts Review,* 16 (Autumn 1975): 698–714.

Grejda, Edward S. *The Common Continent of Men: Racial Equality in the Writings of Herman Melville.* Port Washington, N.Y.: Kennikat Press, 1974.

Griffith, Clark. "Substance and Shadow: Language and Meaning in *The House of the Seven Gables.*" In *The House of the Seven Gables.* By Nathaniel Hawthorne. Ed. Seymour L. Gross. New York: Norton, 1967, pp. 383–94.

Griffith, Cyril E. *The African Dream: Martin R. Delany and the Emergence of Pan-African Thought.* University Park: Pennsylvania State Univ. Press, 1975.

Grimsted, David. "Melodrama as Echo of the Historically Voiceless." In *Anonymous Americans.* Ed. Tamara K. Hareven. Englewood Cliffs, N.J.: Prentice-Hall, 1971, pp. 80–98.

Gross, Seymour L., ed. *The House of the Seven Gables.* By Nathaniel Hawthorne. New York: Norton, 1967.

————, and John Edward Hardy, eds. *Images of the Negro in American Literature.* Chicago: Univ. of Chicago Press, 1966.

————, and Rosalie Murphy, eds. *The Blithedale Romance.* By Nathaniel Hawthorne. New York: Norton, 1978.

Gross, Theodore L. "The Idealism of Negro Literature." In *The Heroic Ideal in American Literature.* New York: Free Press; London: Collier Macmillan, 1971, pp. 125–26.

Gura, Philip F. "Thoreau's Maine Woods Indians: More Representative Men." *American Literature,* 49 (Nov. 1977): 366–84.

Haberstroh, Charles J., Jr. *Melville and Male Identity.* Rutherford, N.J.: Fairleigh Dickinson Univ. Press; London: Associated University Presses, 1980.

Hale, Horatio. *The Iroquois Book of Rites.* New York: AMS Press, 1969.

Hanson, Elizabeth I. "The Indian Metaphor in Henry David Thoreau's *A Week on the Concord and Merrimack Rivers.*" *Thoreau Journal Quarterly,* 10 (Jan. 1978): 3–5.

Harley, Sharon, and Rosalyn Terborg-Penn, eds. *The Afro-American Woman: Struggles and Images*. Port Washington, N.Y.; London: Kennikat Press, 1978.

Haslam, Gerald. "The Awakening of American Negro Literature 1619–1900." In *The Black American Writer*. Vol. II, pp. 41–51. Ed. C.W.E. Bigsby. Deland, Fla.: Everett/Edwards, 1969.

Hayford, Harrison, and Walter Blair, introd. and notes. *Omoo: A Narrative of Adventures in the South Seas*. By Herman Melville. Ed. Harrison Hayford and Walter Blair. New York: Hendricks House, 1969.

Heermance, J. Noel. *William Wells Brown and* Clotelle: *A Portrait of the Artist in the First Negro Novel*. Hamden, Conn.: Shoestring Press, 1969.

Hemenway, Robert, ed. *The Black Novelist*. Columbus, Ohio: Charles E. Merrill, 1970.

Hennelly, Mark. "Ishmael's Nightmare and the American Eve." *American Imago*, 30 (Fall 1973): 274–93.

Henry, Thomas R. *Wilderness Messiah: The Story of Hiawatha and the Iroquois*. New York: William Sloane, 1955.

Herbert, T. Walter, Jr. *Marquesan Encounters: Melville and the Meaning of Civilization*. Cambridge, Mass: Harvard Univ. Press, 1980.

Hetherington, Hugh. *Melville's Reviewers: British and American, 1846–1891*. Chapel Hill: Univ. of North Carolina Press, 1961.

Hewitt, J.N.B. "Iroquoian Cosmology." First Part. Twenty-first *Annual Report of the Bureau of American Ethnology*. Washington, D.C.: GPO, 1903, pp. 127–339.

————. "Iroquoian Cosmology." Second Part. Forty-third *Annual Report of the Bureau of American Ethnology*. Washington, D.C.: GPO, 1928, pp. 449–819.

Hildreth, Margaret Holbrook. *Harriet Beecher Stowe: A Bibliography*. Hamden, Conn.: Shoestring Press, 1976.

Hildreth, Richard. *The Slave; or, Memoirs of Archy Moore*. 2 vols. Boston, 1836. *Wright American Fiction*. Vol. I (1774–1850). Research Publication Microfilm No. 1186, reel H–9. Rev. and retitled *The White Slave; or, Memoirs of a Fugitive*. Boston 1852; rpt. New York: Arno Press, 1969.

Hite, Roger W. " 'Stand Still and See the Salvation': The Rhetorical Design of Martin Delany's *Blake.*" *Journal of Black Studies*, 5 (Dec. 1974): 192–202.

Hoffman, Daniel G. *Form and Fable in American Fiction*. New York: Oxford Univ. Press, 1961.

————. "Myth, Romance, and the Childhood of Man." In *Hawthorne*

Centenary Essays. Ed. Roy Harvey Pearce. Columbus: Ohio State Univ. Press, 1964, pp. 197–219.

Howard, Leon. *Herman Melville: A Biography.* Berkeley: Univ. of California Press, 1951.

Hudson, Theodore R. "In the Eye of the Beholder: The First Black Novelist." *Negro Digest,* 19 (Dec. 1969): 43–48.

Inge, M. Thomas, Maurice Duke, and Jackson R. Bryer, *Black American Writers: Bibliographical Essays.* New York: St. Martin's Press, 1978.

Isani, Mukhtar Ali. "The Exotic and Protest in Earlier Black Literature: The Use of Alien Setting and Character." *Studies in Black Literature,* 5 (Summer 1974): 9–14.

Jackson, Blyden. "A Golden Mean for the Negro Novel." *College Language Association Journal,* 3 (Dec. 1959): 81–87.

_____. "The Negro's Image of His Universe as Reflected in His Fiction." In *Black Voices: An Anthology of Afro-American Literature.* Ed. Abraham Chapman. New York: New American Library; London: New English Library, 1968, pp. 622–31.

_____. "The Ghetto of the Negro Novel." In *The Waiting Years: Essays on American Negro Literature.* Baton Rouge: Louisiana State Univ. Press, 1976.

_____ and Louis D. Rubin, Jr. *Black Poetry in America: Two Essays in Historical Interpretation.* Baton Rouge: Louisiana State Univ. Press, 1974.

Johnson, Claudia D. *The Productive Tension of Hawthorne's Art.* Tuscaloosa: Univ. of Alabama Press, 1981.

Johnston, Johanna. *Runaway to Heaven: The Story of Harriet Beecher Stowe.* Garden City, N.Y.: Doubleday, 1963.

Jones, Louis Thomas. *Aboriginal American Oratory: The Tradition of Eloquence Among the Indians of the United States.* Los Angeles: Southwest Museum, 1965.

Josephy, Alvin M., Jr. *The Indian Heritage of America.* New York: Knopf, 1968.

Karcher, Carolyn L. "Melville and Racial Prejudice: A Reevaluation." *Southern Review,* 12 (Spring 1976): 287–310.

_____. *Shadow Over the Promised Land: Slavery, Race, and Violence in Melville's America.* Baton Rouge: Louisiana State Univ. Press, 1980.

Kaul, A.N. *The American Vision: Actual and Ideal Society in Nineteenth-Century Fiction.* New Haven, Conn.: Yale Univ. Press, 1963.

Kelley, Mary. "At War with Herself: Harriet Beecher Stowe as Woman in Conflict within the Home." *American Studies,* 19 (Fall 1978): 23–40.

Kellner, Robert Scott. "Toads and Scorpions: Women and Sex in the Writings of Herman Melville." Diss. Univ. of Massachusetts 1977.

Kemper, Steven E. *"Omoo:* Germinal Melville." *Studies in the Novel,* 10 (Winter 1978): 420–30.

Kesterson, David B., comp. *The Merrill Studies in The Marble Faun.* Columbus, Ohio: Charles E. Merrill, 1971.

Kimball, Gayle. "Harriet Beecher Stowe's Revision of New England Theology." *Journal of Presbyterian History,* 58 (Spring 1980): 64–81.

Kirkham, E. Bruce. *The Building of* Uncle Tom's Cabin. Knoxville: Univ. of Tennessee Press, 1977.

Kring, Walter D., and Jonathan S. Carey. "Two Discoveries Concerning Herman Melville." *Proceedings of the Massachusetts Historical Society,* 87 (1975): 137–41.

Kroeber, Karl. "An Introduction to the Art of Traditional American Indian Narration." In *Traditional Literatures of the American Indian.* Ed. Karl Kroeber. Lincoln: Univ. of Nebraska Press, 1981, pp. 1–24.

Krupat, Arnold. "The Indian Autobiography: Origins, Type, and Function." *American Literature,* 53 (March 1981): 22–42.

LaFrance, Marston, ed. *Patterns of Commitment in American Literature.* Toronto: Univ. of Toronto Press, 1967.

Larson, Charles R. *American Indian Fiction.* Albuquerque: Univ. of New Mexico Press, 1978.

Lawrence, D.H. *Studies in Classic American Literature.* New York: Viking, 1923.

Leacock, Eleanor. "Class, Commodity, and the Status of Women." In *Women Cross-Culturally, Change and Challenge.* Ed. Ruby Rohrlich-Leavitt. The Hague: Mouton, 1975, pp. 601–16.

Leavis, Q.D. "Melville: The 1853–6 Phase." In *New Perspectives on Melville.* Ed. Faith Pullin. Kent, Ohio: Kent State Univ. Press, 1978, pp. 197–228.

Lebedun, Jean. "Harriet Beecher Stowe's Interest in Sojourner Truth, Black Feminist." *American Literature,* 46 (Nov. 1974): 359–63.

Lebowitz, Alan. *Progress into Silence: A Study of Melville's Heroes.* Bloomington: Indiana Univ. Press, 1970.

Lederer, Wolfgang. *The Fear of Women.* New York: Grune and Stratton, 1968.

Lefcovitz, Allan and Barbara Lefcovitz. "Some Rents in the Veil: New Light on Priscilla and Zenobia in *The Blithedale Romance."* *Nineteenth-Century Fiction,* 21 (Dec. 1966): 263–75.

Lewis, R.W.B. *The American Adam: Innocence, Tragedy, and Tradition in the Nineteenth Century.* Chicago: Univ. of Chicago Press, 1955.

Leyda, Jay. *The Melville Log: A Documentary Life of Herman Melville, 1819–1891.* 2 vols. New York: Harcourt, Brace, 1951.

Liptzin, Sol. *The Jew in American Literature.* New York: Bloch, 1966.
Lorant, Laurie Jean. "Herman Melville and Race." Diss. New York Univ. 1972.
Lovejoy, Arthur O. *The Great Chain of Being: A Study of the History of an Idea.* 1936; rpt. Cambridge, Mass.: Harvard Univ. Press, 1964.
_____. "The Supposed Primitivism of Rousseau's *Discourse on Inequality.*" In *Essays in the History of Ideas.* Baltimore: Johns Hopkins Univ. Press, 1948, 14–37.
_____, and George Boas. *Primitivism and Related Ideas in Antiquity.* Baltimore: Johns Hopkins Univ. Press, 1935.
Lundblad, Jane. *Nathaniel Hawthorne and European Literary Tradition.* New York: Russell & Russell, 1965.
Lynn, Kenneth S., introd. *Uncle Tom's Cabin or, Life Among the Lowly.* By Harriet Beecher Stowe. Cambridge, Mass.: Harvard Univ. Press, 1962.
McConnell, Frank D. "Uncle Tom & the Avant Garde," *Massachusetts Review,* 16 (Autumn 1975): 732–45.
McLuhan, Herbert Marshall. *War and Peace in the Global Village.* New York: McGraw-Hill, 1968.
McNelly, Cleo. "Natives, Women, and Claude Lévi-Strauss." *Massachusetts Review,* 16 (Winter 1975): 7–29.
Male, Roy R. *Hawthorne's Tragic Vision.* Austin: Univ. of Texas Press, 1957.
Malveaux, Julianne. "Revolutionary Themes in Martin Delaney's [sic] *Blake.*" *The Black Scholar,* 4 (July –Aug. 1973): 52–56.
Margolies, Edward. "Ante-Bellum Slave Narratives: Their Place in American Literary History." *Studies in Black Literature,* 4 (Autumn 1973): 1–8.
_____. "Melville and Blacks." *College Language Association Journal,* 18 (Mar. 1975): 364–73.
_____. *Native Sons: A Critical Study of Twentieth-Century Negro American Authors.* Philadelphia: Lippincott, 1968.
_____, and David Bakish, *Afro-American Fiction, 1853–1976: A Guide to Information Sources.* Detroit: Gale Research, 1979.
Marks, Alfred H. "Hawthorne's Daguerrotypist: Scientist, Artist, Reformer." In *The House of the Seven Gables.* By Nathaniel Hawthorne. Ed. Seymour L. Gross. New York: Norton, 1967, pp. 330–47.
_____. "Who Killed Judge Pyncheon? The Role of the Imagination in *The House of the Seven Gables.*" In *The House of the Seven Gables.* By Nathaniel Hawthorne. Ed. Seymour L. Gross. New York: Norton, 1967, pp. 355–69.
Marx, Leo. *The Machine in the Garden: Technology and the Pastoral Ideal in America.* New York: Oxford Univ. Press, 1964.

Matthiessen, F.O. *American Renaissance: Art and Expression in the Age of Emerson and Whitman.* New York: Oxford Univ. Press, 1941.

Mellow, James R. *Nathaniel Hawthorne in His Times.* Boston: Houghton Mifflin, 1980.

Metcalf, Eleanor Melville. *Herman Melville: Cycle and Epicycle.* Cambridge, Mass.: Harvard Univ. Press, 1953.

Miller, Edwin Haviland. *Melville.* New York: George Braziller, 1975.

Miller, Floyd J., introd. *Blake or The Huts of America.* By Martin R. Delany. Boston: Beacon Press, 1970.

Miller, John Chester. *The Wolf by the Ears: Thomas Jefferson and Slavery.* New York: Free Press; London: Collier Macmillan, 1977.

Miller, Perry. "Melville and Transcendentalism." In *Nature's Nation.* Cambridge, Mass.: Harvard University Press, 1967, pp. 184–96.

Miller, R. Baxter, ed. *Black American Literature and Humanism.* Lexington: Univ. Press of Kentucky, 1981.

Mills, Nicolaus. *American and English Fiction in the Nineteenth Century: An Antigenre Critique and Comparison.* Bloomington: Indiana Univ. Press, 1973.

Moers, Ellen. *Harriet Beecher Stowe and American Literature.* Hartford, Conn.: Stowe-Day Foundation, 1978.

————. *Literary Women.* Garden City, N.Y.: Anchor-Doubleday 1977.

Moore, Maxine. *That Lonely Game: Melville, Mardi and the Almanac.* Columbia: Univ. of Missouri Press, 1975.

Moorman, Charles. "Melville's *Pierre* and the Fortunate Fall." In *The Merrill Studies in* Pierre. Comp. Ralph Willett. Columbus, Ohio: Charles E. Merrill, 1971, pp. 30–44.

————. "Melville's *Pierre* in the City." In *The Merrill Studies in* Pierre. Comp. Ralph Willett. Columbus, Ohio: Charles E. Merrill, 1971, pp. 55–58.

Moquin, Wayne, with Charles Van Doren. *Great Documents in American Indian History.* New York: Praeger, 1973.

Mumford, Lewis. *The Human Prospect.* Ed. Harry T. Moore and Karl W. Deutsch. Carbondale: Southern Illinois Univ. Press, 1955.

Murray, Henry A., introd. *Pierre or, The Ambiguities.* By Herman Melville. New York: Hendricks House, 1949.

Murray, Peter B. "Mythopoesis in *The Blithedale Romance.*" In *Critics on Hawthorne.* Ed. Thomas J. Rountree. Coral Gables, Fla.: Univ. of Miami Press, 1972, pp. 106–14.

Nichols, Charles. "The Origins of *Uncle Tom's Cabin.*" *Phylon,* 19 (Fall 1958): 328–34.

Noble, David W. *The Eternal Adam and the New World Garden: The Central Myth in the American Novel Since 1830.* New York: George Braziller, 1968.

O'Connor, William Van. "Conscious Naiveté in *The Blithedale Romance.*" *Revue des Langues Vivantes,* 20 (Feb. 1954): 37–45.

Olsen, Tillie. *Silences.* New York: Seymour Lawrence-Delacorte, 1978.

Ong, Walter J., S.J. "Oral Culture and the Literate Mind." In *Minority Language and Literature: Retrospective and Perspective.* Ed. Dexter Fisher. New York: Modern Language Association of America, 1977, pp. 134–49.

Osofsky, Gilbert, ed. *Puttin' on Ole Massa: The Slave Narratives of Henry Bibb, William Wells Brown, and Solomon Northrup.* New York: Harper & Row, 1969.

Pancost, David W. "Donald Grant Mitchell's *Reveries of a Bachelor* and Herman Melville's 'I and my Chimney.' " *American Transcendental Quarterly,* 42 (Spring 1979): 129–36.

Papashvily, Helen. *All the Happy Endings.* New York: Harper & Brothers, 1956.

Paris, Bernard J. "Optimism and Pessimism in *The Marble Faun.*" In *The Merrill Studies in* The Marble Faun. Comp. David B. Kesterson. Columbus, Ohio: Charles E. Merrill, 1971, pp. 61–78.

Parker, Gail. *The Oven Birds: American Women on Womanhood 1820–1920.* Garden City, N.Y.: Anchor Books, 1972.

Parker, Hershel. "Why Pierre Went Wrong." *Studies in the Novel,* 8 (Spring 1976): 7–23.

Pattee, Fred Lewis. *The Feminine Fifties.* New York: D. Appleton-Century, 1940.

Pearce, Roy Harvey, ed. *Hawthorne Centenary Essays.* Columbus: Ohio State Univ. Press, 1964.

————. *The Savages of America: A Study of the Indian and the Idea of Civilization.* Rev. ed. Baltimore: Johns Hopkins Univ. Press, 1965.

Peyer, Bernd C. "A Bibliography of Native American Prose Prior to the 20th Century." *The Indian Historian,* 13 (Spring 1980): 23–25.

Pommer, Henry F. *Milton and Melville.* Pittsburgh: Univ. of Pittsburgh Press, 1950.

Pops, Martin Leonard. *The Melville Archetype.* Kent, Ohio: Kent State Univ. Press, 1976.

Porte, Joel. *The Romance in America: Studies in Cooper, Poe, Hawthorne, Melville, and James.* Middletown, Conn.: Wesleyan Univ. Press, 1969.

Prior, Moody E. "Mrs. Stowe's Uncle Tom." *Critical Inquiry,* 5 (Summer 1979): 635–50.

Pryse, Marjorie. *The Mark and the Knowledge: Social Stigma in Classic American Fiction.* Columbus: Ohio State Univ. Press, 1979.

Pullin, Faith. "Melville's *Typee:* The Failure of Eden." In *New Perspectives on Melville.* Ed. Faith Pullin. Kent, Ohio: Kent State Univ. Press, 1978, pp. 1–28.

————, ed. *New Perspectives on Melville.* Kent, Ohio: Kent State Univ. Press, 1978.

Radin, Paul. *The Story of the American Indian.* New York: Liveright, 1934.

Rans, Geoffrey. "Inaudible Man: The Indian in the Theory and Practice of White Fiction." *Canadian Review of American Studies,* 8 (Fall 1977): 103–15.

Ransome, Eleanor, ed. *The Terrific Kemble: A Victorian Self-Portrait from the Writings of Fanny Kemble.* London: Hamish Hamilton, 1978.

Redding, J. Saunders. *To Make a Poet Black.* Chapel Hill: Univ. of North Carolina Press, 1939.

Ridge, John Rollin [Yellow Bird]. *The Life and Adventures of Joaquín Murieta: The Celebrated California Bandit.* Norman: Univ. of Oklahoma Press, 1955.

Ridgely, Joseph V. "Woodcraft: Simms's First Answer to *Uncle Tom's Cabin.*" *American Literature,* 31 (Jan. 1960): 421–33.

Rohrlich-Leavitt, Ruby, ed. *Women Cross-Culturally: Change and Challenge.* The Hague: Mouton, 1975.

Rollin, Frank A. [Frances E. Rollin Whipper]. *Life and Public Services of Martin R. Delany.* Boston: Lee and Shepard, 1883.

Rosenberry, Edward H. *Melville and the Comic Spirit.* Cambridge, Mass.: Harvard Univ. Press, 1955.

Rountree, Thomas J., ed. *Critics on Hawthorne.* Coral Gables, Fla.: Univ. of Miami Press, 1972.

Rousseau, Jean Jacques. "Discourse on the Origin and Foundations of Inequality." In *The First and Second Discourses.* pp. 101–81. Ed. with an introd. and notes by Roger D. Masters. Trans. Roger D. Masters and Judith R. Masters. New York: St. Martin's Press, 1964.

Rubin, Louis D., Jr. "The Experience of Difference: Southerners and Jews." In *The Curious Death of the Novel: Essays in American Literature.* Baton Rouge: Louisiana State Univ. Press, 1967, pp. 262–81.

Rugoff, Milton. *The Beechers: An American Family in the Nineteenth Century.* New York: Harper & Row, 1981.

Ruland, Richard. "Melville and the Fortunate Fall: Typee as Eden." *Nineteenth-Century Fiction,* 23 (Dec. 1968): 312–23.

Runden, John P., ed. *Melville's "Benito Cereno": A Text for Guided Research.* Lexington, Mass.: D.C. Heath, 1965.

Runge, Edith A. *Primitivism and Related Ideas in Sturm and Drang Literature.* Baltimore: Johns Hopkins Univ. Press, 1946.

Ruoff, John C. "Frivolity to Consumption; or, Southern Womanhood in Antebellum Literature." *Civil War History,* 18 (Sept. 1972): 213–29.

Ruoff, A. LaVonne Brown. "American Indian Oral Literatures." *American Quarterly,* 33 (Bibliography Issue 1981): 327–38.

——————. Rev. of O-GÎ-MÄW-KWĔ MIT-I GWÄ-KÎ: *Queen of the Woods*, by Simon Pokagon. *American Literary Realism*, 13 (Autumn 1980): 317–19.

Russell, Thomas. "Yarn for Melville's *Typee.*" *Philological Quarterly*, 15 (Jan. 1936): 16–29.

Sanders, Thomas E., and Walter W. Peek, eds. *Literature of the American Indian*. Hollywood, Calif.: Glencoe Press, 1973.

Sayre, Robert F. *Thoreau and the American Indians*. Princeton, N.J.: Princeton Univ. Press, 1977.

Scheick, William J. *The Half-Blood: A Cultural Symbol in 19th-Century American Fiction*. Lexington: Univ. Press of Kentucky, 1979.

Schumacher, Irene. *Gesellschaftsstruktur und Rolle der Frau: Das Beispiel der Irokesen*. Berlin: Duncker & Humblot, 1972.

Scott, Anne Firor. *The Southern Lady: From Pedestal to Politics, 1830–1930*. Chicago: Univ. of Chicago Press, 1970.

Scott, Nathan A., Jr. "Judgment Marked by a Cellar." In *The Shapeless God: Essays on Modern Fiction*. Ed. Harry T. Mooney, Jr., and Thomas F. Staley. Pittsburgh, Pa.: Univ. of Pittsburgh Press, 1968, pp. 139–69.

Sealts, Merton M., Jr. *Melville's Reading: A Checklist of Books Owned and Borrowed*. Madison: Univ. of Wisconsin Press, 1966.

Seelye, John. *Melville: The Ironic Diagram*. Evanston, Ill.: Northwestern Univ. Press, 1970.

Sherrill, Rowland A. *The Prophetic Melville: Experience, Transcendence, and Tragedy*. Athens: Univ. of Georgia Press, 1979.

Silko, Leslie Marmon. "Language and Literature from a Pueblo Indian Perspective." In *English Literature: Opening Up the Canon*. Ed. Leslie A. Fiedler and Houston A. Baker, Jr. Selected Papers from the English Institute, New Series, No. 4. Baltimore: Johns Hopkins Univ. Press, 1981.

Simpson, Eleanor E. "Melville and the Negro: From *Typee* to 'Benito Cereno.'" *American Literature*, 41 (Mar. 1969): 19–38.

Slotkin, Richard. *Regeneration Through Violence: The Mythology of the American Frontier, 1600–1860*. Middletown, Conn.: Wesleyan Univ. Press, 1973.

Smith, Henry Nash. *Democracy and the Novel: Popular Resistance to Classic American Writers*. New York: Oxford Univ. Press, 1978.

——————. *Virgin Land: The American West as Symbol and Myth*. New York: Vintage Books–Random House, 1950.

Smith, William Gardner. "The Negro Writer—Pitfalls and Compensations." In *The Black Novelist*. Ed. Robert Hemenway, Columbus, Ohio: Charles E. Merrill, 1970, pp. 197–204.

Speck, Frank G. *The Iroquois: A Study in Cultural Evolution*. Cranbrook

Institute of Science Bulletin, No. 23. Bloomfield, Mich.: Cranfield Institute, 1945.

Spiller, Robert E., et al. *Literary History of the United States.* 4th ed. rev. New York: Collier Macmillan, 1974.

Stanton, Robert. "The Trial of Nature: An Analysis of *The Blithedale Romance.*" *PMLA,* 76 (Dec. 1961): 528–38.

―――――. *"Typee* and Milton; Paradise Well Lost." *Modern Language Notes,* 74 (May 1959): 407–11.

Starke, Catherine Juanita. *Black Portraiture in American Fiction: Stock Characters, Archetypes, and Individuals.* New York: Basic Books, 1971.

Stein, William Bysshe. *Hawthorne's Faust: A Study of the Devil Archetype.* Gainesville: Univ. of Florida Press, 1953.

Stensland, Anna Lee. *Literature by and about the American Indian: An Annotated Bibliography.* Urbana, Ill.: National Council of Teachers of English, 1979.

Stephens, Ann S. *Malaeska: The Indian Wife of the White Hunter.* New York: John Day, 1929.

Stepto, Robert B. *From Behind the Veil: A Study of Afro-American Narrative.* Urbana: Univ. of Illinois Press, 1979.

Sterling, Dorothy. *Black Foremothers: Three Lives.* Old Westbury, N.Y.: Feminist Press; New York: McGraw Hill, 1979.

―――――. *The Making of an Afro-American: Martin Robison Delany, 1812–1885.* Garden City, N.Y.: Doubleday, 1971.

Stern, Milton R. *The Fine Hammered Steel of Herman Melville.* Urbana: Univ. of Illinois Press, 1968.

―――――. "Melville's Tragic Imagination: The Hero Without a Home." In *Patterns of Commitment in American Literature.* Ed. Marston LaFrance. Toronto: Univ. of Toronto Press, 1967, pp. 39–52.

Stewart, Randall. *Nathaniel Hawthorne: A Biography.* New Haven, Conn.: Yale Univ. Press, 1948.

―――――, ed. and introd. *The American Notebooks.* By Nathaniel Hawthorne. New Haven, Conn.: Yale Univ. Press, 1932.

Stone, Donald D. "Victorian Feminism and the Nineteenth-Century Novel." *Women's Studies,* 1, No. 1 (1972): 65–91.

Stowe, Charles Edward, comp. *Life of Harriet Beecher Stowe, Compiled from her Letters and Journals.* Boston: Houghton Mifflin; Cambridge, Mass.: Riverside Press, 1891.

Stuckey, Sterling. "Through the Prism of Folklore: The Black Ethos in Slavery." *Massachusetts Review,* 9 (Summer 1968): 417–37.

Takaki, Ronald T. *Violence in the Black Imagination: Essays and Documents.* New York: Putnam's Sons, 1972.

Taylor, William R. *Cavalier and Yankee: The Old South and American National Character.* New York: Harper & Row, 1961.

Terborg-Penn, Rosalyn. "Black Male Perspectives on the Nineteenth-Century Woman." In *The Afro-American Woman: Struggles and Images.* Ed. Sharon Harley and Rosalyn Terborg-Penn. Port Washington, N.Y.: Kennikat Press, 1978, pp. 28–42.

Thomas, Brook. *"The House of the Seven Gables:* Reading the Romance of America." *PMLA,* 97 (Mar. 1982): 195–211.

Thomas, William I. "The Mind of Woman and the Lower Races." In *The Sociology of Race Relations.* Ed. Thomas F. Pettigrew. New York: Collier Macmillan, 1980, pp. 10–14.

Thoreau, Henry David. *A Week on the Concord and Merrimack Rivers.* Ed. with introd. and notes by Walter Harding. New York: Holt, Rinehart & Winston, 1963.

Thorp, Margaret Farrand. *The Literary Sculptors.* Durham, N.C.: Duke Univ. Press, 1965.

Todd, Robert E. "The Magna Mater Archetype in *The Scarlet Letter* " *New England Quarterly,* 45 (Sept. 1972): 421–29.

Tompkins, Jane P. "Sentimental Power: *Uncle Tom's Cabin* and the Politics of Literary History." *Glyph* 8, Johns Hopkins Textual Studies. Baltimore, Md.: Johns Hopkins Univ. Press, 1981, pp. 79–102.

Tooker, Elizabeth. *The Indians of the Northeast: A Critical Bibliography.* Bloomington: Indiana Univ. Press, 1978.

Travis, Mildred K. *"Mardi:* Melville's Allegory of Love." *Emerson Society Quarterly,* 43 (Second Quarter 1966): 88–94.

Trent, Toni. "Stratification Among Blacks by Black Authors." *Negro History Bulletin,* 34 (Dec. 1971): 179–81.

Turner, Arlin, comp. *The Merrill Studies in* The Scarlet Letter." Columbus, Ohio: Charles E. Merrill, 1970.

Turner, Frederick W., III, ed. *The Portable North American Indian Reader.* New York: Viking Press, 1973.

Turner, Lorenzo Dow. *Anti-Slavery Sentiment in American Literature Prior to 1865.* 1929; rpt. Port Washington, N.Y.: Kennikat Press, 1966.

200 Years of American Sculpture. New York: Whitney Museum, 1976.

Ullman, Victor. *Martin R. Delany: The Beginnings of Black Nationalism.* Boston: Beacon Press, 1971.

Underhill, Ruth M. *Red Man's Religion: Beliefs and Practices of the Indians North of Mexico.* Chicago: Univ. of Chicago Press, 1965.

Vanderbilt, Kermit. " 'Benito Cereno': Melville's Fable of Black Complicity." *Southern Review,* NS 12 (Spring 1976): 311–22.

Velie, Alan R., ed. *American Indian Literature: An Anthology.* Norman: Univ. of Oklahoma Press, 1979.

Wagenknecht, Edward. *Cavalcade of the American Novel: From the Birth of the Nation to the Middle of the Twentieth Century.* New York: Henry Holt, 1952.

_____. *Harriet Beecher Stowe, the Known and the Unknown.* New York: Oxford Univ. Press, 1965.

Wallace, Anthony F.C. "The Dekanawideh [*sic*] Myth Analyzed as the Record of a Revitalization Movement." *Ethnohistory,* 5 (Spring 1958): 118–30.

Walters, R.G. "The Erotic South: Civilization and Sexuality in American Abolitionism." *American Quarterly,* 25 (May 1973): 177–201.

Ward, John William. *Red, White, and Blue: Men, Books, and Ideas in American Culture.* New York: Oxford Univ. Press, 1969.

Washburn, Wilcomb E. *The Indian in America.* New York: Harper & Row, 1975.

Wasserstrom, William. *Heiress of All the Ages: Sex and Sentiment in the Genteel Tradition.* Minneapolis: Univ. of Minnesota Press, 1959.

Weinmann, Paul L. *A Bibliography of the Iroquoian Literature.* New York State Museum and Science Service, Bulletin 411. Albany: 1969.

Welter, Barbara. "The Cult of True Womanhood, 1820–1860." *American Quarterly,* 18 (Summer 1966): 151–74.

_____. *Dimity Convictions: The American Woman in the Nineteenth Century.* Athens: Ohio Univ. Press, 1976.

West, Ray B., Jr. "Primitivism in Melville." *Prairie Schooner,* 30 (Winter 1956): 369–85.

Whitlow, Roger. *Black American Literature; A Critical History.* Chicago: Nelson-Hall, 1973.

_____. "Black Literature and American Innocence." *Studies in Black Literature,* 5 (Summer 1974): 1–4.

_____. *The Darker Vision: A Socio-Critical History of Nineteenth-Century Fiction Written by Black Americans.* New York: Gordon Press, 1977.

_____. "The Revolutionary Black Novels of Martin R. Delany and Sutton Griggs." *Melus,* 5 (Fall 1978): 26–36.

Wilkins, Thurman. *Cherokee Tragedy: The Story of the Ridge Family and of the Decimation of a People.* New York: Macmillan; London: Collier Macmillan, 1970.

Willett, Maurita. "The Silences of Herman Melville." In *Studies in the Minor and Later Works of Melville.* Ed. Raymona E. Hull. Hartford, Conn.: Transcendental Books, 1970, pp. 85–92.

Willett, Ralph, comp. *The Merrill Studies in Pierre.* Columbus, Ohio: Charles E. Merrill, 1971.

Williams, Joan. "The Reality of the Fair Maidens in Nathaniel Hawthorne's Completed Romances." Diss. Auburn Univ. 1976.

Williams, Kenny J. *They Also Spoke: An Essay on Negro Literature in America, 1787–1930.* Nashville: Townsend Press, 1970.

Wilson, Edmund. *Patriotic Gore: Studies in the Literature of the American Civil War.* New York: Oxford Univ. Press, 1962.

Wilson, Forrest. *Crusader in Crinoline: The Life of Harriet Beecher Stowe.* Philadelphia: Lippincott, 1941.

Winks, Robin W., introd. *Four Fugitive Slave Narratives.* Reading, Mass.: Addison-Wesley, 1969.

Woodcock, George, introd. *Typee: A Peep at Polynesian Life.* By Herman Melville. Harmondsworth, England: Penguin Books, 1972.

Woodress, James. "*Uncle Tom's Cabin* in Italy." In *Essays on American Literature in Honor of Jay B. Hubbell.* Ed. Clarence Gohdes. Durham, N.C.: Duke University Press, 1967, pp. 126–35.

Woods, John A., ed. and introd. *Uncle Tom's Cabin, or, Life Among the Lowly.* By Harriet Beecher Stowe. London: Oxford Univ. Press, 1965.

Woodward, C. Vann. *Mary Chestnut's Civil War.* New Haven, Conn.: Yale Univ. Press, 1981.

Wright, Nathalia. "A Note on Melville's Use of Spenser: Hautia and the Bower of Bliss." *American Literature,* 24 (March 1952): 83–85.

Yates, Norris. "Mask and Dance Motifs in *The Marble Faun.*" In *The Merrill Studies in* The Marble Faun." Comp. David B. Kesterson. Columbus, Ohio: Charles E. Merrill, 1971, pp. 32–35.

Yellin, Jean Fagan. *The Intricate Knot: Black Figures in American Literature, 1776–1863.* New York: New York Univ. Press, 1972.

Zanger, Jules. "The 'Tragic Octoroon' in Pre-Civil War Fiction." *American Quarterly,* 18 (Spring 1966): 63–70.

Index

Direct quotations from secondary works are indicated by the page numbers set in boldface type.

Index

Hawthorne, Nathaniel (*cont.*)
—role of narrator in, 29, 36-37, 195n42
—*The French and Italian Notebooks*, 38, 196n45,n54
—"Grandfather's Chair," 35
—*The House of the Seven Gables*, xvi, 16-28, 37, 181, 194n21
—ending of, 17, 26-28
—*Love Letters of Nathaniel Hawthorne*, 23, 195n30
—*The Marble Faun*, vi, xxi–xxii, 38-54, 92, 182-83, 186, 188
—"The Maypole of Merry Mount," 51
—*Mosses from an Old Manse*, 193n1
—"The New Adam and Eve," 3-4
—"Rappaccini's Daughter," vi, 3-7, 52
—*The Scarlet Letter*, xi–xii, xvii, 7-16, 37, 42, 51-53, 110, 133-34, 163, 181, 183, 188, 190n1
—"The Custom House" in, 193n9
—"Septimius Felton," 52-54
—"The Seven Vagabonds," 51
—*True Stories from History and Biography*, 35, 196n52
—Young Goodman Brown," 22
Hawthorne, Sophia, 3, 23, 52, 57, 195n30, 31
Hayford, Harrison, 190n2
Hayonwatha, xvii, 169-70, 172
healing arts; healing ceremony, 171-72; *see also* ritual
heart, image of, 16, 17, 18, 27
Heermance, J. Noel, 123, 206n9, 207n24, 209n51
Hemings, Sally, 131, 208n32
Hennelly, Mark, 190n2
Henry, Thomas R., 214n15
Henson, 203n17
Herder, Johann Gottfried von, 115-16
hero
—all-black, xxiv, 137, 143, 150-51, 160
—Anglo-Saxon, v
—folk heroes, xvi
—mulatto, 107, 131, 135, 142
heroines
—Anglo-Saxon, 138
—black or mulatto, 111, 116, 124, 126, 135-37
—European, 22, 194n15

heroines (*cont.*)
—Hebrew, 41, 43;
—*see also* women, images of
Hewitt, J.N.B., 187, 216n22
Hiawatha. *See* Hayonwatha; *see also* Longfellow, Henry Wadsworth
Higginson, Thomas Wentworth, 132, 208n35
Hildreth, Richard, *Archy Moore*, 107
Hite, Roger W., 210n2
Hoffman, Daniel G., xvi, xvii, 194n22,n28, 196n44
Holmes, Oliver Wendell, 148
Horatio Alger values, 143, 209n52
horror; terror, 56-57, 63-65, 96
Hosmer, Harriet, 183, 196n53, 215n10
Howard, Leon, 199n26, 201n58
Howe, Irving, 195n41
Hudson, Theodore R., 207n11
Hugo, Victor, 127
Hull, Raymona, 201n72
hunting and gathering tribes, 175,177-78
Hutchinson, Ann, 7

id, the, xiii, 189
idealism, 5, 37, 40, 44, 47, 73, 75, 78, 84, 90-91
Idealism, German, xvii, 191n18
"imperial self." *See* Anderson, Quentin
Indian captivities, xiv
individualism, v, xvii, 16, 71, 119, 164, 177, 180, 189, 194n20
indolence of natives, 65, 68
Inge, M. Thomas, 206n6
instinct, 27, 37-38, 40, 43, 81, 83, 187-88; *see also* primitivism
—versus reason or ideals, xxvi, 6, 53, 65, 73, 189
inversion of traditional images or values, v, xii, 16, 20, 32, 54, 61, 86-87, 122, 164, 182, 200n48, 211n27
irony, 83, 87, 105, 107-10, 112, 122, 124, 140-41, 163
Iroquoian cosmology, 187
Iroquois Confederacy (Iroquois League; Five Nations), xvi, xxv, 169-70; *see also* Dekanawida; Great Law; League of Six Nations
Isani, Mukhtar Ali, 212n37
isolation, alienation, xvi, 8, 10, 56, 69, 72-73, 114, 122, 164, 168, 177-78, 185, 188, 194n26

Index

253

Women, Ethnics, and Exotics was composed on the Mergenthaler Linotron 202N in eleven point Goudy with one point of spacing between the lines. The book was designed by Judy Ruehmann, composed by Williams of Chattanooga, printed offset by Thomson-Shore, Inc., and bound by John H. Dekker & Sons. The paper on which the book is printed bears the watermark of S.D. Warren and is designed for an effective life of at least three hundred years.

THE UNIVERSITY OF TENNESSEE PRESS

KNOXVILLE

254